The Joy of Food

Citrus segm

The Joy of Food
A Celebration of Good Things to Eat

Rory O'Connell

Watercress

Gill Books

Gill Books
Hume Avenue
Park West
Dublin 12
www.gillbooks.ie

Gill Books is an imprint of M.H. Gill and Co.

© Rory O'Connell 2020
978 07171 8984 7

Illustrations by Rory O'Connell
Copy-edited by Kristin Jensen
Indexed by Eileen O'Neill
Printed and bound in Italy by Printer Trento

This book is typeset in Garamond Premier Pro.

The paper used in this book comes from the wood
pulp of managed forests. For every tree felled, at
least one tree is planted, thereby renewing natural
resources.

A CIP catalogue record for this book is available
from the British Library.

5 4 3

For Ruaidhrí

About the Author

Rory O'Connell is founder of the Ballymaloe Cookery School with his sister Darina Allen and is one of its most-loved teachers. He worked for many years with Myrtle Allen as chef at the Ballymaloe House Hotel in Cork as well as with Alice Waters at Chez Panisse in California. In his thirty years of teaching he has taught many of the current stars of the British and Irish cooking scene, including Thomasina Miers, Rachel Allen and Stevie Parle.

Acknowledgements

Thank you to all of the great team at Gill Books – Nicki Howard, Catherine Gough, Teresa Daly and all of the many others there who I never get to meet but are an essential part of the process of getting a book to print.

Thank you to Graham Thew and Bartek Janczak for the super design and for managing to weave my rather naive drawings through the text.

Thank you to Kristin Jensen for editing with patience and humour.

Closer to home, the team at the Ballymaloe Cookery School, farm, gardens and shop is a constant support and I thank you all. Thank you also to Tracie Daly.

My continued inspiration comes from the men and women at home and abroad who grow and produce the food I love to cook with. Without all these committed individuals, many of whom are heroes to me, I would not be able to do what I love to do best: to cook.

To you, the reader, thank you for picking up this book and I hope it brings pleasure to you and the ones you love to cook for.

Contents

Essays

The Joy of Food

Introduction

There are many sounds in the kitchen that I love. One in particular is the almost inaudible sound coming from a stockpot as bubbles gently break on the surface of the liquid. This sound can only be appreciated in a completely silent moment, a solitary moment when all others are gone, the intermittent *plop, plop plop* letting you know that the heat under the saucepan is correct, the level of liquid in the pot is correct, something correct is happening. You have to stand perfectly still to fully appreciate the almost nothingness of it all – even the rustle of an apron can distract. You have to consciously stop to hear the silence punctuated prettily by pleasing little sounds. You have to breathe. Oh, joy.

I suppose we don't associate kitchens with little Zen interludes such as this, but in my life the kitchen is the place that has given me more life-affirming and deeply satisfying, core-penetrating moments than any other place. I have visited many a temple filled with shattering silence that has paled into insignificance in comparison to the particular calm that a kitchen can induce in me.

On the other hand, of course, the kitchen, especially those in busy commercial restaurants, can be fast, furious and unrelenting in the intensity it demands. The curious thing is that a calmness and deep satisfaction can arise from those situations also. If the kitchen is organised, the team happy and focused, the aim of all in that kitchen the same, then a delicious ballet is being performed, every dancer knowing what their move is and when to make it. You could also liken it to an orchestra with the chef conductor silently wielding the baton as the team of cooks makes the music.

It can be the same in one's own kitchen at home, performing solo. You have control, hopefully backed up by confidence, to achieve a deep sense of satisfaction and to cook delicious food. With this food comes joy – the joy of eating, the joy of sharing and the joy of giving pleasure to yourself, but especially to others. In my experience, giving joy through the food I cook is something of a drug. Whether it is the happy reaction from guests in a restaurant dining room or at home – or nowadays, in my working life standing in front of an audience of students who are keen to learn the skills – the nuance, the subtlety, the wherewithal of cooking – the joyful reaction provoked by that response is addictive.

There have been occasions when I have been teaching that I have 'left the room', such is my complete involvement in what I am doing. I will suddenly realise that I have become oblivious of my audience, as I am in an almost trance-like state of focus on the dish I am cooking and the narrative associated with teaching the details of that dish. It becomes just me and the dish. This is an unusual occurrence, and when it first happened I was shocked and shuddered back into the reality of the room and the place I was in. Now I see that happening as a gift, a moment of complete and absolute concentration – if not my Zen moment, then perhaps the zenith of where my level of concentration can take me. This was a gift that my work gave me – the joy of the physical act of cooking.

There is no joy without the food itself, the pleasure of beautiful ingredients. Shivering chervil, glossy basil, sturdy, smoky rosemary, noxious sage, towering fennel, creeping thyme, friendly parsley – my herb family. I look at ingredients almost like friends – some are around a lot and some just make an annual visit. There is hardly an ingredient that does not thrill me. The entire year is punctuated with reunions of sorts and the sheer excitement and wonder of what land and water provide.

Every day can be a day with perfect eggs. Potatoes are good though different depending on the time of year. But what about the moment when you taste your first new season potato with a little sea salt and butter? It is a moment to make a wish, certainly. I always make a wish when I taste the first of a new season ingredient, such as the rhubarb, asparagus, sea kale, gooseberries, strawberries and so on. I have no idea where the little tradition came from, but it certainly allows me to make many wishes throughout the year. My wish is always the same: that I may have the same delightful reunion the following year. If you eat strawberries throughout the year you don't ever get to make a wish, as they are never new and hardly ever a treat; mostly they are entirely forgettable. We all need to remind ourselves how ingredients taste when they are at their best, such as a strawberry picked on a hot day, still warm from the plant, one that has never seen the inside of a fridge, one that has been grown because it has superior flavour – utterly glorious; a whole new world, in fact. You will want to lie down in the strawberry patch, look up at the (hopefully) blue sky and give thanks to the creator of strawberries. You will perhaps ask to have your guilt absolved for eating so many environment-damaging upstarts and promise never to do it again. When you taste the warm plant-ripened berry, you will quickly realise that if allowed, nature can do most of the cooking for you.

Such an approach is not always practicable, but to truly understand food and to really cook well, it is vital to think about ingredients in this way. The more you think and act in this way, the more delicious your food will become. Your strawberry eating could be done on the same evening you picked them up at a farmers market or from a grocer or purveyor who truly cares about taste and provenance. It is also a fact that the better the ingredients you buy, the less intervention – in other words, cooking – is necessary. All the clichés apply here: great vine-ripened tomatoes in September, a few grains of good salt, a drizzle of excellent extra virgin olive oil – yes, eye-widening perfection. Don't try this in March, or April, or, well, for most of the rest of the year. Ingredients have a time and a place. By observing those two tenets, you will eat beautifully and you will have joy at and on your table throughout the year.

I am happy to wait until an ingredient is at its best, and that does not just apply to home-grown ingredients. When the French and Italians decide the time is right to eat peaches or nectarines, that is when I want my supplier to tell me that the same fruit is available here. Equally, I want my summer mackerel from my local fishing village of Ballycotton, as it is the best mackerel experience I can have. Don't try to sell me something at another time of the year that will be a pale imitation.

My problem is that I get offended by inferior ingredients, not because I am a food snob, but because I think they are an insult to our planet and to the environment. I feel that nature and what it provides is our great good fortune and to manipulate it in a way that abuses and exhausts it is to court disaster and dance with a tricky partner. I feel the wonder and the magic of growth deeply and I wish to respect it by treasuring what it produces for our pleasure and nourishment.

This adherence to the rule of using only the best ingredients can be problematic. However, if we keep reminding ourselves that many ingredients are at their cheapest when they are also at their best, and if we use them then, it changes our outlook. This is particularly the case with locally grown and produced food. If we preserve ingredients when they are at their peak by freezing, pickling and so on, we can save a lot of money later in the year when such an ingredient is not environmentally or financially viable. I get great joy, for example, in preserving basil in olive oil in July or August. That job will take me about 20 minutes and I will have beautiful basil to hand for the rest of the year, not to mention the oil it is sitting in. I am also filled with joy at the simple business of freezing lovely ripe tomatoes in September, which takes a matter of minutes, to be used throughout the rest of the year where otherwise they would have come in a tin or a jar from afar. There would not be much point, though, in freezing the best peaches or nectarines, as those fruits don't freeze well and would disappoint. I preserve for flavour, not for sentiment.

If we avoid as much food waste as possible in our kitchens (there is joy to be had in leftovers), we can justify the higher cost of better ingredients and those special purchases that are worth pushing the boat out for. To make this point, I recently had what I call 'my pomegranate moment'. A friend returned from London had kindly brought a gift of a pomegranate, a fruit that I love. It had not come cheap. He had purchased the fruit from a grocer in London, Leila McAllister, whose shop, Leila's, is a beacon for cooks who want to buy in a place that sells only the very best seasonal ingredients, not just from England but also further afield. The pomegranate, which had come from Turkey, looked pretty conventional, but with a healthier, smoother and more lustrous skin than what I can normally get. It had been handled with care. The skin was cherry red, the shade of a slightly racy lipstick. Other than the fact that in appearance the fruit was an unblemished beauty, there wasn't anything to tell me that when I prised open this orb with its little crown on top, what I would see and taste would blow my mind open. The shattered skin revealed nuggets of jewels of pomegranate seeds of an intense ruby colour that I had not previously witnessed. In fact, I think it was the first time I had ever seen such a colour, except perhaps in a crown jewel behind alarmed glass in a museum. I could have stared at the light dancing on the seeds for hours in a sort of reverie. But the real problem here was the taste – a depth of flavour, deeply sweet and deeply sour at the same time, floral and transporting, a turbo-powered magic carpet ride of an experience, speeding me from my own kitchen to a palm-shaded oasis of incomparable beauty. I had reached pomegranate nirvana. Why was this a problem? Surely this is what all cooks wish to find in search of the perfect ingredient? Well, the problem was that it was unlikely that I would be able to find such a prize again in the near future, as I don't live down the street from Leila's in London, the season for that fruit would come and go, and pomegranate shopping trips to Turkey are not very practical on a regular basis. But then, is that not the point here? It's like the first new Irish potato or strawberry – I would have to wait.

So much of my pomegranate moment encapsulates for me the joy in my life of food. Though I might not get to have a similar experience until next year, in the meantime I could look forward to gently tearing open raspberries, as they, too, have a mostly unnoticed shiny jewelled interior under their matt coat, or the sinister-looking black tomatoes would reveal their bloody and delicious innards, while a snapped-open cucumber would reveal a shade of green that would also entrance me.

My year goes along like this from one ingredient to the next – sometimes a great cornucopia, sometimes a smaller choice, always a pleasure. And all the while my physical and emotional involvement with my job feels like a gift, one stumbled upon by accident when the halls of academia failed me (or in truth, I failed them). I feel blessed to have fallen into this life where there is no end to the discoveries, where on any given day I am only scratching the surface of what there is to be learned, where around every corner is another undiscovered ingredient. I can never get to the end of it.

All my senses are in play – the sight, sound, smell, touch and taste of my daily life is a blessing. Not everyone will be charmed by the exquisite curl of a pea tendril, the dizzying smell of a scented rose, the sting of a chilli, the slither of a liver, the noise bread makes as it cools, the feel of a dahlia petal, the snap of an asparagus spear. This is not everyone's symphony of joy, but it is certainly mine.

cauliflower

Cauliflower or Romanesco and Coriander Leaf Soup with Spiced Tomato Oil

When buying a cauliflower, I always choose the one with the most green outer leaves still attached. I find the flavour of the cooked leaves as interesting as the flower itself and the combination of both leaves and flowers gives the most flavoursome result. I wish the growers of this vegetable could send them to market untrimmed, thereby getting more value for the efforts of growing it. It seems a shame to be leaving so much of the vegetable in the field.

I feel the same way about Romanesco, that exotic-looking member of the same brassica family. With its pointy and repeating shell-like clusters of flowers, the Romanesco looks like something that might have grown on the seabed rather than on land. It has become widely available and its delicate green chartreuse colour is a joy. Also known as Roman cauliflower, it is just as versatile as its better-known cousin. From a raw shaved salad to a gratin, Indian-spiced vegetable stew, fried in a simple batter and rolled in grated Parmesan or roasted until nearly charred in a blistering hot oven, the possibilities are endless. It is an ideal vegetable for younger members of the family who might not be too inclined to eat their greens, as when cut apart from the head the individual florets look like perfect little trees, especially at Christmas, when their similarity to our favourite seasonal tree is marked.

In any event, this soup is delicious and comforting and the suggested spiced tomato oil elevates it into something lovely.

I wish the growers of this vegetable could send them to market untrimmed, thereby getting more value for the efforts of growing it. It seems a shame to be leaving so much of the vegetable in the field.

Serves 6–8
— 1 small head of cauliflower or Romanesco, with green leaves if possible
— 50g butter
— 170g diced potato
— 130g finely chopped onion

- 1 garlic clove, peeled and chopped
- 700ml chicken stock (page 319)
- 100ml creamy milk (½ milk, ½ cream)
- 2 tablespoons chopped fresh coriander leaves
- Sea salt and freshly ground black pepper

Remove all the stalks and green leaves from around the cauliflower or Romanesco. Strip the green leaves from the stalks and if the leaves are in good condition, cut them into 2cm pieces. Tender remaining stalks can also be chopped to a similar size and used. Discard the very tough and sometimes stringy stalks. Cut the tough core out of the cauliflower and discard. Break up the florets and chop coarsely into pieces of a similar size to the leaves.

Melt the butter in a heavy-based saucepan and allow to foam. Add the potato, onion and garlic and season with salt and pepper. Toss the vegetables in the butter and cover with a disc of greaseproof paper and a tight-fitting saucepan lid. Cook on a very low heat for about 20 minutes, until the vegetables are beginning to collapse and tenderise.

Add the chicken stock and bring to a gentle simmer. Cover the saucepan and continue cooking until the onion and potato are completely tender. It is crucial that the onion and potato are tender before adding the quick-cooking cauliflower.

Add the chopped cauliflower, leaves and stalks and simmer gently, uncovered, until the cauliflower is tender and cooked.

Add the creamy milk and chopped coriander leaves and purée to a smooth consistency with a hand-held blender or in a liquidiser. If the soup is a little thick for your liking, you can add a little more chicken stock or creamy milk to correct the consistency.

Bring the soup back to a simmer. Taste and correct the seasoning. Serve each bowl of hot soup with a generous drizzle of the spiced tomato oil.

Spiced Tomato Oil
I like to measure out all my ingredients for this recipe before I start cooking, as there is one crucial point during the process where speed is of the essence. Put the ingredients that are added in together into one bowl to facilitate easy additions to the cooking pan.

Makes approx. 450ml
— 1 x 2.5cm piece of fresh ginger, peeled and roughly chopped
— 6 garlic cloves, peeled
— 50ml water
— 3 tablespoons sunflower or extra virgin olive oil
— 2 teaspoons fennel seeds
— 2 teaspoons cumin seeds
— 400g very ripe tomatoes, peeled and chopped, or 1 x 400g
  tin of chopped tomatoes
— 1 tablespoon roasted and ground coriander seeds
— ¼ teaspoon ground turmeric
— Pinch of cayenne pepper
— Pinch of caster sugar
— Sea salt

Put the ginger, garlic and water in a blender and process to a smooth purée.

Heat the oil in a frying pan and allow it to get quite hot. Add the fennel and cumin seeds and **cook and colour for just a few seconds – this happens very quickly.** Immediately add the tomatoes, ginger and garlic mix, coriander, turmeric, cayenne, sugar and salt. Bring to a gentle simmer and cook for 5–8 minutes, stirring occasionally, until the mixture thickens slightly and appears somewhat oily. Taste and correct the seasoning. The oil keeps perfectly for one month in a sealed container in the fridge.

Salad of Shaved Fennel and Kumquat with Goats' Milk Greek-Style Cheese

This is a refreshing combination of ingredients that can be served on its own as a light starter or to accompany grilled meat or fish. It is particularly good with grilled chicken or roast chicken legs. It is vital to shave the fennel thinly, otherwise it may be a bit tough and difficult to eat. It is equally important to take care with the kumquats, as they, too, will be much more delicious when sliced almost paper thin. The flavour of a goats' cheese works well, as its robust taste stands up to the forthright flavour of the other ingredients.

Calling what we used to call 'feta' a Greek-style cheese is rather cumbersome, but the use of the word 'feta' can now only be associated with a sheep's milk cheese made in Greece, hence the longer title. I use one of Jane Murphy's Ardsallagh goats' cheeses from County Cork, which she calls a 'Greek-style salad cheese'. I am certain a sheep's milk cheese in the same style would be good here as well. I have on occasion eaten some of the leftover salad the following day, and though the texture of the fennel had softened somewhat, it was still good.

I like to serve the salad spread out on the plate rather than piled up, as I find the flavours work better that way.

Serves 4
— 1 fennel bulb, about 350g
— 70g kumquats
— 6 tablespoons extra virgin olive oil
— 2 tablespoons freshly squeezed lemon juice
— 1 teaspoon honey
— 1 level teaspoon fennel seeds, toasted and coarsely ground
— 60–80g goats' milk feta cheese
— Sea salt and freshly ground black pepper

Remove any tired outer leaves from the fennel bulb and trim the tops if they are looking a little dry. Save any feathery fennel fronds and flowers for garnishing the dish.

Slice the fennel bulb about 2mm thick, either by hand or using a mandolin. You can slice the bulbs lengthways or sideways. I sometimes do a combination of both.

Cut the kumquats into 2mm-thick slices with a sharp knife and remove and discard any pips as you go. Add to the fennel. I like the kumquats sliced lengthways, but others will be amused by them cut into thin rounds. Removing the pips is a bit tedious but worth the effort.

Whisk the olive oil, lemon juice, honey and fennel seeds together. Season to taste with salt and pepper. Pour the dressing over the fennel and kumquats and mix gently but thoroughly with your fingers. Taste again to see if the seasoning is correct. Allow to sit at room temperature for up to 1 hour before serving.

Serve the salad in a single layer spread out on a large flat plate. Crumble the feta over the salad and garnish with fennel fronds and a few fennel flowers, if available. If I think the oil looks a little scant, I will drizzle a little extra over at the last minute.

Fennel

Mussels with Fennel and Cannellini Beans

This is perhaps an unusual-sounding combination of ingredients, but the finished dish is both light and delicious. I ate something similar in a restaurant in New York a few years ago and this is my interpretation of that dish.

When cooking dried beans it is vital that they are cooked until sufficiently soft, as when undercooked they are unpleasant and difficult to digest. I always use dried beans rather than pre-cooked tinned ones. I find the flavour to be cleaner and more lively. The water left over from cooking the beans, some of which is vital to the recipe, makes a lovely vegetable stock. I usually freeze it if I don't have an immediate use for it.

On the other hand, when cooking mussels it is equally important not to overcook them, as they will lose volume and become tough and rather miserable looking. Mussels are easily available and tremendously good value for money. For some cooks there is a fear associated with the preparation and cooking of mussels. There are a few simple guidelines to follow to remove any of that worry.

The first thing to notice is the smell – really fresh fish smells of nothing at all, and this is the case with mussels. There may be a faint smell of the sea, but honestly that is more to do with the residual smell from the fishmonger's counter than the fish itself. Your fishmonger will have done most of the work in terms of cleaning the shells before you buy them.

Pop the mussels in the fridge when you get them home and keep chilled until you are going to cook them. Give them a quick rinse in cold water before you check that they are all still alive before you cook them. You can remove any loose bits of hair or 'beards', but it is not necessary to tug out the tightly attached ones, as they will be much easier to remove when the fish is cooked.

Lay them out in a single layer on a tray and remove and put to one side any that look open or are not tightly shut. Tap the open shells on the work surface and more often than not they will close, indicating that they are still alive and safe to use. They don't need to shut tightly, though they often do. You just need to ascertain that there is life within. I sometimes tap a reluctant closer three or four times before I get a positive result. If at that stage they still don't close, I discard them. The closed mussels are now safe and ready to cook.

Serves 6–8
Cooking and dressing the beans
— 225g dried cannellini beans
— 1 onion, peeled and halved
— 1 carrot, peeled and halved
— 1 bay leaf
— 4 tablespoons bean cooking water
— 4 tablespoons extra virgin olive oil
— 2 tablespoons freshly squeezed lemon juice
— 1 teaspoon roasted and coarsely ground fennel seeds
— Pinch of chilli flakes
— Sea salt and freshly ground black pepper

Preparing the fennel
— 1 fennel bulb, about 250g
— 3 tablespoons extra virgin olive oil
— 1 tablespoon freshly squeezed lemon juice

Cooking the mussels
— 1kg mussels
— 100ml dry white wine
— Trimmings from the fennel bulb

The sauce
— Mussel cooking liquid
— 4 tablespoons mayonnaise (page 306)

Garnish
— Fennel fronds

Soak the beans in 1 litre of cold water overnight. The next day, discard the water and place the drained beans in a saucepan with the onion, carrot and bay leaf. Cover with fresh cold water and bring to a simmer. Cover and cook gently until tender. The cooked beans should retain their shape. This will take anything from 30 minutes to 1 hour depending on the size and age of the beans. Keep an eye on the cooking water and if necessary top it up with more water to ensure the beans are always covered.

Drain the cooking water from the cooked beans and **reserve**. Allow the beans to cool slightly but not completely, then dress with 4 tablespoons of the reserved cooking water, olive oil, lemon juice, fennel seeds and chilli flakes. Season with salt and pepper to taste. The beans should be glazed but not swimming in a flavoursome coating sauce.

Trim the fennel bulb of any dry or discoloured parts. Reserve the trimmings for cooking the mussels. Slice the trimmed fennel bulb very thinly (about 1mm) from top to bottom or vice versa. Dress with the olive oil and lemon juice and season to taste with salt and pepper.

Place the mussels in a heavy-based pan with low sides and add the wine and fennel bulb trimmings. Cover with a lid, place on a moderate heat and steam open the mussels. Lift the lid every so often to check if any of the mussels have opened, and if so, remove those immediately so as not to overcook them, in which case they would become tough and shrivelled. When all the mussels are cooked and have been removed from the pan, sieve the cooking liquid and replace in the pan. Bring to a simmer and allow to reduce by half its volume. Allow to cool a little, then whisk that liquid gradually into the mayonnaise to attain a thin sauce.

Remove the mussels from the shells and pull out the little hairy beard if still attached. I usually reserve some of the mussels on the half or double shell for garnish, though this is optional.

To assemble the dish, heat the dressed beans until barely warm, then add to the fennel and mix gently. Place on a warm but not hot serving dish and spread it out with your fingers. Scatter on the mussels and drizzle the sauce over the entire dish. Garnish with fresh fennel fronds and serve.

Fig Leaf Panna Cotta with Roasted Figs, Raspberries and Mint

The mention of fig leaves will generally raise a little titter from some quarters, as they are forever associated with their role in protecting male modesty. Many an Adam has been portrayed in art with the leaf performing the role of censor, but if anything drawing attention to the unmentionable area rather than deflecting from it.

Fig trees grow very successfully in Ireland and though the resulting fruit never in my opinion matches up to those from warmer countries like France, Italy and the Balkans, they are still worthwhile. The leaves, however, are for the great part an undiscovered treasure. Even in our temperate climate they achieve a marvellous heady scent, and when treated in the correct way this floral aroma converts beautifully to real flavour. I love the appearance of the trees at all times of the year. In summer the leaves on a healthy tree will look almost Amazonian and in winter the branches denuded of leaves are truly lovely, especially as they are usually decorated with next year's fruit. On a south-facing wall, these trees are no trouble at all and a worthwhile addition to any garden.

The tough and slightly abrasive yet fragrant leaves can be used to flavour sweet creams, such as in this recipe, and are also delicious infused in oils, syrups and in lemonades or drinks. I sometimes use the fresh leaves as a bed for cheeses, especially soft and runny ones, which pick up the magical flavour. They make terrific wrappers for meat, fish, poultry and vegetables and once they hit the heat of a pan or grill, they impart the magic scent onto the ingredient within. The tired leaves are then discarded.

I also dry them on my kitchen counter for using during the winter months. Once thoroughly crisp, they hold on to the exotic notes all through the darkest time of the year. They take on a gorgeous coconut tinge to the flavour when dried like this. I suspect that the small young leaves could also be interesting if pickled, as the sharp liquids would have the effect of tenderising the otherwise inedible tough leaves.

So all in all, as you can see, I most definitely do give a fig for fig leaves.

So all in all, as you can see, I most definitely do give a fig for fig leaves.

Serves 8

Panna cotta
— 600ml cream
— 4–8 fig leaves, depending on size
— Unscented oil, such as sunflower or grapeseed, for brushing
— 50g caster sugar
— 2 leaves of gelatine

Roasted figs
— 4 tablespoons freshly squeezed lemon juice
— 2 tablespoons honey
— 8 ripe figs

To serve
— 250g fresh raspberries
— Fresh mint leaves
— Softly whipped cream

You will need
— 8 x 100ml ceramic, glass or tin moulds

Day 1

Place the cream in a container and add the fig leaves that you have previously gently crushed in your hands. Crushing the leaves allows more of the fig flavour to permeate the cream. Make sure all the leaves are below the surface of the cream. Cover and refrigerate for 24 hours.

Day 2

The next day, brush 8 x 100ml ceramic, glass or tin moulds with unscented oil, such as sunflower or grapeseed.

Place the cream and fig leaves in a saucepan and add the caster sugar. Place over a gentle heat and stir while warming the cream to a bare shiver. Remove from the heat and check that the sugar is completely dissolved.

Place the gelatine leaves in a bowl of water and allow to become collapsed and pliable. Strain the fig leaves from the cream, extracting every drop of cream. Place the cream in a clean saucepan and add the well-drained gelatine leaves. Stir to encourage the gelatine to dissolve completely. If the gelatine is not dissolving, it may be necessary to warm the fig-infused cream slightly. Divide the cream between the oiled moulds and chill for at least 3 hours, until gently set.

To roast the figs, preheat the oven to 180°C.

Place the lemon juice and honey in a bowl and mix well. Prick each fig twice with a pin or a skewer and roll them in the honey and lemon. Place the figs and the juice in a small ovenproof tray or baking dish that they fit into snugly. I use a Pyrex pie dish. Cook in the preheated oven until tender but not collapsed. By now there should be a deep pink slick of fig syrup in the bottom of the dish. The cooking time will depend on the ripeness of the figs. I start checking the figs after 20 minutes, but about 30 minutes should do it. Remove from the oven and allow to cool.

To serve the panna cottas, unmould onto cold plates. It may help to briefly dip the moulds into warm water to help loosen the panna cotta before turning out. They should be just barely set. Place a roasted fig on each plate followed by some raspberries, mint leaves, a spoonful of softly whipped cream and finally a good drizzle of the fig cooking juices. Serve immediately.

Actually

I do give a fig

Roast Slim Jim Aubergines with Dates, Pine Nuts, Sorrel and Mint

This is a light and refreshing dish, perfect as a starter before a more robust main course. Slim Jim, a variety of aubergine that I love, is long and slender, but the larger, more conventionally shaped ones will work perfectly here.

I think some cooks struggle a little when cooking aubergines for the first time, as they are not a vegetable that is part of our food culture, hence they take a little longer to understand. They are a fantastic sponge for all sorts of flavours and the vegetable itself comes in many different guises. Known in other parts of the world as eggplant, this odd-sounding name makes perfect sense when you see one of the varieties that is indeed ovoid or egg shaped and white in colour. They range in size from the thumbnail-sized pea aubergine to the large, shiny, teardrop-shaped ones we are more used to. I have seen up to two dozen varieties laid out side by side on pavement markets in South East Asia and that certainly gave me a good indication as to the range of the different members of this remarkable plant. Some solidly coloured, some streaked and some with vicious little thorns near the stalk, I suppose to ward off predators, a selection of them viewed at once is a lovely sight. The flower of the plant is unexpected and beautiful, with purple petals and a golden centre. All in all, there is much to recommend about the aubergine and it is well worth any moments of doubt associated with the initial experience of cooking it.

Sorrel is a favourite herb of mine, with its astringent and lemony flavour, and I wonder why it is not more widely grown. In my experience, it grows easily and returns each year and spreads a little also. I generally use the domesticated large broad leaf sorrel, which has long, slender, arrow-shaped leaves. It is worth noting that sorrel grows wild and in profusion and I forage for it also. I know it as sheep's sorrel and I find it all along the costal cliff walk near where I live. I have also seen

Sorrel is a favourite herb of mine, with its astringent and lemony flavour, and I wonder why it is not more widely grown. In my experience, it grows easily and returns each year and spreads a little also.

it flourishing inland in lush clumps. This plant is classed as a weed, but to me it is a delight. It is widely used in classic French cooking and many cooks will know the famous sorrel sauce served with salmon created by the Troisgros brothers at their restaurant in Roanne in France. I learned how to cook that dish many years ago as a young chef training with the Ryan brothers, Declan and Michael, at the marvellous Arbutus Lodge in Cork City. It became one of the seminal dishes of the sometimes misunderstood nouvelle cuisine movement in France in the 1960s and 70s, a movement that sought to create a lighter, more delicate cuisine than that associated with classic French cooking.

The other variety of sorrel that many have become familiar with in the last few years is wood sorrel or oxalis. It is very distinctive in appearance, with pretty light green trefoil-shaped leaves. It, too, has the distinctive lemony flavour of other members of the family and was brought into general consciousness as an edible weed by the Nordic food movement, which adopted it with gusto. It is sometimes confused with shamrock because of its slight similarity in appearance to the national Irish flower.

I suppose I would class this dish as modern cooking, but in any event it is a lovely way of showcasing both aubergine and sorrel.

Serves 4
— 2 Slim Jim aubergines or 1 large aubergine
— 1 tablespoon pine nuts
— 2 teaspoons honey
— Squeeze of lemon juice
— 2 tablespoons extra virgin olive oil
— 4–8 fresh mint leaves
— 2 fat Medjool dates, stones removed
— Flaky sea salt and freshly cracked black pepper

Dressing
— 1 large Medjool date, stone removed and finely chopped
— 3 tablespoons extra virgin olive oil
— 2 tablespoons chopped sorrel leaves or a little more lemon juice
— 1 tablespoon freshly squeezed lemon juice
— ⅛ teaspoon honey

Place a wire cooling rack over a medium-low flame. Sit the aubergines on top and roast until the skin is completely charred and blistered and the flesh is utterly tender. If you squeeze the aubergines there should not be the slightest resistance. You will need to move the aubergines and the wire rack to and fro as you go to ensure an even roasting of the vegetables. This process takes between 20 and 30 minutes. Remove the aubergines from the rack and allow to cool. If you don't have a gas flame in your kitchen, you can roast the aubergines under an oven grill element or in a very hot oven.

Gently mix all the dressing ingredients, then taste and correct the seasoning.

Roast the pine nuts in a dry pan over a medium heat until well coloured. The tips of some of the pine nuts can be a dark brown colour. You will need to shake the pan occasionally to ensure a reasonably even colour. Remove from the pan and crush coarsely with a fork. Season with a small pinch of salt.

Halve the cooled aubergines lengthways to achieve four halves in total. If you are using a large aubergine, cut it lengthways into 4 quarters. Place each one on a serving plate and drizzle with a little honey, a few drops of lemon juice and olive oil. Season with salt and pepper. Tear or chop the mint and scatter it over the aubergines along with the crushed pine nuts.

Place half of a date alongside each aubergine and drizzle over the date dressing. Serve immediately.

Sorrel
Loaves.

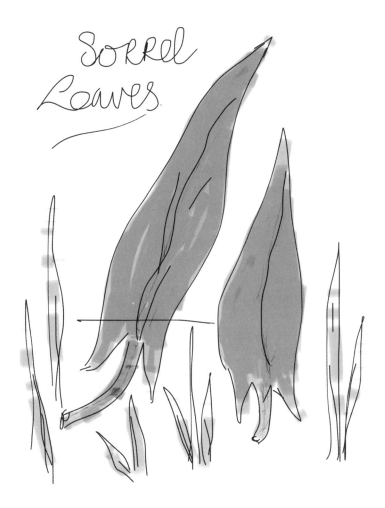

Salad of Shaved Fennel and Radish with Date and Sorrel Dressing

This combination of flavours and textures seems odd at first glance, but it really works well. The rich, sweet date along with the bitter sorrel is a good sweet-and-sour contrast for the peppery radish and cool aniseed-flavoured fennel.

I love dates and though one never thinks of them as a fresh fruit, that is precisely what they are. They are a wonderful ingredient and are delightful in both the sweet and savoury kitchen. They are best stored in a cool place and if you have been too enthusiastic in your shopping, pop them in the fridge and bear in mind that they also freeze very well. Try to find fat, juicy, sweet Medjool dates, as these are the best ones we can get in this part of the world. They come up from Morocco and the new season ones start to appear in autumn. One of the best dates I ever tasted was a variety called Barhi, which I tasted at the farmers market in Berkeley, California, though sadly I have never found it in this part of the world. For this recipe, use a sharp knife to cut the dates into neat, crisp dice.

If you fail to find sorrel, then I have suggested you up the lemon juice quantity by 1 tablespoon. I am in the fortunate position of having plenty of sorrel in my garden – it grows easily and seems to withstand our mild winters – and also to be able to forage it in the wild close by to where I live. I find it both on a cliff walk overlooking the sea and also on the edge of farmland meadows.

I serve this salad as a light and refreshing starter or as a salad to accompany grilled chicken or lamb.

Serves 4
Salad
— 2 small fennel bulbs
— 4 fat radishes
— 2 fat Medjool dates, stones removed and chopped into 1cm pieces

I love dates and though one never thinks of them as a fresh fruit, that is precisely what they are. They are a wonderful ingredient and are delightful in both the sweet and savoury kitchen.

— Flaky sea salt and freshly ground black pepper

Dressing
— 2 large Medjool dates, stones removed and finely chopped
— 6 tablespoons extra virgin olive oil
— 4 tablespoons chopped sorrel leaves or 1 extra tablespoon lemon juice
— 2 tablespoons freshly squeezed lemon juice
— ¼ teaspoon honey

Garnish
— 4 fennel fronds
— A drizzle of extra virgin olive oil

Mix all the dressing ingredients gently but thoroughly. Taste and correct the seasoning.

Trim any tough and discoloured outside leaves from the fennel and slice thinly (approx. 1mm) from root to tip with a mandolin. Place in a large bowl with the radishes sliced to a similar thickness. Add the chopped dates and season with salt and pepper.

Divide the vegetables between four large plates, spreading them out into a single layer rather than a pile.

Spoon over the well-mixed dressing and finish each salad with tiny pinches of fennel fronds and a small drizzle of extra virgin olive oil.

Hazelnuts

Every year when we were growing up, we would pick wild
hazelnuts. The time was the same every year – a few weeks
after we went back to school in September, when the air had
chilled slightly and the sweet smell of summer had been
replaced by the heavier, earthier smell of autumn. We had
put on our jumpers again and summer shorts had been
packed away until next year and replaced with long trousers.
We would head off with bags, baskets, buckets, bowls or
whatever receptacle we favoured ourselves. The volume of
the crop varied each year, as is the way in the wild, and we
understood at a young age not to take a large bounty for
granted.

Off we would go, unaccompanied and unafraid, a small
little troupe usually made up of my nearest brother, Richard,
and nearest sister, Elizabeth. My older siblings would all
have returned to boarding school or college by then. The
house was quieter. My mother would have been busy
running our home and our business.

We had various places that we knew where the hazel
trees grew. There were some hedgerows about a mile
from our home, but our favourite spot was on Cullohill
Mountain, which was a two-mile walk or so from where
we lived. I have no recollection of what we chatted about
as we walked along – childish matters, no doubt – but we
probably stopped for a few blackberries on the way. We
definitely passed an unused lime kiln and the castle, ruined
remains of a monumental fifteenth-century tower house.
It was built by the MacGillapatricks around 1425 and was
destroyed by Cromwellian forces in the mid-seventeenth
century. We would have craned our necks to look up at
the wonderful sheela na gig on the east wall. We may have
looked into the field across the road, where a row of damson
trees grew conveniently close to a beautiful stone wall. The
wall raised us to the perfect damson-picking height, which
was right up in the branches. These were also on our radar
for a delicious harvest. A couple of fields further on was

another ruin, this time of a church, roofless since the middle of the seventeenth century. It had been the private chapel of the Catholic lords of Upper Ossory. We loved that our tiny village had such storied buildings and they fuelled our imagination. We thought Cromwell was a horrible creature for bringing our castle down.

The 'mountain', as we called it, was a series of low hills that divided our part of County Laois from north County Kilkenny. To us little things, it was a towering, uninhabited wilderness that had mostly been colonised by wild hazels. Underfoot was mossy and slightly mysterious. Thin little streams trickled down the hills. Golden leaves floated down and silently hit the ground. Dappled light flickered through the not-yet-bare trees and lit our way. It was not eerie, but it was darkly atmospheric and a perfect environment for our easily moulded minds to play with the innocent stories of our childhood, which gave credence to fairies, leprechauns and the little people.

We never strayed too far apart, yet at the same time maintained a speechless and solitary harvesting regime. Some branches drooped and yielded the nuts easily, while others required a tiptoed stretch or a hop and a jump to catch a prize that was just out of reach. We knew the golden, ripe nuts that came off the branch easily from the hesitant, green, unready ones. Those were left for another day.

Some of the trees were suitable for climbing onto and for stretching on precariously, as the rather supple limbs melted slightly under our skinny weight. Occasionally a branch would break and we would check to see that the others were intact. It was a disaster to be too brave or careless and accidentally empty the contents of the baskets onto the ground, where the nuts almost immediately disappeared into nature's camouflage. I can still remember the particular earthy smell of the floor of the steep mountain: greasy and wet after rain and sweetly fermenting as leaves, moss, twigs and branches decomposed in a spongy natural cycle that we did not think about but somehow loved. There was virtually no sound apart from fallen nature breaking under our feet, a frustrated snort at an out-of-reach cluster of nuts or a startled bird making a hasty exit. The chattering would recommence on the walk home.

Unlike other foods we picked in the wild, such as the aforementioned damsons as well as the occasional wild plum, mushrooms, crab apples and blackberries, these nuts were for our own delectation. We did not present these to our mother; these were to be eaten in a solitary manner. Our individual personalities exhibited themselves in our approach to eating the nuts. I was an instant and hungry eater and would crouch on the ground while still on the mountain, find two suitable stones and crack a few to eat as I went along. I couldn't wait. Richard would save all his until we got home and carefully crack them into an egg cup, and as soon as the little cup was full, he would shoot the lot of them into his mouth and be rendered speechless for several highly contented minutes. He would then repeat the process. Elizabeth, if my memory serves me, fell somewhere between my greedy approach and Richard's controlled elegance.

Our mother would watch us as she cooked supper, happy, I think, in the knowledge that we were doing something that she, too, had done as a child. My brothers and sisters have continued the practice with their children and grandchildren and memories continue to be created. You could ask me what Santa brought me all those years ago and I would have difficulty remembering any of the presents, but those simple hours gathering nuts on the side of a hill are a vivid memory and as precious a gift as I have ever received.

Hazelnuts.

Chopped Cauliflower Salad with Red Onion and Semi-Dried Tomatoes

What I find interesting here is how the cauliflower is completely changed by chopping it when it is cooked, not only in terms of the texture, but also the flavour. The vegetable takes on a more sophisticated appearance and a more comforting texture. I think it is a revelation and I sometimes chop cousins of the cauliflower, such as Calabrese and purple or white sprouting broccoli, in the same way.

The red onions should not be too darkly cooked, as too strong of a caramel flavour will trample over the other flavours here.

When buying sun-dried or semi-dried tomatoes, do try to find the best quality. None of us are under the illusion that the vast majority of these dried and preserved tomatoes were allowed to relax and dehydrate on a terracotta-tiled roof in a sylvan setting in Italy before they got to us, though of course, that is precisely how small batches of the tomatoes will be preserved. But those are generally reserved, and quite rightly too, for the person who made the journey up to the roof with the glut of the sliced and seasoned tomatoes. In any event, choose dried fruit with a good deep colour and a firmer rather than softer texture.

This salad is delicious on its own as a light and refreshing starter with perhaps some thick natural yoghurt and warm flatbread. I also serve it as a side dish with grilled or slow roast pork or lamb.

Serves 4–6
— 1 head of cauliflower
— 2 tablespoons extra virgin olive oil
— 1 red onion, peeled and thinly sliced
— 100g semi-dried tomatoes, coarsely chopped
— 1 teaspoon roasted and coarsely ground cumin seeds
— 1 level teaspoon ground turmeric

When buying sun-dried or semi-dried tomatoes, do try to find the best quality. None of us are under the illusion that the vast majority of these dried and preserved tomatoes were allowed to relax and dehydrate on a terracotta-tiled roof in a sylvan setting in Italy before they got to us.

— 1 lemon
— Sea salt and freshly ground black pepper

Remove the outer green leaves from the head of cauliflower and chop across the stalks into pieces 1cm wide. Break the head into large florets while removing any tough core or stalks. Place the leaves in a saucepan and barely cover with cold water. Add a pinch of salt and bring to a simmer. Now sit the florets on top of the leaves. Cover, bring to a simmer and cook until the florets are just tender. Strain and discard the cooking water and spread out the cooked vegetable to cool slightly.

Heat the olive oil in a frying or sauté pan and add the sliced onion. Toss in the oil and cook, uncovered, until tender and a little golden. Remove from the heat and add the chopped tomatoes, cumin and turmeric. Mix well and adjust the seasoning with salt and pepper.

Chop the cauliflower coarsely and place in a bowl. Add the onion and the tomato and spice mixture and mix gently. Correct the seasoning. Spread out on a flat serving dish and finally grate a little lemon zest over.

Coffee Granita with Coffee Caramel Sauce and Blood Oranges

This is a refreshing end to a meal with lovely flavours and colours. I love icy granitas and in the case of blood oranges, I look forward to their arrival every year. I start looking out for them after Christmas, particularly the varieties that come from the volcanic areas of Sicily. There, this fruit is revered not just for its refreshing juice, but it is also regarded as a health food and the variety they search out is the Tarocco. The bloody flesh of the oranges makes a rather sinister-looking juice and when segmented, the pieces of orange look like chunks of unpolished precious stones with their rich veined colour. Sicilians also love granita and will take the opportunity to eat it at any time of the day, and that includes at breakfast time, when they may also serve brioche on the side and whipped cream on top.

The cook can be quite organised with this pudding, as all the elements can be made ahead. The granita sits happily in the freezer, the sugared blood oranges will keep for several hours in the fridge and the coffee caramel sauce keeps for months. The assembly of the dish is definitely a last-minute one, but I enjoy putting this type of dish together, where one is intently focused on getting the correct balance and proportion of ingredients onto each plate.

Serves 6

Coffee granita
— 400ml warm, strong filter coffee
— 70g caster sugar

Coffee caramel sauce
— 225g caster or granulated sugar
— 100ml water
— 225ml warm, strong filter coffee
— 1 tablespoon whiskey (optional)

Blood oranges
— 6 blood oranges
— 2 teaspoons caster sugar
— 2 teaspoons chopped fresh mint (optional)

To serve
— 6 tablespoons softly whipped cream

Mix the coffee and sugar and stir with a whisk to dissolve the sugar granules completely. Place the liquid in a freezerproof container and freeze. As soon as the mixture starts to freeze around the edges, use a fork to dislodge the frozen ice and mash it up into the rest of the liquid.

Refreeze and continue this process a further four or five times. Eventually the ice will be a collection of small, icy, coffee-flavoured shards. When the granita has reached this shard-like texture, it is best to cover it. If you taste the ice at this stage it may seem a little under-sweetened, but when the dish is assembled for serving, the addition of the coffee caramel sauce adequately sweetens the entire dish.

While the sweetened coffee is freezing, make the coffee caramel sauce. Place the sugar and water in a heavy-based saucepan with low sides and put on a gentle heat. Stir occasionally until the sugar is dissolved, then remove the spoon. Increase the heat to bring the syrup to a boil and cook to a rich, deep caramel. If the syrup caramelises unevenly, which it probably will, don't stir it with a spoon, but rather gently tilt the saucepan to and fro to draw the deeper-coloured caramel into the paler syrup to achieve an evenness of colour.

When the caramel is the required chestnut colour, draw the pan off the heat and immediately add the warm coffee and whiskey (if using). The liquids will spit and splutter a bit, so keep your hands away from the saucepan. Replace on a gentle heat and allow the now-thick caramel and thin coffee to cook together to a single consistency. A small amount of the caramel may stay in a thick slick on the bottom of the pan – if so, don't stir it and don't worry about that, as there will be plenty of flavour in the sauce and the small amount left behind in the saucepan will not have a significant effect on the consistency.

Bear in mind that the sauce will thicken somewhat as it cools, so don't cook it down too much. Remove from the heat and allow to cool completely. The cooled sauce will keep for months in the fridge.

Segment the blood oranges neatly to achieve individual segments with no skin or membrane attached. Sprinkle with the sugar and chopped mint (if using) and keep chilled until ready to serve.

To serve, place a tablespoon of the granita in the centre of six deep bowls. Scatter the orange segments and some of their juice around the granita and top each serving with a tablespoon of softly whipped cream. Drizzle 1 tablespoon of the coffee caramel sauce over the cream. Finally, drizzle with any remaining juice from the oranges and a few more shards of granita and serve immediately.

Salmon Wrapped in Nasturtium Leaves with Nasturtium Butter

These little parcels are both pretty and delicious. There is something rather special about presenting each person at the table with their own little serving, almost looking like a carefully wrapped and decorated gift.

The combination of salmon and peppery nasturtium is great, but it is also worth trying this dish using fat Dublin Bay prawns instead of the salmon. In that case, I cook the prawn tails in the shell first in boiling salted water and then shell them, allowing three prawns per parcel.

The parcels can be assembled ahead of time and chilled for cooking later. At first glance, the technique of wrapping the salmon in leaves seems both retro and difficult. Well, wrapping bits of food in leaves before frying may have gone off the radar, but it is still utterly worthwhile and, especially in this case, not difficult to do.

Finding nasturtiums may be your only difficulty here. All gardeners will know that they are the most simple of all garden plants to grow and once established in the ground or container, they will scamper off in all directions. Once you get to know the sweet and spicy taste of the leaves, flowers and seeds, you will be hooked and will add them to salads, vegetables, oils and so on. If you don't have them growing yourself, there is a strong possibility that they might be in a neighbour's garden or window box just waiting to be a colourful and cheering addition to your table.

Serves 4
— 4 large nasturtium leaves with long stalks attached
— 4 X 75g escalopes of salmon
— A little plain butter and a few drops of extra virgin olive oil, for frying
— Sea salt and freshly ground black pepper

There is something rather special about presenting each person at the table with their own little serving, almost looking like a carefully wrapped and decorated gift.

Nasturtium butter
— 50g butter, at room temperature
— 1 lemon
— 2 tablespoons very finely chopped nasturtium leaves and flowers
— Freshly ground black pepper

Garnish
— Nasturtium leaves and flowers
— Lemon wedges (optional)

For the nasturtium butter, cream the butter in a bowl. Grate a little lemon zest, about ¼ teaspoon, onto the butter. Add the chopped nasturtium leaves and flowers, a few twists of the black pepper mill and a few drops of lemon juice. Mix well and taste the tiniest bit to see if more lemon or pepper are required. Place the butter on a piece of greaseproof paper and roll into a neat log, twisting the ends to secure it. It should look like a little Christmas cracker filled with a green and red flecked butter.

Bring a medium-sized saucepan of water to the boil and have a bowl of iced water ready. Hold each nasturtium leaf by the stalk and immerse it into the boiling water for 2 seconds. Do not allow the leaf to drop into the water, so keep holding it by the stalk and drop into the iced water. Repeat this with the remaining leaves. Lift the leaves out of the iced water and lay out on a clean kitchen towel.

Take one leaf and spread it out with the stalk side down. Place a piece of salmon on the leaf and season with salt and pepper. Place a very thin slice of nasturtium butter on the salmon and fold the leaf over the fish to create a neat square parcel with the fish and butter completely enclosed. Place the parcels on a baking tray lined with non-stick baking paper and refrigerate until ready to cook.

Heat a sauté pan over a moderate heat and add a little plain butter and olive oil. When the butter is gently foaming, place the parcels in the pan. Cook carefully on each side for 3 minutes, being vigilant with the heat so that the leaf does not scorch. Place the cooked parcels on hot plates and garnish each one with another thin slice of nasturtium butter, a flower and a couple of tiny leaves. I usually also serve lemon wedges separately.

Nasturtium

Bramley Apples Baked with Chocolate, Hazelnuts and Sultanas

Gosh, how times have changed. When we were growing up, we were occasionally allowed to bring a Bramley apple in from the orchard, slice it thinly and dip the cold pieces in granulated white sugar before eating it. Mind you, my mother did keep an eye on us to make sure we did not eat too many of these wincingly bittersweet treats, as she knew – and indeed, we knew – that too many slices could definitely lead to 'a pain in my tummy'. I vividly remember the crunchy texture of the sugar and the almost lemony tang of the bitter apple. It was without doubt what would nowadays be called a taste sensation. I wonder how many children taste such a thing these days – not too many, I suspect, in a world full of terrifying and mixed messages about food. We must not forget the joy of food, the joy of remembered moments around the table, the joy of sharing and of memories made.

There is something rather lovely about a baked apple though. They have a retro appeal, certainly, but much more importantly, when properly cooked at the correct time of the year, they are a joy. The best time as far as I am concerned is when the apples are either still on the trees or shortly afterwards. When they are fresh off the tree, they are full of juice and this yields the fluffiest and lightest baked apple. The apple I always bake is the crimson variety of the Bramley, which has the most delicate pink hue to the steaming froth within.

The timing of a baked apple is all-important. The flesh of the cooked apple needs to be cooked through and almost like froth, and at the same time the apple should look as plump as a pigeon at harvest time. An overcooked baked apple is a sad, shrivelled and dishevelled sight. I am still as amused by the pale marshmallow-pink midriff of the cooked apple just beginning to ooze out of the stretched and shrinking skin as I was when I watched them coming out of the oven at home as a child.

There is something rather lovely about a baked apple though. They have a retro appeal, certainly, but much more importantly, when properly cooked at the correct time of the year, they are a joy.

By the time these apples are cooked, the chocolate will have melted into a sauce that combines beautifully with the juices in the bottom of the roasting dish, with the sultanas and hazelnuts adding further texture and flavour. I like cold softly whipped cream with the hot apples, which I serve on hot plates. Others will perhaps like thin custard.

Serves 4
— 4 Bramley apples
— 6–8 teaspoons Barbados soft dark brown sugar
— 40g chocolate (54% cocoa solids), chopped into small pieces
— 30g butter, diced
— 50g hazelnuts
— 30g sultanas or raisins
— 200ml apple juice

To serve
— Chilled softly whipped cream

choc stuffed apple

Preheat the oven to 180°C.

Using an apple corer, punch a hole right down though the core of each apple. If the hole looks a little narrow, I sometimes punch a second hole to make plenty of room for the filling. Now you need to score an incision about 1mm deep all around the belly of the apple. This allows the skin to shrink during cooking and prevents the apple from bursting.

Place the apples in an ovenproof baking dish. The apples should be snug but not touching each other.

Start filling each apple with 1 teaspoon of sugar followed by some chocolate, then some butter, hazelnuts and sultanas. Use a little force, such as your thumb, to press the ingredients into the opening, pushing in as much as you can. Scatter all the chocolate, hazelnuts and sultanas that won't fit in the hollowed apples around the apples in the dish. Top each stuffed apple with the remaining sugar and pour the apple juice over and around the apples.

Cover the dish with a piece of dampened non-stick baking paper. Bake in the preheated oven for about 30 minutes, until the apples are completely tender but still holding their shape.

Serve the apples as soon as possible on hot plates and spoon over the juices, fruit and nuts from the baking dish. Chilled softly whipped cream is the perfect accompaniment.

Asparagus with Coolea Fonduta, Lemon and Marjoram

The classic Italian fonduta sauce is made from Fontina, a wonderful melting cow's milk cheese from Val d'Aosta in Piedmont. Here I am using Coolea, a marvellous Irish cow's milk cheese from County Cork, which is rather more local to me and I think it is glorious. The vegetable featured here, asparagus, definitely deserves glorification.

The long slender growing habit of the asparagus adds to the grandness that surrounds this aristocrat of the soil and exaggerates that lofty position. It emerges from the ground, tall and haughty, looking like a weapon, hence the word 'spear' best used to describe its shape.

It occupies a particular period in the calendar, generally May and June, in this part of the world, though with temperatures changing, these times are definitely going to change too. It is one of the ingredients that I most look forward to over the course of the year, mainly because it is utterly delicious when locally grown, recently harvested and properly cooked. It falls into the category of ingredients that I eat only when it is in season here in Ireland. There is of course wonderful asparagus grown in other countries, but generally by the time it gets here, it is a pale imitation of what it can be like when local and fresh. It starts to lose sweetness very soon after being harvested, so in an ideal world it must be treated like a local ingredient.

It can be eaten cooked or raw. When raw, it is shaved very thinly before being dressed. I like it best cooked and I cook it in boiling salted water until tender. Traditionally it was often tied into bunches before cooking and placed in tall, narrow saucepans so that most of the vegetable was cooked by the steam rather than the water. I never felt that this way of cooking was any advantage, as the spears simmering loose in boiling water always works better for me.

It falls into the category of ingredients that I eat only when it is in season here in Ireland. There is of course wonderful asparagus grown in other countries, but generally by the time it gets here, it is a pale imitation of what it can be like when local and fresh.

The sauce is undeniably rich, so it is crucial to serve just the correct amount. I like to serve hot toast or grilled sourdough bread on the side. If the seasonal stars align, a bowl of freshly cooked new potatoes would also be lovely and would make the dish into a meat-free main course. This sauce is also good served with sea kale, in which case I replace the marjoram with fried sage leaves.

Serves 4
— 600g asparagus spears (this will yield approx. 450g after trimming and peeling)
— 100ml cream
— 100g Coolea cheese, grated
— 1 tablespoon fresh marjoram leaves
— Zest of 1 small lemon
— Sea salt and freshly ground black pepper

To serve
— Toast, grilled bread or new potatoes

Prepare each spear of asparagus separately by snapping off the tough bottom of each stalk where it naturally breaks when gently encouraged. Using a swivel peeler, peel any remaining tough skin from the base of the spears to ensure there will be no unpleasant stringy bits.

Bring a large saucepan of water to a rolling boil and salt generously. Add the asparagus and poach, uncovered, until tender. This will take about 5 minutes, but may take longer depending on the thickness of the spears.

While the asparagus is cooking, bring the cream to a simmer in a small saucepan and allow to bubble very gently for 3 minutes. You don't want the cream to visibly thicken or change colour. Add the grated cheese and gently melt it into the sauce while stirring with a wooden spoon and return to a bare simmer. Remove from the heat and add salt and pepper to taste. The sauce can be made ahead of time and reheated over a gentle heat later. If you plan to reheat the sauce later, I find that adding a tablespoon or two of the asparagus cooking water helps to bring the sauce back to its original silky-smooth consistency.

Drain the cooked asparagus well and place on hot plates. Drizzle over the bubbling hot sauce and sprinkle the marjoram leaves and grated lemon zest over each serving. Serve immediately with either toast or grilled bread on the side or new potatoes if a more robust dish is required.

Mackerel Cakes with Spiced Tomato Oil

Mackerel is without doubt one of my favourite fish and I will eat it almost any way it is prepared. My only caveat in the case of this wonderful fish is that it is really fresh. The fresh fish will be firm and shining in appearance, with the eyes clear and the gills pink and pert. The firm texture of the mackerel is ideal for these cakes and makes cooking them rather easy, as they hold their shape perfectly in the pan. The ginger and green chilli are lovely with the meaty flavour of the fish, as they freshen up the flavour. The couscous coating adds a nice crunch to the outside of the cakes and allows you to form them into perfect shapes.

There are so many sauces and salads that will be good with the crisp cooked cakes. The suggested spiced tomato oil is perfect, as tomatoes and mackerel are a wonderful match. I might even serve a plain mayonnaise as well as the oil. The spices in the tomato oil will complement the chilli and ginger well. The aubergine and ginger pickle on page 229 is another obvious match, as is the Mexican courgette salad on page 70. A salad of seasonal leaves will always be pleasing.

My only caveat in the case of this wonderful fish is that it is really fresh. The fresh fish will be firm and shining in appearance, with the eyes clear and the gills pink and pert.

Serves 4
— 500g mackerel fillets, skin on and deboned
— Zest of 1 lemon
— 2 garlic cloves, peeled and crushed to a paste
— 1 tablespoon chopped fresh coriander leaves
— 2 teaspoons finely chopped fresh green chilli
— 2 teaspoons finely grated fresh ginger
— Couscous, to coat
— 1 tablespoon extra virgin olive oil
— 10g butter
— Sea salt and freshly ground black pepper

To serve
— Spiced tomato oil (page 8)

Cut 250g of the mackerel into 1cm pieces. Place the remaining 250g in a food processor and use the pulse button to render it to a coarse purée. This takes only a matter of seconds.

Mix the diced and puréed mackerel in a bowl with the lemon zest, garlic, coriander, chilli and ginger and season with salt and pepper. Fry a tiny piece of the mixture in a pan until cooked and taste to check the seasoning.

Shape the mixture into four neat round cakes with straight sides and flat on the top and bottom. Roll in the couscous to coat the top, bottom and sides. The cakes can be refrigerated until later if necessary.

Heat the oil and butter in a small pan until foaming, then add the cakes. Reduce the heat somewhat and cook on both sides until golden in colour and firm to the touch.

Serve the cakes on hot plates with spiced tomato oil.

Mackerel

Chanterelle Mushrooms

Chanterelle Mushroom Custards with Tarragon Toasts

These delicate little savoury custards make an elegant starter or supper dish. The chanterelle mushroom is one of the glories of all wild foods and much sought out by foragers and cooks alike. Also known as girolles, they are delicious with so many different savoury foods. White poultry such as chicken, guinea fowl and turkey sit brilliantly with them. They are also good with fish. In fact, one of my favourite dishes of the year is a big fat summer plaice simply baked and served with butter melted with thyme leaves, parsley, fennel and chives and the sautéed mushrooms folded through. Heaven. A big pile of them straight from the pan and piled onto hot buttered toast is easy to achieve and also a joy. I fold them through scrambled eggs with a little cream and Parmesan and pop those on toast as well for a fabulous treat.

The mushrooms need a little preparation with a dry brush and a small sharp knife before cooking. I cut off the very base of the stalk and brush off any detritus remaining from the ground where they grew. It is best to avoid washing them, as they soak up the water and cook out to a rather soggy consistency. In fact, when buying chanterelles, it is best to try to find ones that look as if they have been picked during dry weather. Remember that the water or rain they may have absorbed will be adding weight on the scales, hence adding to the cost.

Many years ago I spent some time working in the kitchen at Le Manoir aux Quat'Saisons in Oxford, cooking with the marvellous Raymond Blanc. When we were preparing these mushrooms there, we would delicately pare the skin off the stalk to reveal a beautiful butter-coloured stalk. This undoubtedly added to the elegance of their appearance, making the pared stalk look like a long, fine heel of a lady's shoe. The effect was purely cosmetic, though, and this level of detail is not necessary at home.

The mushrooms need a little preparation with a dry brush and a small sharp knife before cooking. I cut off the very base of the stalk and brush off any detritus remaining from the ground where they grew. It is best to avoid washing them, as they soak up the water and cook out to a rather soggy consistency.

I have cooked these custards in all manner of receptacle, ranging from heatproof glasses or classic ceramic dariole moulds to espresso cups. All that matters is that they are the correct size and of course can bear the heat of the oven. I usually sit them on a saucer lined with a paper doily and serve a teaspoon as the appropriate cutlery. I should mention that I have a love–hate relationship with paper doilies, mostly hate, but in this case the rather fussy little lacy paper prevents them from slipping and sliding around the saucer as you dip your spoon in and out of the gorgeous set custard.

Serves 8
Mushrooms
— 10g butter, plus extra melted butter for greasing
— 1 tablespoon extra virgin olive oil
— 1 garlic clove, peeled and finely chopped
— 200g chanterelle mushrooms, cleaned and coarsely chopped into 2cm pieces
— 2 tablespoons chopped fresh flat-leaf parsley
— Sea salt and freshly ground black pepper

Custard
— 300ml cream
— 2 eggs
— 1 egg yolk
— 50g grated Parmesan cheese

Tarragon toasts
— 50g butter, at room temperature
— 1 heaped tablespoon chopped fresh tarragon
— 8 slices of white yeast or sourdough bread

You will need
— 8 x 100ml ovenproof containers

Preheat the oven to 180°C. Lightly brush 8 x 100ml ovenproof containers with melted butter.

To cook the chanterelles, melt the butter and olive oil in a sauté pan and allow to foam. Add the chopped garlic and stir for

5 seconds. Add the prepared mushrooms and season with salt and pepper. Stir to mix with a wooden spoon and sauté over a moderately hot heat until the mushrooms are wilting and tender. Do not fry them at too fierce a heat, as this can toughen their delicate texture. Remove from the pan and allow to cool. When slightly cooled, stir in the chopped parsley. If the mushrooms exude a lot of liquid in the cooking, leave it in the pan after removing the cooked mushrooms, bubble that liquid until thick and syrupy in consistency and add to the cooked mushrooms. This concentration of the cooking juices adds greatly to the flavour.

To make the custard, whisk the cream, eggs and egg yolk, Parmesan and some salt and pepper together. Divide the cold mushrooms between the buttered containers and pour over the custard to fill the containers about three-quarters full.

Place the custards in a deep roasting tray or ovenproof dish such as one you might use for a lasagne. Place in the oven and pour water from a just-boiled kettle to come halfway up along the sides of the receptacles. Cover with a piece of dampened greaseproof or non-stick baking paper.

Cook in the preheated oven for 20–25 minutes, until the custards are just set. You will know they are cooked when the custard has set to a wobble rather than an undercooked ripple.

To make the tarragon toasts, mix the butter and chopped tarragon. Toast the slices of bread on both sides. Remove the crusts, then spread with the tarragon butter. Cut each slice into four to six soldiers.

Remove the custards from the oven and allow to cool for 5 minutes before serving with a teaspoon for each guest and soldiers of tarragon toast.

Light a Candle

I nearly always light a candle in the evening before I sit down to eat. This may seem like a pretentious little happening, but whatever it is about igniting a little flame, it amuses me. Somehow it is like drawing a breath for oneself, the briefest moment of introspection at the end of the day and a moment to give thanks for what we are about to receive. Candles are everywhere nowadays and I think their function as a source of light is rarely the reason for lighting them anymore. Growing up, candles appeared at birthdays and at Christmas. People of my mother's generation who had lived through the time before electrification must have been relieved to be able to enter a room and illuminate the entire space with the flick of a switch. It must have been liberating indeed not having to deal with the messy old oil lamps that also bolstered the wax and wick. I vaguely remember my mother cautioning us as to the dangers of candles as a fire hazard, and my romance with the atmospheric, if somewhat superfluous, glow created was brought into sharp relief by tales of houses burned to the ground.

Candles in church were another thing altogether, and growing up that was where most of them were. There, they took on a rather more mysterious appearance, their effect exaggerated by the dim lighting and swirling noxious smoke from the thurible, that rather blingy piece of church paraphernalia that belched out highly scented emissions. Speaking of noxious scents, I have never met a scented candle I wanted to dine with. It's a simple unscented altar candle on the table and occasionally a coloured version of the same, but no fruits of the forest or Caribbean breezes swirling about my food. That is not to say that I don't like scented candles in other parts of the house – one of my favourite ones, from a chi-chi Parisian company, is chosen especially for its capacity to evoke a feeling of being in front row seats in St Peter's Basilica in Rome. I can also tolerate the scent of bay or tuber roses, but never at the table. No smell, please, just the glow.

Asparagus Mousse with Chervil Sauce

This is a delicate, elegant and refined little mousse, which I like to prepare a couple of times during the asparagus season. The combination of asparagus and chervil is a classic one and works beautifully.

Chervil is that rather trembling little herb with a faint aniseed flavour. Related to parsley, but oh so much more refined looking than the sturdy parsley, it looks wonderful growing, as its very light stems and stalks will be shaken by even the mildest breeze to create a hazy, shimmering appearance. It is simplicity itself to grow and I have often popped a few seeds into a flower pot, where it makes a lovely companion to more colourful plants. If you cannot find chervil, you could replace it with a small pinch of chopped tarragon or mint, both of which will pair well with the vegetable.

I like to serve the mousse in small portions, as it is quite rich. The uncooked mousse will keep perfectly in the fridge for 12 hours, so this is a dish you can get organised with.

The technique for the light and flavoursome sauce is really useful and the suggested asparagus and chervil here could be replaced another day with fresh peas and mint or cucumber and fennel.

The technique for the light and flavoursome sauce is really useful and the suggested asparagus and chervil here could be replaced another day with fresh peas and mint or cucumber and fennel.

Serves 8

Mousse
— 850ml water
— 225g asparagus, weighed after peeling and trimming
— 140g chicken breast
— 1 egg
— 1 egg yolk
— 150ml milk
— 4 sprigs of fresh chervil, chopped, plus extra leaves for garnish
— 200ml cream
— Melted butter, for brushing

— Sea salt and freshly ground black pepper

Sauce
— 4 tablespoons asparagus cooking water
— 110g butter, diced and chilled
— 8 peeled, trimmed and fully cooked asparagus spears, cut into 3 or 4 pieces at an angle
— 1 tablespoon chopped fresh chervil
— Squeeze of lemon juice

You will need
— 8 heatproof ramekins, approx. 100ml each

Preheat the oven to 180°C.

Bring the water to the boil. Add a pinch of salt and the prepared raw asparagus spears and cook, uncovered, for 4 minutes. **Reserve 4 tablespoons of the cooking water for the sauce.** Strain the asparagus and refresh in iced water. Drain and place on a tea towel and pat dry.

Cut the chicken breast into small dice and place in the bowl of a food processor. Purée the chicken breast briefly, just to break it up. Chop up the cooked asparagus and add to the chicken with the egg and egg yolk, milk, chervil and a pinch of salt. Purée again until quite smooth. Add the cream and blend once more until a fine, smooth purée is achieved. Strain the mixture through a fine-mesh sieve, pushing hard to get as much of the mixture through as possible. The more of the mixture you manage to push through the sieve, the better the flavour will be.

Brush eight heatproof ramekins with a little melted butter and place a disc of non-stick baking paper in the bottom of each mould. This will make turning out the cooked mousse easier and neater. Fill the moulds, then tap them on the countertop to ensure there are no air bubbles and smooth the surfaces to ensure a neat finish. The uncooked mousse can now be chilled and will sit happily in the fridge for 12 hours or longer.

When ready to cook, place the mousse in a bain-marie where the simmering water comes halfway up the sides of the ramekins. I use an ovenproof dish or tray about 8cm deep for the bain-marie, pop in the ramekins and half fill the container from a kettle that has just gone off the boil. Cover with a sheet of parchment paper and cook in the preheated oven for 20–25 minutes, until just set. When the mousse is cooked, it will feel gently firm to the touch of your finger. Catching the mousse when it is just cooked and set is vital, as if it cooks for too long, it will become too firm and spongy and will lose its tender charm. Turn off the heat in the oven and the mousse will sit there quite happily while you make the sauce.

To make the sauce, put the reserved asparagus cooking water in a small saucepan and bring to a simmer. Over a low heat, whisk in the cold butter a couple of bits at a time. Keep whisking and gradually the sauce will thicken lightly. Continue until all the butter has been incorporated. Add the asparagus and warm through for 2 minutes, then remove from the heat. Add the chopped chervil and a squeeze of lemon juice. Taste and correct the seasoning.

Unmould the mousse onto hot plates, not forgetting to remove the disc of baking paper, and spoon the sauce and asparagus over. Serve garnished with chervil leaves.

Compote of Cherries

Is there a prettier sight than a cherry tree in full blossom or indeed laden down with glossy fruit later in the year? Is there a more delicious moment than when you bite the first shiny cherry off the stalk when the new season fruit arrives? As far as I am concerned, that first taste is one of the year's highlights and reminds me to be thankful for nature's extraordinary bounty. Wild cherry trees flourish all over Ireland, but it is usually the birds that get to eat these generally out-of-reach, slightly tart and wildly flavoured fruits. It is only in the recent past that cherries have been grown commercially here, and what a joy to be able to get baskets of the now locally grown fruit.

Many years ago when I was cooking in Paris, a bag of cherries nearly landed me in hot water. A friend and I decided it was great fun to throw the cherry stones at each other as we walked down the rather grand Rue Saint-Honoré. Well, a haughty gendarme thought that this was not the slightest bit amusing. Even with my slim grasp of the language, I was able to discern that he was calling both of us savages and that we should take more care to be respectful of the streets of his beloved city. Deeply embarrassed at our youthful tomfoolery and as red faced as the cherries themselves, we scuffled around on the ground to retrieve the cherry stones and scuttled off to eat the rest in subdued silence. That rather took the shine off that particular bag of cherries.

This recipe is a masterclass in simplicity. Four ingredients all cooked together at a very gentle heat produce a pure, delicious flavour. I like to serve the cherries in several different ways. When served warm with ice-cold pouring cream, they are something of a revelation. You can also imagine how well the hot fruit would pair with a chocolate ice cream or sorbet. They are also good with an almond praline ice cream; almond pairs well with almost any stone fruit. When chilled, they will usually be an accompaniment to a rich confection such as crème brûlée or panna cotta.

This recipe is a masterclass in simplicity. Four ingredients all cooked together at a very gentle heat produce a pure, delicious flavour.

Serves 4
— 450g cherries, with stones left in
— 110g caster sugar
— 2 tablespoons kirsch
— 1 tablespoon freshly squeezed lemon juice

Place the cherries, sugar, kirsch and lemon juice in a small low-sided saucepan. Cover and place on a very gentle heat. The sugar needs to melt and the cherries need to soften slightly. If the heat is too high, the juice that leaks from the cherries will be cooked off and you will not end up with a ruby-coloured syrup. They take about 20 minutes to cook until just tender but still holding their shape. The cherries can be served warm or chilled.

Salted Hake with Roast Pepper and Basil Oil

Salting fish has been used as a way of preserving fish for time immemorial. Many people will have seen large fillets of heavily salted fish in European markets or further afield. They are quite a sight when hard as a board, hanging or stacked high, they look like an ingredient from times past and the uninitiated may be perplexed.

At first glance, it seems almost impossible that this rather odd-looking ingredient could be transformed into something delicious to eat. Personally, I find them intriguing to observe and quite beautiful in an unconventional way. There is a quality to their presentation that would not seem out of place in a gallery displaying modern contemporary art. The appearance of the dried and salty fillets suggests great age even though they are sometimes just weeks old. I remember seeing fillets of salted fish hanging on a clothesline near the fishing village of Ballycotton in Cork – an extraordinary sight for a young boy from the landlocked Midlands.

The fish in this recipe is salted not to preserve it, but to change the texture and flavour for gentle poaching at a later stage. The process gives the fish a toothsome quality, combining heightened flavour and a firmer texture. Many fish can be salted, but here I am using hake, which produces a beautifully white and firm result, but cod is also wonderful. Less glamorous species such as pollock and ling are greatly improved by a light salting, in my opinion.

The garlic cream and the roast pepper and basil oil can be prepared ahead for this dish, making the final assembly rather easy. Serve with fluffy mashed potatoes or boiled new potatoes and a green vegetable.

Serves 4 as a main course or 8 as a starter
Salted hake
— 50g flaky sea salt
— 4 x 150g pieces of hake, filleted and skinned
— 75ml cream

The fish in this recipe is salted not to preserve it, but to change the texture and flavour for gentle poaching at a later stage.

— 50ml extra virgin olive oil
— 1 garlic clove, peeled and crushed to a paste

Roast pepper and basil oil
— 1 large red pepper
— 2 tablespoons extra virgin olive oil, plus extra for rubbing
— 1–2 teaspoons vino cotto or balsamic vinegar
— 6–8 fresh basil leaves
— Sea salt and freshly ground black pepper

Scatter half of the flaky sea salt over the base of a dish that the hake will fit into snugly. Put the hake on top and scatter with the remaining salt. Pat the salt onto the surface of the fish. Cover and chill for 4 hours. While the fish is salting, prepare the pepper and basil oil.

Preheat the oven to 220°C.

Place the red pepper on an oven tray, rub all over with a little olive oil and season with salt and pepper. Roast in the preheated oven for about 30 minutes. The pepper should be well coloured and starting to collapse and the skin should be blistered. Remove from the oven, place in a bowl and seal tightly with cling film and allow to cool. When cool, peel off the skin and remove the seeds. Cut the pepper flesh into neat 0.5cm dice. Season with salt and pepper and dress with the olive oil and a few drops of vino cotto or balsamic vinegar. Chop or tear the basil finely and immediately stir through the peppers and oil. Retain at room temperature.

After the salting period, remove the fish and rinse off the salt thoroughly under a cold running tap. Place the fish in a saucepan, ensuring a snug fit, and cover with cold water. Bring to a simmer and cook gently for 6–10 minutes, until the fish is just cooked through. Pour off the cooking water, draining it well, leaving the fish in the pan.

In a separate small saucepan, heat the cream, olive oil and garlic to just under the boiling point, then pour over the fish. Bring the fish and cream back to a bare simmer.

To assemble the dish, transfer the fish to a large heated serving dish or individual plates. Pour the hot cream over the fish and drizzle the peppers and some of the basil-infused oil over the top. Serve immediately.

Leek Mousse with Mussels and Sauce Bretonne

This mousse is rich and should be served in small portions. The mussels can be replaced with shrimp or lobster. I have also served the mousse as a vegetable accompaniment with roast chicken and guinea fowl and firm-textured fish like sole, monkfish, turbot and brill. The mousse can be prepared early in the day and cooked later.

The Bretonne sauce is an excellent sauce to serve with the fish mentioned above. Refer to the recipe for mussels with fennel and cannellini beans on page 12 for detailed instructions on how to cook the mussels.

Serves 6–8
— 36–48 fresh mussels

Mousse
— 20g butter, plus extra melted butter for brushing
— 450g leeks, sliced and washed
— 3 eggs
— 300ml cream
— Sea salt and freshly ground black pepper

Sauce
— 2 egg yolks
— 1 teaspoon Dijon mustard
— ½ teaspoon white wine vinegar
— 110g butter
— 1 tablespoon chopped fresh herbs (chives, parsley, thyme, chervil, tarragon)

You will need
— 6–8 ceramic or metal moulds, approx. 100ml each

Preheat the oven to 170°C. Brush the moulds with melted butter and line the bottoms with a disc of non-stick baking paper.

This mousse is rich and should be served in small portions.

Melt the butter in a small low-sided saucepan and allow to foam. Add the leeks, toss them in the butter to coat and season with salt and pepper. Cover with a disc of greaseproof paper and a tight-fitting lid. Cook on a very gentle heat until the leeks are just tender. Drain the leeks and press off all the excess liquid. Allow to cool for a few minutes, then place in a blender and add the eggs and cream. Purée until smooth and taste to correct the seasoning. Place the mousse mixture in the prepared moulds, filling the moulds to the top.

When ready to cook, place the mousse in a bain-marie where the simmering water comes halfway up the sides of the moulds. I use an ovenproof dish or tray about 8cm deep for the bain-marie, pop in the moulds and half fill the container from a kettle that has just gone off the boil. Cover tightly with a sheet of parchment paper and cook in the preheated oven for about 20 minutes, until the mousse is just set. Remove from the oven and keep warm.

Place the mussels in a clean frying pan, cover with a lid and place on a low heat. They will gradually start to pop open and release their own cooking juices. Remove the shells from the pan as soon as they open. Reserve the cooking liquid. When all the mussels are cooked, remove the beards and carefully remove the mussels from the shells, then add them to the cooking liquid.

Place the egg yolks in a Pyrex bowl with the mustard and vinegar. Melt the butter and bring to a boil. Slowly drizzle the boiling butter onto the egg yolks, whisking all the time. The sauce will gradually begin to thicken. Continue until all the melted butter has been added. Add the chopped herbs. Add the cooked mussels and some of their cooking juices to the sauce. The sauce should be quite thin.

To serve, unmould the mousse onto warm plates. Drizzle a little sauce and some mussels around and over each mousse. Garnish with a relevant herb, such as fennel fronds, dill or chervil. Serve immediately.

Leek Mousse Shrimps

Almond Tuiles

Almond tuiles are a classic French biscuit, shaped immediately after cooking to look like an old-fashioned curved terracotta roof tile. A corrugated metal tray or tuile pan is usually used to shape the cooked tuiles, but a rolling pin or even a bottle will also achieve the required shape.

The almonds in the recipe can be replaced with other thinly sliced nuts, such as hazelnuts or Brazil nuts, and other flavourings, such as orange or lemon zest, can be added to the uncooked batter, but I am using a classic version of the recipe here. I serve these with coffee after dinner, but honestly they are delicious at any time of the day. Served alongside a bowl of perfectly ripe pears or peaches, they combine to make a simple but rewarding dessert. They are also good served with ice creams or sorbets. I occasionally zest an orange or lemon over the cooked and cooled tuiles just before serving.

Makes 12
— A little sunflower or grapeseed oil, for brushing
— 70g egg whites
— 115g caster sugar
— 20g plain flour
— Pinch of salt
— 25g butter, melted and cooled
— 125g flaked almonds

Preheat the oven to 180°C. Line a baking tray with non-stick baking paper. Brush the paper with a little tasteless oil such as sunflower or grapeseed.

Place the eggs whites in a mixing bowl, then add the sugar, flour and a pinch of salt. Combine well with a whisk, then add the melted butter and whisk again to achieve a batter-type consistency. Add the flaked almonds and gently mix them through the batter. This uncooked batter will keep in the fridge for several days if you don't wish to use it all in one go.

Using a teaspoon, spread the mixture into flat round discs about 8cm in diameter on the lined tray. The batter will look thin on the paper, but that is the key to light and crunchy tuiles. The mixture does not spread in the cooking, so several will fit on a standard oven tray. A word of caution, though, as you have to act quickly when the tuiles are cooked and still soft, so I think it is better to cook them in batches of four.

Bake in the preheated oven for 8–10 minutes, until golden brown. The edges will colour more quickly than the centres, but hold your nerve to get a good colour on the centres of the tuiles too, otherwise you may end up with a soft-centred, chewy result, which is not what you want here. If your oven cooks unevenly, change the positioning of the tray during the cooking time.

Immediately after the tuiles are cooked and acting quite quickly, remove one at a time with a fish slice from the baking paper and place it nutty side facing down on a tuile tray or nutty side facing up if draping them over a wooden spoon or bottle. They will be soft while hot and will solidify on cooling. When the tuiles are cool and crisp, store in an airtight box lined with kitchen paper.

Dust off your baking paper and save it for another day.

Mango and Cucumber Gazpacho

This recipe came about as a result of a trip to South East Asia. During a big freeze in Europe, I was fortunate to be dipping my toes in the warm waters of the Andaman Sea and eating delicious exotic foods. The alarming and regular messages from home of icy roads, snow drifts and frozen pipes only added to the luxuriant feeling I was having. One warm and balmy evening we were served little shots of what was called a mango and cucumber gazpacho. It was great, and when I came home I started experimenting immediately and this is the result. The addition of a drizzle of olive oil and chopped mint at the end is my own and is optional. However, if you have a really good bottle of olive oil, few dishes will showcase it as well as this one.

You will need to think ahead, and indeed shop ahead, in the case of the mango. It needs to be ripe and juicy. The way to test a mango for ripeness is to press on the flesh with the heel of your thumb – if the flesh yields gently and your thumb leaves a little dent or impression in the surface of the fruit, then generally it is ripe and ready to use. Mangos fall into the same category as avocados in that they are either perfect to eat or not suitable at all. There is no grey area with this fruit. I tend to buy them slightly under-ripe and then allow them to come to a state of perfection sitting on my kitchen counter for a few days.

The most revered mango of the year is the Alphonso, which generally appears around April and continues until June. We associate that variety of the fruit with India, but of course it is grown in many other countries also. The best mango I have ever eaten was in Mexico, where street vendors peel the fruit, then mount it on a pronged fork and you can walk along the street eating it just as you would an ice cream. The only downside of this exercise is that the eater tends to get covered in sticky mango juice from ear to ear. Not a terrible price to pay for such a pleasure-filled experience. I find the variety called Kent to be reliable in this part of the world. In any event, finding that ripe and juicy fruit is key to the success of this recipe.

The way to test a mango for ripeness is to press on the flesh with the heel of your thumb – if the flesh yields gently and your thumb leaves a little dent or impression in the surface of the fruit, then generally it is ripe and ready to use.

Serves 4
— 1 ripe mango, about 425g
— 1 cucumber
— 1–2 teaspoons caster sugar
— Pinch of salt
— Zest and juice of 1 lime
— 2 teaspoons chopped fresh mint
— Extra virgin olive oil, for drizzling (optional)

Peel the mango with a swivel peeler. Slice the flesh off the stone and place in a bowl. Purée with a hand-held blender or in a liquidiser until completely smooth.

Peel and halve the cucumber lengthways. If there are lots of seeds, remove them with the aid of a melon baller or a teaspoon and purée to a smooth consistency. Fold the two purées together. Season with 1 teaspoon of sugar and a pinch of salt. The remaining sugar may be needed – the sweetness of the mango will determine this. Add the lime juice to taste. Mix well and taste and correct the seasoning, adding a little more lime juice, salt or sugar as needed. Cover and chill well.

Serve the gazpacho in small portions with a grating of lime zest, a pinch of chopped fresh mint and a drizzle of extra virgin olive oil (if using).

My Doodles

Like many people, I have always doodled. Whether in the margin of the page I am working on or on a scrap of paper nearby, I am almost always scribbling. Mostly these doodles were mindless (not to be confused with mindfulness) with no particular theme, rhyme or reason. However, over the years, and by accident, I have concentrated a bit more to elevate these shabby grotesques into recognisable images with a purpose rather than just a distraction.

When I started cooking professionally, I started keeping notebooks to act as an aide-mémoire for ideas, perhaps just a combination of ingredients to be experimented with in the future or definite recipes that had been tried and tested and then sometimes little illustrations to memorise a particular presentation. Occasionally I coloured in the drawings, though this was not the norm. This was a time before we had camera phones at our disposal to record every possible image we might or might not need to refer to in the future. There are zillions of those pictures in my phone and allegedly they are also safe in some cloud or other, but that is a concept I don't in any way understand.

I still use a notebook on a daily basis, mostly for the compilation of lists. I think I always will, but now my little drawings are done on my phone or tablet. I discovered this possibility when adding to a smartphone note one day. I decided to press the little pencil emoji and lo and behold, a new world of sketching possibilities opened up to me. Using my finger, I was able to mark down crude sketches that to a greater or lesser extent reflected what I was trying to record.

I started to get more interested in the possibility of the images when I found that some of them had personality and as much impact as the written word, and in some cases actually made a much stronger point. If in a recipe I am suggesting that the cook should stir vigorously, curiously, a simple sketch of just that seems to jump off the page rather than perhaps being skipped over and not taken seriously in the reading of the text. What fascinates me, though, is how some emotion seems to be transferred from my finger, through the device and into the image. It allows me to transfer some of the pleasure and the sheer joy I get from cooking, teaching and feeding people onto a page that I could never do with the manual use of pen, pencil, paint or paper. I find it fascinating that somehow a crude and rather ham-fisted sketch of an old-fashioned grater as suggested as the better tool to grate Parmesan cheese can be impactful.

In any event, these images are not the result of years spent mastering the art of drawing. I have not pursued the challenging path of the artist who spends countless hours, days, months and years honing an ancient craft. I have no illusions about my skill in this métier. Drawing is not my craft. These expressions are a conflux of passion, technology and a single digit and their purpose is to explain some of my craft or my love for my craft: cooking. If they please or ring a visual bell, that's great. If not, well, that's okay too.

Mexican Courgette Salad

This is a clean and fresh-tasting salad that is best made with really fresh and quite small courgettes. Large courgettes tend to be watery and not nearly as crisp as the little ones and this salad partly relies on that crispness for its charm. As a general rule, I serve very small courgettes raw in salads such as this, medium-sized ones I cook quickly over a high heat until tender and the largest ones are cooked slowly to a more collapsed texture. The vegetable has merit at all the different stages of growth, but seasonings and cooking methods change according to its size.

It is also worth mentioning that courgettes have a distinctive perfume, especially when freshly picked and ideally having never seen the inside of a fridge. Excessive refrigeration has a detrimental effect on many vegetables and also fruit. The difference between the flavour and texture of a vegetable or fruit that has been recently picked and never chilled (ideally still slightly warm from the plant in the case of summer fruit and vegetables) and one that has languished in chilly surroundings is huge. We sometimes forget to smell vegetables and though it is fair to say that not all vegetables will have you waxing lyrical when held and inhaled under the nose, there are certainly a few that I like to stop and enjoy their perfume. Tomatoes and cucumbers are a good case in point, as are beans, peas and asparagus.

The flavours here are both hot and cold at the same time, the heat coming from the chilli and the coolness coming from the lime. The final addition of the freshly chopped herbs adds a floral note. The salad is delicious as a refreshing summer starter and I also serve it with simple grilled or roast chicken legs or grilled fish such as mackerel or hake. A dab of nasturtium butter (page 36) on the meat or fish also works well with all the flavours.

Serves 4–6

— 4 small to medium-sized courgettes (about 15cm long, not too big and watery; smaller courgettes can also be used, you may just need a couple more)

— Juice of 1 lime (you may not need all the juice, so add to
  taste)
— 4–6 tablespoons extra virgin olive oil
— 1 fresh red chilli, deseeded and finely chopped
— 20 fresh mint leaves, torn or chopped just before using
— 2 tablespoons chopped fresh coriander leaves or flat-leaf
  parsley
— Sea salt and freshly ground black pepper

Cut the courgettes into 2cm dice, thick slices or into more
random angular shapes but of a similar size. Toss in the lime
juice, olive oil and chilli and season to taste with salt and pepper.

The courgette salad needs to sit for 30 minutes before eating
and is quite happy sitting for an hour. Just before serving,
add the chopped or torn herbs and fold them through the
courgettes. Serve immediately.

Simple Summer Cake with Raspberries and Lemon Basil

This cake is a joy to cook and a joy to eat. It is without doubt best eaten on the day it is made. It will of course be good the next day, but this type of sponge is best when it never gets a chance to become cold. When it becomes chilled, the loose and light sponge seizes somewhat, yielding a firmer and less tender texture. The flavour is also dulled by chilling and I think that the very best way to eat this is before the cake has even had a chance to become chillier than room temperature, almost retaining a whisper of heat from the oven.

The simple technique of briefly blending the raw cake ingredients could not be easier. This is not a cake you walk away from when blending, as prolonged mixing can toughen or even curdle the mixture. I use the pulse button on my food processor so it is almost impossible for me to overmix it.

The lemon glacé icing is also very easy, but you need to carefully watch the amount of lemon juice being added to the sugar so that you don't end up with an icing that is too thin and runny. A thin icing will not coat the top of the cake neatly, but rather will run away with a mind of its own, out of your control.

The decoration of raspberries and lemon basil is delicious and looks so pretty. The unsweetened red raspberries, which I like to cut crossways to reveal their interiors, look like a sparkling ruby ring and are a good foil for the sweetness of the cake and the icing. I like to see the berries cut in this way as it is a different view than one normally gets when they are generally presented whole.

This is a cake I would serve with a cup of tea or coffee, but in my opinion when freshly made and iced, it is perfectly lovely and appropriate served after lunch or dinner as a dessert, in which case I would serve a bowl of softly whipped cream alongside.

The very best way to eat this is before the cake has even had a chance to become chillier than room temperature, almost retaining a whisper of heat from the oven.

Serves 8–10

Cake
— 175g butter, at room temperature, plus extra for greasing
— 175g self-raising flour, plus extra for dusting
— 150g caster sugar
— 3 eggs, preferably free-range

Lemon glacé icing
— 160g icing sugar
— Finely grated zest of ½ lemon
— 2–3 tablespoons freshly squeezed lemon juice

Decoration
— 15 firm fresh raspberries
— 15–20 small lemon basil leaves

To serve
— Softly whipped cream

You will need
— 1 x 20.5cm sandwich tin

Preheat the oven to 180°C. Brush a 20.5cm sandwich tin with melted butter, flour the base of the tin and line with a disc of non-stick baking paper.

Put the soft butter, flour, sugar and eggs into the bowl of a food processor. Whizz for a few seconds to amalgamate. You may need to run a spatula around the sides and bottom of the processor bowl to loosen and integrate any unmixed mixture and pulse briefly again. Once the mixture comes together, that's it. Turn the mixture into the prepared tin and smooth the top.

Bake in the preheated oven for 25–30 minutes, until golden brown and well risen. The cooked cake will have shrunk very slightly from the edge of the tin and a skewer inserted into the cake will be dry and clean when retracted.

Cool in the tin for 10 minutes before carefully removing and cooling on a wire rack, paper side down.

Meanwhile, make the icing. Sieve the icing sugar into a bowl. Add the lemon zest and use a wooden spoon to beat in just enough lemon juice to make a soft icing that will spread hesitantly.

Once the cake is cool, remove the disc of paper and place the cake bottom side down on a pretty plate. Spread the icing over the top of the cake and use a palate knife to encourage it to drip gently over the sides. Use a sharp knife to cut the raspberries crossways to achieve little rings about 0.5cm thick. Dot these and the lemon basil leaves over the top of the cake. Serve with softly whipped cream.

Sauce Malaga (Roast Almond, Egg and Anchovy Sauce)

You find inspiration for new recipes and dishes in many different places. It might be a combination of ingredients that rings a bell when glimpsed in an article in a weekend food supplement, it might be a photograph on Instagram, a dish in a restaurant or sometimes an idea just pops into your head. Markets where lots of different ingredients are displayed side by side are also a likely spot to spark an idea. I find this particularly to be the case in markets in countries warmer than our own, such as France, Italy and Spain, where the range of ingredients is generally wider than at home. Markets in more exotic places, such as India or South East Asia, are also a potential treasure trove for ideas, but I tend to spend a lot of my time in those markets asking what a strange-looking ingredient is and how it is used. This can be a frustrating exercise, as often the craziest-looking ingredients may not be available at home, so they are not suitable for adding to a recipe in this part of the world. Of course, not all ideas are good ideas and not all tested dishes yield a palatable result, though it is very pleasing to come up with a new dish that you know will give pleasure not just to oneself but also to others.

This recipe came about as a result of a conversation with a friend who had eaten a dish in a tapas bar in Malaga. All he could tell me was that the dish – or was it a sauce? – was great and had contained hard-boiled eggs and almonds. That is not a lot to go with, but I roasted some almonds, hard boiled some eggs and the rest of the ingredients just seemed to make sense and ended up being pounded together with my pestle and mortar.

This combination may sound unusual, but it is really delicious. I serve the sauce with grilled or roast chicken or slow roast lamb and also roast vegetables such as carrots or beetroot. The technique for making the sauce may also sound strange, but mashing and pounding the ingredients with the pestle and mortar gives the sauce a very particular consistency.

This particular recipe came about as a result of a conversation with a friend who had eaten a dish in a tapas bar in Malaga. All he could tell me was that the dish – or was it a sauce? – was great and had contained hard-boiled eggs and almonds.

Makes enough sauce for 8–10 servings
— 50g unskinned almonds
— 2 eggs
— 4 anchovies, coarsely chopped
— 4 tablespoons extra virgin olive oil
— 1 tablespoon freshly squeezed lemon juice
— Sea salt and freshly ground black pepper

Preheat the oven to 180°C.

Place the almonds on an oven tray and roast in the preheated oven for about 20 minutes, until the almonds are richly coloured, starting to split and some of the skins are starting to lift off. Remove from the oven and allow to cool completely.

Place the eggs in a saucepan of boiling salted water and cook for exactly 10 minutes. Remove immediately and cool in a bowl of cold water. When cool, peel off the shells.

Place one-third of the cooled almonds, a pinch of ground black pepper and the anchovies in the mortar and start pounding. As the almonds start to break down, add another third of the almonds and a little olive oil as you go to loosen the mixture. When the final third of almonds has been added and the mixture is looking mushy, add in the whole hard-boiled eggs and pound those into the mixture. Add the remaining olive oil in increments to achieve a sauce that is slightly coarse yet creamy in consistency, somewhat similar to but not quite as refined as a pesto sauce. The sauce will need all the olive oil and the lemon juice can now be added to sharpen the flavour. I occasionally add a few drops of cold water while making the sauce and also when all the ingredients have been added to achieve the required soft and somewhat creamy consistency. The sauce rarely needs salt, as the anchovies are quite salty, but do taste just in case a few grains are needed.

Refrigerate until needed, but serve at room temperature.

Hot Smoked Salmon with Labneh and Watercress Oil

This is a lovely combination of flavours and textures and creates a stylish-looking dish.

The various elements of the dish can be prepared ahead for last-minute assembly. The lightly cooked texture of hot smoked salmon works well with the labneh and the vivid watercress oil adds sparkle and great flavour to the dish. If you have never made labneh before, perhaps this is the moment. It is simplicity itself and is useful in so many different ways. The recipe is on page 321.

The technique for making the watercress oil is also easy, but is perhaps one of those recipes that is hard to believe until you have actually made it once. The resulting flavoured oil is wonderful and a truly fabulous shade of green. When you have made it for the first time, you will quickly realise that many other leaves will also work brilliantly. I make it with chives, wild garlic, rocket and basil with terrific results, all of which would be good here.

This dish can be served family style, passing the salmon, labneh and oil separately for guests to serve themselves. It also looks great with the labneh spread on a large platter with a dip in the centre to hold a pool of the verdant oil. The pieces of smoked salmon can then be draped over the edge of the labneh to handsome effect. If you prefer to arrange individual plates, care needs to be taken to assemble the ingredients in the correct proportion. If you can't find coriander flowers, sprigs of watercress or leaves appropriate to your oil of choice will be perfect.

I usually serve brown bread and butter alongside this dish.

Serves 4
— 320g labneh (page 321)
— 300–350g hot smoked salmon
— 4–6 tablespoons watercress oil (see the next page)
— 4 pinches of chilli flakes
— Fresh coriander leaves and flowers
— Sea salt and freshly ground black pepper

The technique for making the watercress oil is also easy, but is perhaps one of those recipes that is hard to believe until you have actually made it once. The resulting flavoured oil is wonderful and a truly fabulous shade of green.

Divide the labneh between four plates. Season with salt and pepper.

Using a wet tablespoon, make a shallow depression in the back of each mound of labneh. Place a piece of salmon beside the labneh. Drizzle on the oil, making sure some of it rests in the little depression. Scatter a pinch of chilli flakes over each plate, followed by the coriander leaves and flowers. Serve immediately.

Watercress Oil
This will yield more oil than you will need for the recipe, but it keeps perfectly in a sealed container for a month. I drizzle it over grilled meats, poultry, fish and vegetables or use it in a vinaigrette.

— 200g watercress leaves or tender stalks or spring onion greens
— 320ml sunflower oil

Roughly chop the greens and blend with the oil in a liquidiser or blender on full speed until completely smooth. Strain the oil through a square of muslin. You will have to squeeze the muslin to extract the green oil, otherwise if you have time you can hang it up over a bowl and allow it to drip overnight.

Freeze the strained oil. Once the oil is frozen, scrape the frozen oil into a new container, leaving behind the frozen water residue, which you can discard. This process will give you perfectly clear green oil.

RAMSONS

Chicken Braised with Wild Garlic and Lemon

This dish is fairly simple to prepare and quite delicious to eat. The quantity of wild garlic may seem excessive, but when cooked this way the green garlic flavour is subtle and sophisticated. The volume of sauce is scant, but the depth of flavour is such that it is sufficient.

The arrival of the wild garlic is a delightful moment for all cooks, a sure sign that spring has arrived or at least is close at hand and that nature is providing us with a much-needed tonic of this green goodness. It has so many different uses in soups, sauces, herb relishes and pestos, broths, stews, with almost any fish and shellfish you can think of, braised and roast poultry and meat ... the list goes on and on. It is tremendous stuff and it is everywhere.

The first wild garlic to appear as early as January is the slender-leaved *Allium triquetrum*, also known as three-cornered leek. The leaves, with a similarity to a daffodil leaf, are distinctive on close inspection, as each leaf indeed has three distinct corners. Each stem produces a little bunch of bell-like flowers, also delicious, and these pretty little blossoms are part of the reason why the plant is sometimes confused with white bells, a relation of the bluebell and definitely not edible, and why to some the plant is also known as snowbell. Every part of the plant is edible, including the tiny little garlic-like bulbs and even the roots attached that grow and anchor the plant beneath the soil. The bulbs can be pickled in a simple brine for using at other times of the year. Once you become familiar with the growing habit of the plant, you will start to notice it everywhere and will perhaps wonder how you could possibly have missed seeing it all along. It seems to be as comfortable in urban as rural settings and generally it prefers the sunny side of the road.

The later garlic, a lover of a shady wooded spots, is *Allium ursinum* and is easy to tell apart from its skinnier cousin by its much broader leaves and star-shaped clusters of flowers. Known widely as ramsons, I once cooked this treasure in plenty of Irish

The arrival of the wild garlic is a delightful moment for all cooks, a sure sign that spring has arrived or at least is close at hand and that nature is providing us with a much-needed tonic of this green goodness.

butter on a Cherokee Indian reservation in North America to accompany an equally wild trout. Now that was a memorable meal. This is used in exactly the same way as the early garlic and prolongs the season for longer. It is marvellous, really, as it is a bridge between the end of last year's normal bulbs of garlic and the arrival of the new season's crop.

Serves 6
— 1 organic or free-range chicken
— 60g butter, at room temperature.
— 500ml wild garlic leaves, finely chopped (measure the wild garlic in a measuring jug)
— 1 lemon
— 120ml white wine, such as Chardonnay
— 120ml chicken stock (page 319)
— Sea salt and freshly ground black pepper

Garnish
— Wild garlic flowers (if available)

Preheat the oven to 160°C.

Heat a heavy-based cast iron casserole on a gentle heat. Dry the breast side of the chicken with kitchen paper. Rub the breast with 10g of the butter. Place the chicken breast side down in the heated casserole and allow to colour gently until both breasts are golden. You will have to move the chicken about a bit to get an even result, but don't worry if it is not the same colour all over.

Turn the chicken breast side up in the casserole and season with salt and pepper. Mix half of the chopped wild garlic with the remaining 50g of butter and spread it all over the chicken. Zest the lemon with a Microplane grater directly over the chicken. Pour in the wine and chicken stock and cover with a tight-fitting lid. You need the tight-fitting lid to prevent the steam escaping from the chicken as it cooks. If the steam escapes, you will end up with less cooking juices that will be too concentrated in flavour.

Cook the chicken in the preheated oven for about 90 minutes. To ensure that the chicken is fully cooked, check that the juices between the leg and the breast are running clear, with no trace of pink. When cooked, scrape any of the chopped garlic still sitting on the chicken breast into the juices in the bottom of the casserole. Remove the chicken and keep warm in an oven set to 100°C.

Place the casserole on a low heat on the hob, add the remaining chopped garlic leaves and bring the juices to a simmer. Cook for 5 minutes, then taste and adjust the seasoning. The juices may take on a slightly syrupy consistency, which is perfect, but don't over-reduce or the flavour will be too strong and the quantity too scant. I sometimes add a few drops of lemon juice to freshen up the flavour. I don't degrease the cooking juices, as I think they are an important part of the sauce.

Carve the chicken neatly onto a hot serving dish and pour over the bubbling hot sauce or pass separately in a heated sauce boat. If some of the wild garlic flowers are available, they make the prettiest and most delicious garnish when sprinkled over the entire dish.

3 CORNERED LEEK

Wild garlic

Casserole Roast Pheasant with Jerusalem Artichokes and Indian Spices

I love a traditional roast pheasant with all the time-honoured trimmings, but this recipe, with the use of an Indian spice mixture, is a way to ring the changes with this bird. Pheasants are generally excellent value for money and this technique of casserole roasting produces a very juicy result and is my favoured method of cooking this bird, which when roasted can sometimes be a little dry.

The joy of this dish, apart from the flavours, is that when you remove the casserole from the oven the ingredients have produced a sauce created by the juices of both the pheasants and the artichokes, then all you have to do is carve the birds and bring it to the table.

Jerusalem artichokes, which curiously are a member of the sunflower family, are getting easier to find every year as they become better known and valued for their taste and as a wonderful food for the gut. Gardeners will know that they are utterly easy to grow – when you plant them once, you will have them for ever more, as they come back year after year. The knobbly tubers sometimes require peeling, which is definitely tedious, but in this recipe they just need careful scrubbing. The vegetable can be eaten raw or cooked and is extremely versatile. They make a silky soup and a lovely purée and are delicious when roasted to a rich colour or slowly braised in chicken stock. There are countless flavours that it will accept and in this book I also pair them with mussels and saffron in a soup (page 158).

The spice paste as listed will make twice what you need for this recipe, but I find it so useful that I make the full quantity and keep it in the fridge for up to a week or freeze it. I use it with other birds, such as chicken, quail and guinea fowl, and it makes a fantastic paste for roast chicken wings.

The joy of this dish, apart from the flavours, is that when you remove the casserole from the oven the ingredients have produced a sauce created by the juices of both the pheasants and the artichokes, then all you have to do is carve the birds and bring it to the table.

Serves 4–6
— 2 oven-ready pheasants
— 20g butter, at room temperature
— 650g Jerusalem artichokes, scrubbed and sliced in half
   lengthways
— 1 tablespoon chopped fresh coriander leaves
— Sea salt and freshly ground black pepper

Spice paste
— 2 large garlic cloves, peeled and crushed to a paste
— Juice of 1 lemon
— 2 tablespoons extra virgin olive oil
— 1 tablespoon lightly roasted and finely ground cumin seeds
— 1 tablespoon sweet paprika
— 1 tablespoon ground turmeric
— 1 level teaspoon cayenne pepper
— 1 teaspoon caster sugar
— 1 teaspoon salt
— 1 teaspoon freshly ground black pepper

Preheat the oven to 180°C.

Mix all the ingredients for the spice paste together and reserve.

Heat a heavy-based casserole large enough for the two birds on a gentle heat until quite hot. Dry the skin of the birds, then smear the butter over the breasts and legs and place them breast side down in the heated casserole. The breasts should sizzle on contact with the casserole – if they don't, remove and allow the casserole to become hotter. Equally, however, you don't want to burn the birds, so make sure your heat is not too high. Allow the breasts to become a golden brown colour, then remove the birds from the casserole and turn off the heat. Do not wash out the casserole at this point unless it has overheated while browning the birds.

Place half of the artichokes in the casserole and season with salt and pepper. Smear **half of the spice paste** over the breasts and legs of the birds and also a little into the cavity, then return the birds to the casserole. Reserve the rest of the spice paste for another use. It will keep covered in the fridge for a week or it freezes well. Place the remaining artichokes around the birds, season and cover with a tight-fitting lid.

Place the casserole in the preheated oven and cook for 1 hour 15 minutes. Test to see if the birds are cooked by checking to see if the juices run clear between the thigh and the breast. I loosen the leg a little and push in a teaspoon to collect some of the juices so that I can accurately judge the colour. If the juices are a little pink, I usually pop the covered casserole back into the oven for another 10 minutes and test again.

The dish is now finished and ready to serve with the tender artichokes and delicious cooking juices as the sauce. If you wish you can spoon off the small amount of fatty juices from the surface of the sauce, but I often leave them in.

Carve the birds onto hot plates or a serving dish. Surround with the artichokes and pour over the bubbling hot juices and a sprinkle of chopped coriander. I love to serve simple boiled green cabbage or curly kale with this dish. York is a wonderful variety of winter cabbage.

Jerusalem Artichokes

Large Pot of Boiling WATER

French Beans with Nasturtium Butter

Many people will have nasturtiums flourishing in their gardens but perhaps don't realise that the leaves, flowers and indeed seeds of the cheerful and trouble-free plant are all edible and quite delicious. Their flavour is peppery and sweet. In my kitchen they appear in the salad bowl and chopped into a butter or oil to serve with grilled or roast fish, lamb and pork. I add them to a classic preparation of egg mayonnaise to add an intriguing flavour and here I toss them with butter into hot French beans. The yellow, orange and red flowers and the green leaves look very pretty when chopped and glistening through the buttery beans.

In my experience, French beans require more salt in cooking than any other green vegetable to ensure a good flavour.

This nasturtium butter is also great with boiled new potatoes.

Serves 4–6
— 450g French beans, round or flat
— 25g butter
— 70g nasturtium leaves and flowers, chopped
— Sea salt and freshly ground black pepper

Top and tail the beans and cut them into 2–3cm pieces. I usually cut them at an angle to create a more interesting effect.

Bring a large saucepan of water to the boil and salt generously. Add the beans and cook at a boil, uncovered, until they are tender. I like beans, and indeed all green vegetables, to be cooked through, so no squeaky beans here unless that is particularly to your taste.

As soon as the beans are cooked, immediately strain them, discarding the cooking water, and return to the saucepan. Add the butter, chopped nasturtiums and some freshly cracked black pepper and stir through. Serve immediately.

The yellow, orange and red flowers and the green leaves look very pretty when chopped and glistening through the buttery beans.

Grilled Radicchio with Crab Mayonnaise

I love everything about bitter radicchio. It is a wonder the way it braves the winter weather, producing tightly formed heads of leaves of an intense crimson streaked with brilliant white veins. It is no surprise that a paint colour has been named after this member of the chicory family. I love its somewhat sour and sharp flavour, which is something of an acquired taste, but it stealthily sneaks up on you and when that point is reached you will just long for it. Grilling the bitter heads of the intensely coloured leaves adds a depth of flavour, and while mellowing the bitterness a little, it also adds a little smokiness, which is great.

In the case of the crab meat, I prefer a combination of the milder-tasting white meat from the claws and the stronger, darker meat from the body. One can buy pre-cooked crab meat and when fresh it can be delicious, but nothing compares to buying a few whole crabs, cooking them yourself and extracting the fresh, slightly warm meat. In that case, you have a bonus of the crab shells for a sweet-tasting stock, perfect for soups and sauces.

The textures in this dish are lovely. The rich and sweet-tasting crab meat pairs perfectly with the grilled leaves and the toasted crumbs add a gentle crunch.

Serves 4
— 2 heads of radicchio, about 150g each
— 3 tablespoons extra virgin olive oil
— 220g cooked crab meat
— 2 tablespoons mayonnaise (page 306)
— 1 medium-hot fresh red chilli, deseeded and finely chopped
— 1 tablespoon chopped fresh coriander leaves, plus extra leaves for garnish
— 1 small onion
— Pinch of English mustard powder
— A few drops of freshly squeezed lemon juice
— 3 tablespoons crustless fresh white breadcrumbs
— Sea salt and freshly ground black pepper

I love its somewhat sour and sharp flavour, which is something of an acquired taste, but it stealthily sneaks up on you and when that point is reached you will just long for it.

Radicchio

Heat a heavy-based cast iron grill pan until quite hot but not smoking. Trim any loose and tattered leaves off the radicchio, then depending on size, cut in half or quarters down through the stalk. The stalk will loosely hold the pieces together while cooking. Toss gently in 2 tablespoons of the olive oil and season with salt and pepper. Place on the hot grill pan – they should sizzle slightly on contact. Allow to get nicely coloured before turning and continue cooking until the leaves are tender. You will lose the rich red colour of the leaves as they cook and take on a rusted appearance.

Mix the crab, mayonnaise, chilli and coriander in a bowl. Grate the onion on an old-fashioned box grater onto a plate. You will end up with a juicy, mushy onion mixture and that is precisely what you want. Add all this and the mustard powder to the crab with a few drops of lemon juice and mix gently. Taste and correct the seasoning, adding a few more drops of lemon juice if necessary, but the mixture should not taste distinctively of lemon.

Heat the remaining tablespoon of olive oil to a shimmer in a small frying pan, then add the breadcrumbs. Stir continuously over the heat until the crumbs are crisp and golden. Remove from the pan immediately.

To assemble, place the radicchio on warm plates. Spoon the crab alongside and sprinkle over the crumbs. Garnish with a few coriander leaves and serve immediately.

Roast Chicken Salad with French Beans and Tarragon

A chicken salad can be a glorious thing and I am very happy with this version, which combines the bird with bright green summer beans. I would also be happy to use the green bean known as the Romano bean or flat green bean, which is as delicious as its pencil-shaped cousin. However, I only ever cook and eat both of these beans during the summer and early autumn months when they are grown and in season in this part of the world. I find the imported and out-of-season beans utterly forgettable and a very pale imitation of the locally grown ones.

This salad is definitely best when assembled while the roast chicken is still slightly warm. That way you get a particularly lovely flavour and texture from the bird. Cooked meats become firmer and drier as they cool and lose some of their loveliness. However, the remains of yesterday's roast chicken will also produce a delicious result. The chicken cooking juices from the roasting tray, both fatty and lean, are crucial for adding deep, lip-smacking flavour to the salad – in fact, I would go so far as to say that they are the making of it or certainly are the element that raises this salad to a level above many chicken salads that I have eaten. The herb of choice here is tarragon, which is of course a classic with chicken. Its perfumed taste ties the flavour of the beans in beautifully.

The addition of a lemon to the chicken while roasting adds freshness and its acidity cuts through the richness of the dish and lifts the flavour of all the ingredients it comes in contact with. I chop up the cooked and collapsed lemon and pass it separately for any eaters who love a hit of bitterness with the salad. In this case, the roasted lemon performs the role that a salted preserved lemon might perform in another dish. I love it and the lip-puckering, eye-closing, cheek-hollowing reaction that it provokes.

Texture is added to the salad with the thin slivers of crisp mild garlic. The breadcrumbs, fried in the oil left after cooking the garlic, also add a nice crunch. A little heat is added with the

This salad is definitely best when assembled while the roast chicken is still slightly warm. That way you get a particularly lovely flavour and texture from the bird. Cooked meats become firmer and drier as they cool and lose some of their loveliness.

addition of chilli flakes, while the richness comes in the form of mayonnaise.

I usually serve a tray of roast tomatoes, still warm from the oven, and a bowl of just-boiled new season potatoes to accompany the salad.

Serves 8
— 1 free-range chicken, about 1.75kg in weight
— 2 large sprigs of fresh tarragon or thyme
— 1 lemon, pricked 6–8 times with a skewer
— 10 tablespoons extra virgin olive oil
— 4 large garlic cloves, peeled and thinly sliced
— 160g crustless fresh white breadcrumbs
— 600g French or scarlet runner beans, cut at an angle into 3cm pieces
— 6 tablespoons mayonnaise (page 306)
— Large pinch of chilli flakes
— Sea salt and freshly ground black pepper

Preheat the oven to 180°C.

Season the chicken with salt and pepper and insert the herb sprigs and lemon into the cavity. Place on a roasting tray that it fits into snugly and roast in the preheated oven for about 90 minutes. If the roasting tray is too large, the precious cooking juices evaporate during the cooking and are lost. I baste the chicken several times during the cooking by spooning the juices over the surface of the chicken to enhance the flavour and colour of the bird.

Meanwhile, heat 8 tablespoons of the olive oil in a heavy-based frying pan until it begins to shimmer. Add the sliced garlic and fry until golden while stirring all the time to separate the slices of garlic. This happens very quickly, so have a perforated spoon ready to lift the garlic out quickly as soon as it is crisp and golden brown. Place the garlic on a piece of kitchen paper to drain.

Immediately add the breadcrumbs to the oil, again stirring constantly, allowing them to become a rich golden colour. Remove straight away to a separate piece of kitchen paper to drain. Save the garlic-flavoured oil for another day. As long as you have not allowed it to burn, it is perfectly safe to use again.

When the chicken is cooked, remove it from the oven and allow to cool to the point where it is still warm but at the same time comfortable to handle. To ensure that the chicken is fully cooked, check that the juices between the leg and the breast are running clear, with no trace of pink.

While the chicken is cooling, bring a large saucepan of water to the boil and salt generously. Add the prepared beans and cook until tender. Drain the beans and spread out to allow them to cool slightly. When the beans are cool enough to mix with your fingers but still warm to the touch, dress with the remaining 2 tablespoons of olive oil and some freshly ground black pepper.

To assemble the salad, remove the legs and breasts from the chicken and cut or tear into bite-sized pieces. Place in a large bowl and add all the cooking juices, including the fat, from the roasting tray. Add the beans, mayonnaise and chilli flakes and stir gently but thoroughly to mix. Taste and correct the seasoning and add a little more mayonnaise if needed, but don't make the salad too rich.

Place on a large serving dish and scatter over the crumbs followed by the fried garlic. I usually cut up the lemon that was cooked in the cavity of the chicken into 12 pieces and pass that on a separate dish for anyone who would like a lemony hit with the salad.

Chicken, Garlic and Watercress Broth

What is it about a broth that seems to nourish in a way that some other soups do not? It is surely the nutrients in the chicken stock that is pushing some internal button of pleasure and satisfaction.

This is a quick and simple recipe and the watercress, which adds such a fresh green flavour to the dish, can be replaced with other green leafy ingredients. The finely chopped leaves (omit the stalks) of spinach and chard would be lovely, as would wild garlic leaves.

This is light but still full of flavour. If I want a richer taste, I grate some Parmesan cheese directly into each bowl of broth and drizzle on a little olive oil. Serve really hot.

This is a quick and simple recipe and the watercress, which adds such a fresh green flavour to the dish, can be replaced with other green leafy ingredients.

Serves 4 as a starter
— 25g butter
— 4 garlic cloves, peeled and finely chopped
— Pinch of chilli flakes (optional)
— 150g chicken breast, skin removed and cut into 1cm dice
— 150g watercress, finely chopped
— 450ml chicken stock (page 319)
— Sea salt and freshly ground black pepper

To serve
— A grating of Parmesan cheese (optional)
— A drizzle of extra virgin olive oil (optional)

Melt the butter over a moderate heat in a small saucepan. Add the garlic and chilli flakes (if using) and cook very gently for 5 minutes. You are trying to mellow out the strong taste of raw garlic. Add the diced chicken and stir to coat the pieces in the garlicky butter. Season with salt and pepper and cook, covered, on a very low heat for 5 minutes. Add the watercress and stir again. Increase the heat slightly and cook until the green juices start to come out of the watercress. Add the chicken stock and bring to a simmer. Maintain at this heat for 5 minutes. The chicken should be cooked through now, but pick out a piece and cut it in half to determine that it is indeed cooked, with no trace of pink juices visible. Check the seasoning.

Serve bubbling hot in hot bowls. If you are adding the Parmesan and olive oil, add it now.

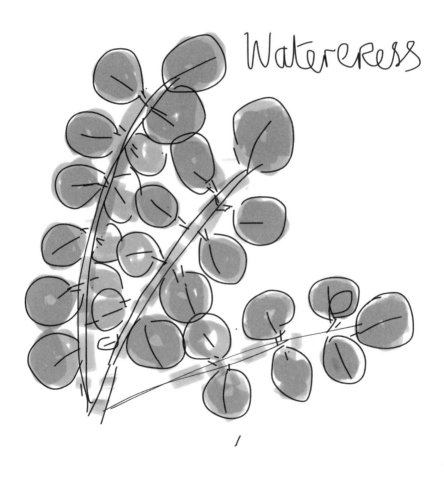

Watercress

Cucumber & elderflower

Cucumber and Elderflower Granita

I think granitas are great for the home cook, as they are so easy to make and bring a little of the smartness we expect in restaurants to your own family table. This delightful version seems to suit either the beginning or the end of a meal, depending on what else you are serving. Various decorations can be added when serving, such as fresh elderflower blossom when in season or the leaves and petals of the Tagetes marigold later in the summer. If you can find the whimsical-looking tiny cucumber called cucamelon, then one of those on each serving would be a definite conversation starter. At Christmas a few pomegranate seeds or myrtle berries would be an appropriate addition.

The amount of juice you can extract from a cucumber varies throughout the year and without doubt large home-grown summer cucumbers yield more juice than the somewhat more slender imported varieties, so perhaps it is worth having a little extra cucumber to hand to ensure you end up with the 350ml of juice required in the recipe.

The process of making the icy granita is simplicity itself and just requires a little commitment from you to return to the freezer to give the ice the occasional stir.

Serves 6–8
— 500g cucumber
— 115ml elderflower cordial
— 3 tablespoons lime juice

Optional decorations
— Elderflower blossoms
— Tagetes marigold leaves or petals
— Cucamelons, very thinly sliced
— Pomegranate seeds
— Myrtle berries

The process of making the icy granita is simplicity itself and just requires a little commitment from you to return to the freezer to give the ice the occasional stir.

Peel the cucumber and cut into rough dice. Place in a blender and purée until smooth. Pass the cucumber purée through a fine-mesh sieve, pushing to extract the juice and fine pulp – you should end up with 350ml of the strained juice and pulp. Discard any extra. Add the elderflower cordial and lime juice to the cucumber and mix well.

Place the juice in a Pyrex bowl, place in the freezer and freeze until nearly set. Break up the partially frozen ice with a fork or a whisk until it looks rather slushy, then return to the freezer. Refreeze and repeat the process three more times to achieve a flaky, shard-like consistency. The granita is then ready to serve or can be stored until you want to serve it. I keep the granita covered in the freezer to protect the delicate flavour.

Serve the granita in chilled bowls or glasses just as it is or with some of the suggested decorations.

Use a fork to stir up the granita!

Blackberry and Sweet Geranium Posset

A classic lemon posset or set cream is a simple and lovely thing and my version here, with blackberries and sweet geranium leaves, is a delicious variation on the theme. It is remarkable how easy this is to make and how the mixture sets into a tender chilled pudding without the aid of eggs or gelatine. I like the possets served straight from the fridge, nice and chilly.

I often make this during the winter months using wild blackberries that I have frozen in the late summer or early autumn. If you are using frozen berries, use them straight from the freezer. I never cease to be amazed by the value one gets from a few bags of frozen fruit when fresh local fruit is simply not an option due to the season.

If you don't have the lemon- or rose-scented geranium, you can just leave it out. The fragrant leaves do, however, bring a magical element to the dish. The plants are easily found at good garden centres and can be treated as a houseplant, living on a bright windowsill, or if the weather is mild where you live, they can spend spring, summer and autumn out of doors in a sheltered sunny spot. I can't imagine not having one of these plants for the ravishing flavour they bring to certain dishes. In fact, it is the sort of magic that one receives from this rather innocuous-looking leaf that humbles and mesmerises me and reminds me every time I use it how astonishing nature is and how fortunate I am that my career has brought me down a path where I can handle these treasures all the time.

A little softly whipped cream is the perfect accompaniment along with a fresh organic or crystallised rose petal. The combination of rose and blackberry is a marriage made in heaven, so I might be tempted to add just a few drops of rosewater to the cream when whipping. A thin lacy biscuit such as the nougatine biscuits on page 297 would also be good here.

The possets can be served in little cups or glasses or the prettiest receptacle you like to use. The portions are quite small, as this is a rich little dish, but I always think it is better to be

I often make this during the winter months using wild blackberries that I have frozen in the late summer or early autumn.

longing for one more spoonful rather than being faced with too much food.

Serves 8
— 100g fresh or frozen blackberries
— 90g caster sugar
— 5 leaves of lemon- or rose-scented geranium
— 400ml cream
— 50ml freshly squeezed lemon juice

To serve
— Softly whipped cream
— Fresh or candied rose petals (page 332)
— Nougatine (page 297)

Place the blackberries, sugar, geranium leaves and cream in a small saucepan and bring to a bare simmer. Stir occasionally to encourage the sugar to dissolve. Maintain that bare simmer for 5 minutes. If the cream boils hard, the texture and consistency of the posset will be spoiled.

Remove the saucepan from the heat and stir in the lemon juice. You will notice the colour of the cream improving dramatically as soon as the lemon juice goes in. Now strain the cream through a fine-mesh sieve to remove the geranium leaves and at the same time push as much of the blackberries through as possible.

Pour the strained cream into eight little cups or glasses and allow to cool before placing in the fridge for 3 hours to set. The posset will keep perfectly in your fridge for several days. I like to cover them to protect the delicate flavour.

Serve with a little softly whipped cream and if you have them, a fresh or candied rose petal and a nougatine biscuit.

Blackberries

Chocolate and Sour Cherry Cake

This is a marvellously easy and delicious cake. All the cake ingredients are briefly whizzed in a food processor and the cherries are gently folded in. The icing is a simple chocolate ganache. It really is that simple.

The dried sour cherries used here are a million miles away from the lurid candied cherries, most of which never had the pleasure of hanging from the branch of a cherry tree. I like Amarena cherries from Italy, which are sufficiently tart to exert their flavour against the chocolate in this recipe.

When the cherry blossom is in season, I sprinkle some of the petals over the iced cake. Small rose petals can also make a pretty garnish, and if you can find a few fresh violets, you can imagine how gorgeous that would look too.

Serves 8
Cake
— 150g butter, at room temperature, plus extra melted butter for greasing
— 125g caster sugar
— 125g self-raising flour, plus extra for dusting
— 25g unsweetened cocoa powder
— 3 eggs
— 75ml full-fat buttermilk
— 1 teaspoon vanilla extract
— 75g dried sour cherries, chopped into 0.5cm pieces

Icing
— 100ml cream
— 100g chocolate (52% cocoa solids), roughly chopped
— ½ teaspoon vanilla extract

Decoration
— 10–20g dried sour cherries, cut in half or quarters
— Rose petals or cherry blossoms, when available

The dried sour cherries used here are a million miles away from the lurid candied cherries, most of which never had the pleasure of hanging from the branch of a cherry tree.

To serve
— Softly whipped cream or crème fraîche

You will need
— 1 x 21cm cake tin

Preheat the oven to 180°C. Brush a 21cm cake tin with melted butter and dust lightly with flour. Shake off any excess flour and line the base of the tin with a disc of non-stick baking paper.

Place the butter, sugar, flour, cocoa, eggs, buttermilk and vanilla in the bowl of a food processer. Pulse briefly to achieve a soft cake batter. This takes only a matter of seconds. I usually run a rubber spatula around the sides and base of the bowl of the food processer just in case any flour or cocoa have become trapped there and pulse again for 2 seconds.

Add the cherries and pulse for 1–2 seconds to just mix them through the cake batter. It is crucial you do not break up the chopped cherries.

Scrape the batter into the prepared cake tin and make a little dip in the centre of the cake with the back of a spoon to encourage an even rise.

Bake in the preheated oven for 25–30 minutes. Insert a skewer into the cake to check it is properly cooked – the skewer should be completely clean when removed from the cake. The cooked cake will also have shrunk fractionally from the edge of the tin. Allow the cake to sit in the tin for 5–10 minutes before removing it to a wire rack to cool completely.

To make the icing, place the cream in a small saucepan and bring to a simmer. Remove from the heat and allow to cool for 5 minutes. Add the chocolate and vanilla and stir until a smooth, glossy sauce is achieved. Allow to cool until completely cold.

Remove the paper disc from the cake and place on a plate. Spread the ganache over the top of the cake right out to the edge. I allow it to drip down the sides of its own accord. Sprinkle on the remaining chopped cherries and flower petals (if using).

Serve the cake with softly whipped cream or crème fraîche.

Setting the Table

There is something reassuring about placing a knife and fork on the table, a placemat, a side plate, a water or wine glass – just making the decision to create a little order in which to enjoy what we are about to receive. Of course, setting the table can be taken to Olympian levels of intricateness and extravagance depending on the enthusiasm of the setter or the nature of the meal being taken. That's all very fine, but generally the object of the exercise for me is the conscious preparation of a space in which I can enjoy the food I have prepared.

It's a pity that in some apartments and houses these days the dining table is almost a thing of the past, along with the kitchen itself, soon to become a twee memory of less busy times. Many people just have no idea how to cook and as a result are daunted and scared by the very thought of it. I understand this fear and I can understand how as a result, creating a little civilised moment and environment in which to eat the food they are afraid of could well be seen as somewhat superfluous.

Just ask me to sort out a problem under the bonnet of the car and see what would happen – nothing is precisely what would happen, as I would have no idea what I was doing. So it is with cooking. I was lucky to get a grounding at my mother's apron strings and by the age of 10 would have been able to cook sufficiently well to feed myself. The days of most people learning how to cook like that are pretty much gone. This lack of an essential life skill has been thrown into the sharpest focus all over the world in recent times. When isolated behind closed doors in times of quarantine, we have to rely almost solely on ourselves to cook, to nourish and sustain, but it is extremely difficult to do so without the adequate skills.

In the modern lives we live, where for the most part and by necessity there is no one at home during the day to cook or to share the skills if they do have them, we need to radically rethink how we teach ourselves how to cook.

Just
one
candle
can
create
an atmosphere

Set the table

Thank you
for a lovely
dinner - R x

The obvious place, of course, is in school. Food and the table need to be a part of the curriculum, a subject that is rewarded with academic points just as you are for maths, French, chemistry and so on. I think this new subject should be called 'Table', and what a subject it could be. Cooking skills would be the primary focus, of course, but think of all the related subjects as the topic is expanded to study and explore where our food comes from, how and where it is grown and produced, the history and geography of food, from caveman to confined man – it could be a thrilling journey of joy-filled learning.

During the Covid-19 confinement, as internet cooking classes thankfully proliferated, it can only have brought the table and its place at the centre of all homes back into if not the middle of the room, then into the middle of the conversation. The time when families ate together regularly has been eroding over the past decades as our increasingly hectic lifestyles have made it all but impossible for most family units to get all their members in the same place at the same time. Meals are taken in the car, in the bus, on a high stool, on the way to the gym, on the way home from the gym, slumped on the sofa watching television (which can't be good for digestion) – anywhere except sitting at the table. Where on earth is the joy in that? And is that not what our eating and communing together is supposed to be about? A little joy in the hectic helter-skelter of modern living, not to mention nourishment for our bodies and balm for the soul?

Breaking bread is such a symbolic gesture, but in many ways the way that we break bread nowadays is broken. Many of the systems in place have failed us; we need to cease taking our daily bread for granted. We need to be thankful for and respectful of the planet and the people who toil to bring us clean, safe food and a regular supply of it to put on our tables. We need to put the joy back into the table. We need to reset the table.

Mozzarella en Carozza with Chicken or Turkey, Semi-Dried Tomato and Preserved Basil

I had eaten tiny, elegant versions of this fried Italian sandwich at bars in Turin and Milan long before fully understanding its title. This sandwich is a classic Italian offering believed to have originated in Campania, which is logical enough given that that region is regarded as the home of mozzarella. The word 'carozza' refers to a carriage, which seems a rather grandiose description of the fried bread that surrounds and transports the mozzarella to your mouth. The notion that the strings of melted mozzarella resemble the reins of a horse and carriage is plausible enough, though other versions of the origin of the name refer to Neapolitan bread used to make the sandwiches that resembled the wheels of carriages.

The word 'carozza' refers to a carriage, which seems a rather grandiose description of the fried bread that surrounds and transports the mozzarella to your mouth.

The classic version has just the cheese in the centre, but my version is a little more adventurous. I don't often like to play around too much with a classic timeless dish, but at least my additions are in the same spirit as the original in that it was a way to use up leftover bread and here I am adding a few other little leftovers, but all in the spirit of the original in not wanting to waste a scrap of food.

As with any sandwich, proportion is important (see my rant on the subject on page 222–223). When I was eating these alongside my Negroni at Caffe Torino in Turin, the delicate little mouthfuls were a masterclass in sandwich building that allowed me to eat that piece of food with the elegance demanded by sitting on the edge of one of the most beautiful squares in the world, the Piazza San Carlo. I was thankful for the delicate nature of the offering, as you don't want to be seen struggling with an oafish amount of food as elegant Italians stroll past looking every inch the thoroughbreds born to decorate this beautiful place, with their apparently uncontrived and unstudied demeanour. There, this is most definitely a finger sandwich.

Serves 4
— 200ml milk
— 100g plain flour seasoned with salt and pepper
— 4 eggs, beaten
— 3 tablespoons sunflower oil
— 1 tablespoon extra virgin olive oil
— 8 slices of good-quality white yeast bread with crusts on
— 1 ball of mozzarella, thinly sliced
— 70g shredded cooked chicken or turkey, seasoned
— 50g semi-dried tomatoes
— 4 pinches of chilli flakes
— 8 fresh basil leaves

Preheat the oven to 140°C.

Place the milk, flour and beaten eggs in three separate wide bowls or deep plates. Heat the sunflower and olive oil in a cast iron frying pan on a medium heat.

Lay four slices of the bread on a board and cover with the mozzarella, not going quite out to the edge of the bread. Add the chicken or turkey, then scatter over some semi-dried tomatoes, pinches of chilli flakes and freshly torn basil. Finish each sandwich by topping with the final layer of bread. Press on the top of the bread to firmly stick the two slices together.

Taking one sandwich at a time, dip firstly in the milk to coat the top, base and sides, moving next to the flour, again coating the top, base and sides, and finally finishing by dipping the top, base and sides in the beaten eggs. Place in the preheated frying pan – you should have enough space in your pan to cook two sandwiches at a time. A gentle medium heat is needed in order to melt the cheese, heat the centre and seal the crust of the sandwiches, so allow a few minutes per side. Remove when a rich golden colour is achieved and the bread has become crisp. Remove from the pan and drain on kitchen paper. Keep warm in the moderately hot oven while you fry the two remaining sandwiches.

The sandwiches are best served hot and I like to cut them into old-fashioned triangles before serving. A piquant chutney, mayonnaise or tomato salsa make a perfect accompaniment. A hot tomato chilli salsa would also complement these sandwiches brilliantly.

Courgette Soup with Basil and Garlic, Chilli and Fennel Oil

There has been a trend over the last few years for soup to be served with a very thick consistency and the notion of a bowl of soup as a meal has changed people's perception and understanding of this dish. There are certainly some soups that should be robust, such as an Italian bean soup or a tangle of noodles in a spiced broth in a South East Asian bowl, but it would be a pity to forget about a refined smooth soup with a creamy consistency, which is seen as one course in a meal rather than the main event.

This is fresh tasting and delicious with a zing of heat and spice from the garlic, chilli and fennel oil. Medium or even larger green courgettes are perfect here and generally with those, the soup is a lovely green colour. It is fun, though, to make this soup with yellow courgettes, as it produces a golden-coloured result. It is perhaps the effect of the basil that is most surprising here – the leaves are torn into the soup just before it goes to the table and as a result the floral scent of the herb is obvious and immediate.

Failing the garlic, chilli and fennel oil, I am happy to serve this soup garnished with a little softly whipped cream or just a drizzle of plain unseasoned extra virgin olive oil and a restrained sprinkle of chilli flakes. Should you happen to get a few of the beautiful flowers with the courgettes, those are good torn into bite-sized pieces and scattered over the bowls of soup just before they go to the table.

This is fresh tasting and delicious with a zing of heat and spice from the garlic, chilli and fennel oil.

Serves 6
— 25g butter
— 1 tablespoon extra virgin olive oil
— 170g peeled and diced potato
— 130g chopped onion
— 600ml chicken stock (page 319)
— 500g courgette, cut into 0.5cm dice

— 50ml cream (optional)
— 8–12 fresh basil leaves
— Sea salt and freshly ground black pepper

To serve
— Garlic, chilli and fennel oil (see below)

Heat the butter and olive oil in a saucepan and allow to foam.
Reduce the heat and add the potato and onion. Season with salt
and pepper and toss the vegetables in the fat. Cover with a disc
of greaseproof paper and a tight-fitting lid and cook over a very
low heat for 10 minutes, allowing the vegetables to sweat and
begin to tenderise.

Add the chicken stock and bring to a simmer. Cook, covered,
until the potato and onion are completely tender. Add the
diced courgette and simmer, uncovered, until the courgette is
also tender. Add the cream (if using), return to a simmer briefly
and purée the soup to achieve a silky-smooth consistency.
(The consistency (thickness/thinness) of soup is down to the
individual – more or less stock will achieve that.) Taste and
correct the seasoning.

Serve the soup in hot bowls with a drizzle of the garlic, chilli
and fennel oil and some torn basil leaves.

Garlic, Chilli and Fennel Oil
— 4 tablespoons extra virgin olive oil
— 2 fat garlic cloves, peeled and very thinly sliced
— 1 rounded teaspoon fennel seeds, coarsely ground
— Pinch of chilli flakes
— Sea salt

Heat the olive oil in a **small pan** on a moderate heat. Add the
thinly sliced garlic – it should sizzle on contact with the oil.
Stir for a minute or two, until crisp, golden and completely
cooked through. Now take the saucepan off the heat (err on the
side of caution with the level of heat, as garlic can burn quickly
and easily). Immediately add the coarsely ground fennel seeds,
a pinch of chilli flakes and a pinch of sea salt. Stir and decant
straight away into a small bowl to stop the cooking.

Courgettes & Flowers

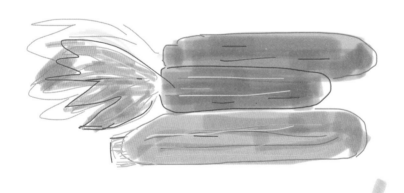

Flash-Grilled Haddock with Roasted Cherry Tomatoes and Black Garlic Aioli

This is a simple technique for cooking fish and one that I use all the time when a speedy supper is required. I am suggesting haddock or whiting here, but you could also use hake, pollock or mackerel. If you don't have a grill element in your oven, you could just roast the fish in the highest heat your oven will muster.

You will need to keep a close eye on the fish as it cooks, as the thickness of the fillets you are using will determine the exact cooking time. The cooked fish will have turned a pearly white and be just slightly firm to the touch. The suggested cooking time in the recipe is a guideline rather than a definitive statement. This is often the way when cooking individual pieces of fish or indeed meat. The weight may be the same, but the part of the fish the fillets came from will determine its thickness and that in turn determines its cooking time. A minute or two too long under the grill might just tip the fish from being perfect to being a little overcooked. These challenges make us better cooks and by watching what is happening and what the results are, we learn and our store of knowledge is increased.

The flavour of the sweet tomatoes pairs well with the black garlic in the aioli.

Serves 4
— 30g butter
— 1 tablespoon extra virgin olive oil
— 4 x 150g portions of skinned haddock or whiting
— 350g cherry tomatoes
— 2 sprigs of fresh thyme, leaves stripped
— Pinch of caster sugar
— 4 generous sprigs of fresh flat-leaf parsley, chopped
— Sea salt and freshly ground black pepper

You will need to keep a close eye on the fish as it cooks, as the thickness of the fillets you are using will determine the exact cooking time.

To serve
— 2 tablespoons black garlic aioli (page 306)
— Lemon wedges

Preheat the grill.

Melt the butter and olive oil in a small saucepan. Place the skinned fish on a baking tray lined with parchment paper and paint each piece of fish with some of the melted butter and olive oil. Season with salt and pepper.

Roll the cherry tomatoes in the remaining butter and olive oil, then scatter over the thyme leaves and season with salt, pepper and a tiny pinch of sugar. Scatter the coated tomatoes around the fish.

Roast under the grill for about 10 minutes, until the fish is just firm to the touch and cooked through. Keep the fish warm while you finish the sauce.

Place the black garlic aioli in a small bowl and add just enough of the cooking juices from the tray to loosen the sauce to the consistency of softly whipped cream.

Serve the fish, tomatoes and any remaining cooking juices on hot plates scattered with a little chopped parsley. Pass the aioli and lemon wedges separately.

Lamb Shanks with Tomatoes and Almonds

This recipe has its origins in the wonderful cooking of North Africa. The large quantity of tomatoes combined with the gentle combination of spices are cooked down to a rich, sumptuous sauce. I cook this dish when fresh vine-ripened tomatoes are readily available. I think that is when the dish is at its best, as the perfume and depth of flavour of tomatoes that have come to their prime on the branch is reflected in the finished dish. I have also used frozen tomatoes with excellent results, though the juicy nature of those requires a longer cooking time to reduce the sauce to a thick coating consistency. It may seem strange to grate rather than chop the onions, but this process yields a softer edge to the cooked onions, which then disappear into the sauce. The addition of honey and ground cinnamon at the end of the cooking is when the dish really starts to sing, and though the quantity of both may seem excessive, it really is needed to bring all the aromatic flavours together.

The shanks can of course be served whole, but I now prefer to slide the softly tender meat off the bone back into the sauce and serve less to match the changing tastes in relation to my consumption of meat. I usually leave one of the shanks whole as part of the presentation of the dish. You will know what is required at your table. The dish would be perfect served with fluffy couscous or buttery, smooth mashed potatoes. I also serve a bowl of dark green crispy leaves tossed in a simple vinaigrette to accompany.

The dish reheats perfectly, in which case you may need to add a few drops of water to loosen up the consistency.

The addition of honey and ground cinnamon at the end of the cooking is when the dish really starts to sing.

Serves 5–8
— 5 lamb shanks
— 75g butter
— 160g onion, peeled and coarsely grated
— 2 garlic cloves, peeled and finely chopped
— 1 cinnamon stick

- 1 teaspoon ground ginger
- 1 level teaspoon saffron threads
- 2 tablespoons tomato purée
- 1.4kg ripe tomatoes, peeled and chopped
- 3–4 tablespoons honey
- 1 teaspoon ground cinnamon
- 200g skinned almonds
- 2 tablespoons chopped fresh flat-leaf parsley leaves
- Sea salt and freshly ground black pepper

To serve
- Couscous or mashed potatoes
- Crisp green salad

Place the shanks, sitting sideways rather than standing up, in a heavy-based casserole. Add 50g of the butter along with the onion, garlic, cinnamon stick, ginger and saffron. Mix the tomato purée with 450ml of water, whisking it well, and pour it over the contents of the casserole. Add more water to barely cover the shanks. Season with salt and pepper. At this point I like to taste the rather unappetising-looking liquid just to check how the seasoning is going. I find that by doing this I will have a greater understanding of the progression of the flavour of the dish from start to finish and it teaches me a lot about how flavours change, blend and mature over a particular cooking time.

Cover the casserole with a tight-fitting lid and simmer very gently for about 2 hours, until the meat is nearly ready to fall off the bones with a gentle push of a fork. It is vital that the lid of the saucepan is a tight fit to prevent the liquid from evaporating too quickly. It this does happen, top up the level of water again, though I find this rather dilutes the flavour of the finished dish. Alternatively, the casserole can be cooked in an oven heated to 160°C for a similar length of time.

When the meat is cooked, remove it and the cinnamon stick from the casserole. Add the chopped tomatoes and cook over a moderately high heat until the liquid from the tomatoes has all but evaporated. You will need to stir the casserole occasionally with a flat-bottomed wooden spoon to prevent scorching. The objective is to end up with just the meat juices, now richly flavoured with the concentrated tomato. If you wish to serve the meat off the bone, you could gently push it off the bones while the tomatoes are cooking. I usually leave one shank whole as a presentation piece. Now add the honey and ground cinnamon and simmer for a moment longer to allow the flavours to mingle. Taste and correct the seasoning.

Melt the remaining 25g of butter in a sauté pan and allow to cook to a pale hazelnut colour. Add the almonds and a pinch of salt and fry until they colour very lightly. Lift them out of the butter with a slotted spoon.

Reheat the lamb and tomatoes as necessary and place in a heated serving dish. Scatter over the almonds and parsley and serve with couscous or buttery mashed potatoes and a salad of crisp leaves on the side.

Upside-Down Blackberry, Apple and Geranium Cake

This is a classic combination of two autumnal fruits and that is when I think it tastes best. The flavour of sweet apples fresh off the trees with their perfumed scent and wild berries from the hedgerows is utterly wonderful. From early August onwards, native sweet apples will be in season and plentiful and are a revelation in terms of their depth and complexity of flavour. There are several varieties that would be suitable here, such as Cox's Orange Pippin, Egremont Russet or Irish Peach. The sweet apple holds its shape better during cooking than the bitter Bramley, which tends to collapse to a fluff.

The blackberries can of course be cultivated, in which case they will be bigger and fatter than their wild cousins. However, if you freeze some foraged wild berries, the cake becomes a possibility at any time of the year.

The scented geranium leaves lend their magical perfume, though I have cooked the cake without the leaves and it was just as lovely.

This type of cake is undoubtedly best eaten on the day it is cooked while still warm from the oven, though if gently reheated the next day, it is still very pleasant.

The perfect accompaniment for the warm cake is a thin vanilla custard and softly whipped cream perhaps enlivened with a few drops of calvados.

From early August onwards, native sweet apples will be in season and plentiful and are a revelation in terms of their depth and complexity of flavour.

Serves 8

Caramel
— 125g caster or granulated sugar
— 2 tablespoons water

Fruit
— 225g fresh or frozen blackberries
— 2 eating apples, peeled, cored and cut into 1cm dice

Cake
— 150g butter, at room temperature
— 150g caster sugar
— 200g self-raising flour
— 3 eggs
— 2 large or 4 medium lemon- or rose-scented geranium leaves
— 1 vanilla pod, very finely chopped

To serve
— Thin vanilla custard
— Softly whipped cream

Preheat the oven to 170°C.

Put a low-sided ovenproof 20cm sauté pan on a low heat and add the sugar and water. Stir gently and bring to a simmer. Try to ensure that the sugar dissolves before the water comes to a boil by occasionally stirring with a wooden spoon. Continue cooking until a hazelnut-coloured caramel is reached. If the sugar is cooking unevenly, do not stir, but rather gently tilt the pan to and fro, allowing the dark caramel to travel into the pale and vice versa. As soon as you have an even-coloured caramel, immediately remove the pan from the heat and scatter in the blackberries and apples in an even layer.

Put the butter, caster sugar and flour in a food processor and blend for a few seconds. Add the eggs and process very briefly, until smooth and blended. It may be necessary to run a spatula around the bowl of the processor to loosen any flour or dry mixture. Add the geranium and vanilla and pulse for a further 2 seconds. The key here is not to blend the mixture for too long, as it can curdle or toughen the texture of the cooked cake.

Spread the batter evenly over the blackberry and apple base in the pan. Place the pan in the preheated oven and bake for about 80 minutes. The cooked cake will be well coloured and will have shrunk very slightly from the edge of the pan. A skewer inserted into the cooked cake should come out clean when retracted. If the skewer is not clean, cook for a further 5–10 minutes and repeat the process.

Allow the cake to cool a little in the pan for 10 minutes before carefully inverting it onto a plate. Be careful, as some of the hot juices may leak out when you are turning it out of the pan. Remember, this is an upside-down cake.

The cake is best served warm with a thin vanilla custard and softly whipped cream, though either on their own would be lovely. It is also good served at room temperature or gently reheated the next day.

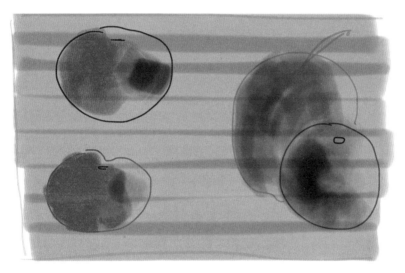

HERitage Apples

Chicken Livers with Blackberries, Cumin and Pomegranate Molasses

It seems to me that chicken livers have gone out of fashion, as one rarely sees them on restaurant menus any more except in the guise of a pâté. They are a terrific ingredient and immensely versatile. I always cook organic livers and I like to serve them just cooked through rather than pink. I also use turkey, goose and duck livers, all of which work perfectly here. It is worth noting that raw livers freeze very well, so there is no need to waste a liver from a Christmas turkey, duck or goose when it can be saved for a meal early in the new year.

For most of the year I use frozen blackberries, which are perhaps the most undervalued berry of all. From early August into September and right the way through until the end of October in this part of the world, the hedgerows are groaning with the jewel-like fruit and an hour or two spent collecting the fruit, for using fresh or for freezing, are some of the most pleasant hours of my year. To be able to harvest such a useful and delicious food on the side of the road is pure joy. Though mostly thought of as a berry as part of a sweet dish, they are very useful in the savoury kitchen.

I do seem to have used quite a bit of pomegranate molasses in this book, but I make no apology for that fact. The rich concentrated juice is a wonderful condiment and is a perfect match here with the blackberries and roasted cumin seeds. I am also aware that if you go out and buy a bottle of the molasses, it is useful to have several recipes to hand to get the most value from your purchase.

You will neetd some fresh crusty bread to mop up the juices from your plate.

I do seem to have used quite a bit of pomegranate molasses in this book, but I make no apology for that fact. The rich concentrated juice is a wonderful condiment and is a perfect match here with the blackberries and roasted cumin seeds.

Serves 4
— 250g organic chicken livers
— 1 level teaspoon cumin seeds
— 1 tablespoon extra virgin olive oil
— 80g fresh or frozen blackberries
— 2 tablespoons pomegranate molasses
— 4 dessertspoons crème fraîche
— 2 tablespoons fresh coriander leaves
— Sea salt and freshly ground black pepper

To serve
— Crusty bread or grilled or toasted sourdough bread

Preheat the oven to 180°C.

Wash the livers carefully in cold water and trim off any stringy membranes or discoloured flesh. Divide each liver into the two separate lobes if they are still attached, once again being careful to remove any stringy membranes. Dry thoroughly on kitchen paper.

Heat a dry heavy-based cast iron frying pan on a medium heat, then add the cumin seeds. Cook briefly to raise the colour of the seeds or until a little vapour and aroma rise from the pan. Remove the seeds immediately and grind to a coarse powder with a pestle and mortar or in a spice grinder.

Replace the pan on the heat (no need to wash) and add the olive oil. Allow the oil to heat, then add the dried chicken livers. Sauté the livers, allowing them to become richly coloured. Be careful with the heat here, as if the pan is too hot the livers will burn and get a tough crust, which is not pleasant to eat. I like the livers cooked through until no trace of pink remains, but do be careful not to overcook them to the point where they become dry and dull. They can be both cooked through and wonderfully plump and juicy if you maintain a good eye on the heat of the pan.

As soon as the livers are cooked through, add the ground cumin and turn the livers in the spice. Cook for a further minute like this. Add the blackberries and some salt and pepper. Press a few of the berries with a fork to crush them to create a small amount of juice. Add 1 tablespoon of the pomegranate molasses and allow to bubble just once, then **remove the pan from the heat immediately** and taste the juices, which should by now be syrupy and delicious. Correct the seasoning if necessary.

Spoon the livers, juices and berries onto hot plates. Top each serving with a dessertspoon of crème fraîche and a drizzle of the remaining pomegranate molasses. Scatter over some fresh coriander leaves and eat immediately with crusty bread or grilled or toasted sourdough bread.

Roast Pumpkin or Squash and Brussels Sprouts with Pumpkin Seed Praline, Pomegranate Molasses and Crème Fraîche

This is a good combination of ingredients for an autumn or winter meal, though I hope the inclusion of both pumpkin and squash in the recipe title is not confusing. All pumpkins and squashes are members of the greater cucurbit family and either can be successfully used in this recipe.

Ingredients that we traditionally thought of as being firmly of the winter season are now appearing earlier – no doubt climate change playing its tricks on us again. The Brussels sprout, for so long associated with Christmas meals, is now appearing months ahead of its festive deadline. Pumpkins and squashes are also getting ahead of themselves. Whereas I do think the early, small and tightly formed sprouts are fresh tasting and lovely, I think the squashes are considerably better after being exposed to some cold frosty nights. There is no doubt in my mind that as climate change tightens its grip on changing temperatures in this part of the world, it will cause a shift in our associations of certain ingredients with certain times of the year. The silver lining of that rather depressing conversation is the possibility that there may be plants that could flourish here in a way that was not possible due to our weather in the past. It would be nice to be able to grow lemons with a degree of success!

I serve this dish at room temperature either as a standalone lunch or supper dish or as an accompaniment to roast lamb or pork. The rich flavour of the pumpkin is great with the lightly roasted Brussels sprouts and the crunchy praline. The final drizzles of pomegranate molasses and crème fraîche elevate the dish.

Ingredients that we traditionally thought of as being firmly of the winter season are now appearing earlier – no doubt climate change playing its tricks on us again.

Serves 8 as a starter or an accompaniment to roast meat or 4 as a main dish
— 750g pumpkin or squash
— 2 tablespoons extra virgin olive oil
— 250g Brussels sprouts
— 200g crème fraîche
— 1 teaspoon honey
— 2 tablespoons pomegranate molasses (approx.)
— Sea salt and freshly ground black pepper

Pumpkin seed praline
— 25g pumpkin seeds
— 15g caster sugar

Preheat the oven to 200°C.

To make the praline, line a small tray with non-stick baking paper. Place the pumpkin seeds and sugar in a very small saucepan and cook over a moderate heat. Allow the sugar to caramelise to a chestnut colour and don't be afraid to stir the caramel and seeds if it seems to be cooking unevenly. As soon as the rich caramel is achieved, remove from the saucepan and pour out onto the paper. Allow to cool completely to become crisp.

Place the pumpkin or squash on a chopping board and carefully cut it in half. The skin of some pumpkins and squashes can be quite slippery, so you may need to exert force to cut it open, hence always have your knife pointing away from you so that if it slips, it will hit the chopping board and not you. Remove the seeds and carefully peel off the skin with a knife.

Cut the prepared pumpkin or squash into eight wedges and place in a bowl. Add the olive oil and season with salt and pepper. Place on a parchment-lined tray, leaving a little space between the pieces. I usually sit them upright like little boats on the paper, though I don't think this is crucial. Reserve the oily bowl for later. Roast in the preheated oven for 30 minutes.

While the pumpkin or squash is roasting, peel any unsightly outer leaves from the Brussels sprouts and cut each one into six thin pieces straight down through the vegetable rather than crossways. Put these into the oily bowl and season. Scatter them over the pumpkin or squash after 30 minutes of cooking and return to the oven to cook for a further 10 minutes. The cooking time of pumpkins and squash varies somewhat, so do test the flesh for tenderness by inserting a skewer – there should be no tough resistance. The sprouts will have begun to tenderise but will not be soft. Remove from the oven.

Mix the crème fraîche with the honey.

To serve the dish, place the pumpkin wedges and Brussels sprouts on a warm wide, flat platter or divide between individual warm plates. Place a generous dollop of crème fraîche on each wedge and retain the remaining crème fraîche for serving separately. Drizzle the pomegranate molasses over and finally break the pumpkin seed praline over each serving. Serve as soon as possible.

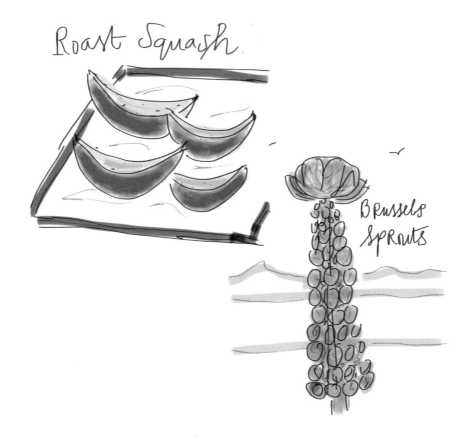

Roast Squash.

Brussels Sprouts

Rustic Turkey or Chicken Pie with Swiss Chard and Tarragon

It is very satisfying as a cook when you manage to extract another dish from the seemingly scant or almost non-existent remains of a previous meal. In a way, that is what this pie is all about. The cold turkey or chicken I refer to can be from any part of the cooked carcass from a previous roast, but the little scraps that are stuck right in against the bones – the bits you have to work hard to extract as a result of their proximity to the bones of the bird; the most flavoursome (and probably most nutritious) morsels – are the bits I love. The uninitiated will look at a seemingly well-picked carcass of a cooked bird and maybe see stock, while the more experienced and thrifty cook will see another meal as well as stock or broth. I like to cook organically reared poultry and it is important to extract as many meals from the expensive bird as possible. This is the sort of mindful housekeeping that previous generations of cooks understood in a time when it was regarded to be a sin to waste food, a time when a chicken or turkey was a treat, a time when the true value of food was understood. So don't think of this just as a way of adding interest to the palate jaded by a few days of eating turkey or chicken, but as an exercise in responsible eating that at the same time produces a truly delicious dish. When I speak of the joy of cooking, this is some of the joy that I refer to.

The vegetable, chard, that I suggest is a favourite of mine, but if that leafy beauty with its muscular stalks is not available, spinach is an excellent substitute. The spinach stalks are truly delicious, so don't discard them but use them exactly the same way as I have suggested using the chard stalks – more joy.

This is a great technique for making an open-face pie or perhaps some might like to call it a tart. In any event, the process can be used for many other ingredients other than those suggested here. The pastry is simple to make and easy to work with. It is an ideal vehicle for making the very best of leftovers

The uninitiated will look at a seemingly well-picked carcass of a cooked bird and maybe see stock, while the more experienced and thrifty cook will see another meal as well as stock or broth.

such as roast chicken or turkey. The pastry freezes well, so this makes getting organised all the easier.

I like to serve the pie with a salad of crisp leaves or a green vegetable such as purple sprouting broccoli or peas.

Serves 6–8

Pastry
— 175g cold butter, cut into 1cm dice
— 275g plain flour, plus extra for dusting
— Pinch of salt
— 50ml sour or fresh cream

Filling
— 450g Swiss chard or spinach
— 25g butter
— 1 medium onion, peeled and finely chopped
— 1 large garlic clove, peeled and crushed to a paste
— 1 egg
— 1 egg yolk
— 25g grated Parmesan cheese
— 150ml cream
— 1 tablespoon chopped fresh tarragon
— 150g cold leftover roast turkey or chicken, pulled or cut into 2cm pieces
— A little beaten egg, to glaze the pastry
— Sea salt and freshly ground black pepper

To make the pastry, in a large bowl rub the cold butter into the flour with a pinch of salt to resemble fine breadcrumbs. Add the sour or fresh cream and bring the mixture together with your hands. Sprinkle a little flour on the worktop and turn out the pastry. Dust the pastry with a little flour and knead gently to form a smooth mass. Flatten the pastry into a neat 2cm-thick disc. Wrap the pastry in parchment and chill until completely cold. The pastry can also be frozen at this point.

To make the pie filling, begin by cutting or pulling the stalks from the chard. Cut the stalks into 1cm-thick pieces and gently pull the leaves into 3cm pieces. Bring a large saucepan of water to the boil and season well with salt. Add the chard stalks to the

Rainbow Chard

boiling water and cook, uncovered, for 3–4 minutes. Add the leaves and cook for a further 2 minutes, by which time the stalks and leaves should be tender. Drain immediately and press on the drained vegetable to extract as much water as possible. Spread out the chard on a flat dish to cool.

Melt the butter in a small saucepan and when it foams add the onion and garlic. Turn in the butter to coat and cover with a piece of parchment paper and a tight-fitting lid. Cook on a very gentle heat to soften but not colour the vegetables. When cooked, remove from the heat and cool.

Whisk together the egg and yolk, Parmesan, cream and tarragon and season with salt and pepper.

Mix the cooled onions and garlic, chard and turkey together and season to taste.

Preheat the oven to 180°C. Line an oven tray with non-stick baking paper. If the tray has raised sides, turn it over and put the paper on the flat side, as the edges can impede removing the cooked tart neatly from the tray.

To assemble the pie, dust your worktop with flour. Remove the pastry from the fridge and if very firm, don't be afraid to knead it slightly. Alternatively, just allow it to sit on the worktop for 5 minutes to become a little more manageable. Roll the pastry out to a 35cm circle. This sounds and may even look too big – it is not. Wrap the pastry around your rolling pin and transfer to the paper-lined oven tray.

Place the turkey or chicken filling in the middle of the pastry, allowing a 6–8cm clear border all the way around. Fold the pastry border in over the filling to create an open-face pie. The effect of the overlapping pastry will be rather rustic – that's fine. Pinch and push the pastry where necessary to achieve a round tart. Paint the surface of the pastry with a little beaten egg. Now pour the cream and Parmesan mixture over the filling, being careful to allow it to travel down through the filling. I use a thin-bladed knife or skewer to help this to happen.

Cook the tart in the preheated oven for 35–45 minutes. The filling should be gently bubbling and the pastry beautifully coloured.

Allow to rest for 5 minutes before slipping it onto a serving dish and bringing it to the table.

Parmesan and Lemon Crackers

These are a simple cracker suitable for serving with cheese or when a crisp and cheesy bite is needed.

If I am serving the crackers as a nibble, I sometimes add a pinch of chilli flakes or lightly roasted cumin seeds to the raw mixture. If the crackers are being served with cheese, I tend to leave them plain. I love them generously buttered and topped with thinly sliced radishes as a simple snack, but almost anything that sits well with cheese can be popped on top. A single slice of tomato seasoned with a pinch of sea salt, a few drops of olive oil and a basil leaf is easy and refreshing.

If I am serving the crackers as a nibble, I sometimes add a pinch of chilli flakes or lightly roasted cumin seeds to the raw mixture.

Makes approx. 40 crackers
— 115g plain white flour
— 115g finely grated Parmesan cheese
— 55g butter, chilled and cubed
— Zest of 1 lemon
— 2 teaspoons coarsely ground black pepper
— 1 teaspoon sea salt
— 2 tablespoons cold water

Place all the ingredients **except the water** in a food processor and blend until somewhat smooth. Add the water and pulse briefly until it resembles fine breadcrumbs. Remove the mixture to a bowl and bring together by hand to form a smooth dough.

Place the dough on a piece of parchment paper and roll into a cylinder 20cm long. Using the same parchment, wrap the cylinder neatly and tightly and refrigerate for 2 hours or freeze for use at a later date.

Preheat the oven to 190°C. Line a baking sheet with non-stick baking paper.

Once fully chilled, remove the dough from the fridge, cut into 3mm-thick discs and place on the lined baking sheet. Bake in the preheated oven for about 8 minutes, until the edges of the crackers are golden brown. It may take slightly longer in your oven. Remove from the oven and allow to cool slightly on the tray before moving to a wire rack to cool completely.

Store in an airtight container.

Old fashioned grater is best for parmesan

A Bunch of Flowers for the Table

Few things say as much as a bunch of flowers on the table. In the same way as I like to set the table before I sit down to eat, I also like to always have a little pot of blooms, leaves, twigs or a mixture of all of the above to brighten up the scene and to bring some nature into the house. The flowers seem to complement the act of sitting down to eat. The flowers don't need to be a grand arrangement, but could just as easily be a bunch of foraged wild blossoms.

Ruby Beets

Beetroot Tartare with Goats' Cheese Snow, Hazelnut Praline, Honey and Mint

I was very tempted to title this salad 'oh no, not another goats' cheese and beetroot salad'. However, I feel it deserves its inclusion here as it is really good and very fresh tasting indeed. I think there may be some cooks who believe that all beetroot needs cooking before it makes its way to the table, but this is not the case. The vegetable can be simply washed and if necessary peeled, then grated, sliced or diced and it is ready to go. Younger summer (and hence quick-growing) beets taste best for a salad like this, where the flesh is sweeter, tender and less earthy than the later and older autumn or winter beets.

It may seem unusual to be adding a hazelnut praline to this salad, but the proportion here is less sugar laden than a praline you would find in the pastry kitchen and the texture and flavour it brings to the beets are lovely.

If you can find some of the beautifully coloured golden beetroot, you could use those. The less recognisable shade of that beet should cause some confusion hopefully followed by amusement at the table.

The snowy effect created by the grated frozen goats' cheese is pretty and delicious. A ewes' milk cheese would be excellent here also. The various elements of this dish – the goats' cheese snow, the hazelnut praline and the grated beetroot – can all be prepared in advance, making the last-minute assembly of the salad an easy and pleasant task.

It may seem unusual to be adding a hazelnut praline to this salad, but the proportion here is less sugar laden than a praline you would find in the pastry kitchen.

Serves 4–6
— 150g goats' cheese, such as St Tola or Ardsallagh
— 300g beetroot
— 6 tablespoons extra virgin olive oil
— 2 tablespoons freshly squeezed lemon juice

— Drizzle of honey
— 24–36 small fresh mint leaves
— Sea salt and freshly ground black pepper

Hazelnut praline
— 25g blanched hazelnuts
— 15g caster sugar

Place the goats' cheese in a container and freeze for several hours or overnight. Once the cheese is firmly frozen, grate it into a 'snow' using a medium-coarse box grater or Microplane grater. Cover and replace in the freezer immediately.

Place the hazelnuts and sugar in a very small saucepan and place over a moderate heat to caramelise. The sugar will probably cook unevenly, so don't be afraid to give it a little stir to even out the cooking. When the sugar has melted and cooked to a chestnut colour, stir it well to coat the nuts, then remove immediately from the heat and spread out on a sheet of non-stick baking paper. Allow to cool completely and set – the praline will harden within 1 hour. As soon as it is hard, place it on a chopping board and chop coarsely. This can all be prepared several hours ahead of serving the salad.

Remove the stalks and tail from the beetroot and peel with a vegetable peeler. Grate the beet on the coarsest part of a box grater. Place in a bowl and dress with the olive oil and lemon juice and season to taste with salt and pepper.

When ready to serve, spread the beetroot out flat on a large serving dish or individual plates. Drizzle some honey over the beetroot, then a sprinkling of hazelnut praline and mint leaves. Drizzle any of the remaining beetroot dressing over the salad. Remove the cheese from the freezer and dust it all over the plates. Serve quickly before the snow melts.

Salad of Kohlrabi with Shiso, Grilled Mackerel, Egg and Japanese Mustard Dressing

There are two ingredients in this refreshing salad recipe that some cooks may not be familiar with, but both are worth searching out. The kohlrabi and shiso sound a little eccentric, but once you get a handle on the appearance, textures and flavours of both, they are quite delicious.

At first sight the odd-looking kohlrabi appear somewhat alien. The word 'sputnik' is often used to describe this member of the brassica family with its funny antennae-like growths. The strangeness of its appearance comes only from the fact that kohlrabi is unfamiliar to us. Once you have seen it a few times, it seems perfectly normal and entirely entitled to be growing in your garden. Let's face it, if you had never seen a carrot before, you might think the orange-coloured, rocket-shaped, green-haired thing was positively nuclear. Kohlrabi, which needs to be heavily peeled to remove the tough skin, can be eaten raw or cooked and has a delicate flavour akin to broccoli or kale stalks. When really fresh it is refined and lovely. I have served it gently cooked with warm lobster and a light butter sauce and a shivering of chopped chervil to general satisfaction. If you are serving it raw it needs to be either very thinly sliced, grated, finely diced or cut into neat thin julienne strips.

Shiso, from the *Perilla* family, is related to mint and has a curious flavour somewhat reminiscent of cinnamon and cloves. When I smell it, for whatever reason it also reminds me of potato crisps. It is used in many sushi dishes and loves the heat and flavour from wasabi and horseradish, hence its presence in this recipe. It is now visible on restaurant menus, as is the aforementioned kohlrabi, and the plant itself is easy to grow, loving a sunny spot or partial shade. In my experience it also loves the heat of a windowsill, tunnel or glasshouse.

At first sight the odd-looking kohlrabi appear somewhat alien. The word 'sputnik' is often used to describe this member of the brassica family with its funny antennae-like growths.

Shiso, from the Perilla family, is related to mint and has a curious flavour somewhat reminiscent of cinnamon and cloves.

The oily mackerel is the perfect finishing touch for this salad. A bowl of steaming hot new potatoes is all that is needed to accompany the salad to make a pleasing meal.

Serves 4
Salad
— ½ cucumber, peeled, deseeded and cut into 0.5cm dice
— 1 kohlrabi, peeled to remove the tough outer skin
— 2 organic eggs, hard-boiled for 10 minutes and peeled
— 4 mackerel fillets
— Plain flour seasoned with salt and pepper
— 1 dessertspoon extra virgin olive oil
— 2 tablespoons finely chopped shiso leaves
— 1 teaspoon finely chopped and deseeded fresh red chilli
— Sea salt and freshly ground black pepper

Japanese mustard dressing
— Juice of ½ medium lemon
— 3 tablespoons soy sauce
— 1 tablespoon Barbados soft dark brown sugar
— 2 teaspoons mustard powder
— 1 teaspoon extra virgin olive oil

Make the dressing by whisking all the ingredients to combine. Taste and correct the seasoning. It is unlikely to need extra salt.

Place the diced cucumber in a bowl, add 1 tablespoon of the dressing and stir to coat.

Slice the peeled kohlrabi as thinly as possible. I use a Japanese mandolin to do this. Toss the thin slices in 2 tablespoons of the dressing.

Cut the hard-boiled eggs into neat quarters.

To cook the mackerel, place a heavy-based cast iron grill or sauté pan on a medium heat. Dry the mackerel fillets and dip both sides in the seasoned flour, shaking off any excess flour. Paint the skin side of the fish with the olive oil and as soon as the pan is hot, place the fish skin side down in the pan. The fish should sizzle on contact with the pan. If it does not, quickly remove the fillet and wait a moment longer until your pan is hot enough. Cook the fillets for 4–5 minutes, by which time the skin should be blistered and crisp. Turn over and cook for a minute or two on the other side. Remove and keep hot while you assemble the salad.

To assemble the salad, scatter the diced cucumber over a large flat serving plate. Position the eggs randomly on the plate. Add the kohlrabi slices and twist and turn them a little to give the dish a little height. Sprinkle on the finely chopped shiso and the chilli. Place the fillets of hot grilled mackerel over the salad and serve immediately.

Plums

Roast Plums with Pomegranate Molasses and Crème Fraîche

This is a wonderfully simple and delicious dish. I love the intensity of flavour that is created by roasting fruit, particularly stone fruit. Leaving the stones in the halved fruit during the cooking adds a terrific depth of flavour and also means you don't have to wrestle with resistant ones before cooking. Once the fruit is tender, the stones come away from the flesh easily or you can, as I do, leave them where they are for guests to remove them as they eat. The variety and ripeness of plum will affect the flavour and also the cooking time of the dish. I like plums for roasting to be a day away from being perfect to eat as a raw plum, if that makes sense. If they are too ripe, they tend to collapse a bit in the cooking. If they are too under-ripe and hard, they take a long time to cook and the delicate flavour becomes a little too strong for my taste. The deeper and bloodier-looking the raw plums are, the more suitable they are for this dish. The richly coloured shiny cooking juices blend visually with the pomegranate molasses.

The pomegranate molasses that we buy is made from the juice extracted from bitter varieties of the fruit, as opposed to the sweet pomegranates that we like to deseed and sprinkle onto our sweet and savoury dishes. You can juice a pomegranate from the shops with a citrus juicer with relative ease and then reduce that juice to make your own molasses. It's jolly good but does not have the cheek-hollowing sharpness of the bitter varieties grown specifically for that purpose.

The crème fraîche that I suggest serving with the fruit is better than a conventional whipped fresh cream. The sharpness of the combination of plum and pomegranate would just trample over the mild fresh cream, whereas the acidity in the crème fraîche holds its ground very well with the flavours involved. A sprinkling of coarse almond or hazelnut praline (page 139) would be good here too and I often serve this alongside labneh ice cream (page 237) for a gorgeous combination of flavours.

The deeper and bloodier-looking the raw plums are, the more suitable they are for this dish. The richly coloured shiny cooking juices blend visually with the pomegranate molasses.

Serves 4–6
— 8 blood plums
— 1 lemon
— 110g caster sugar
— Crème fraîche
— A drizzle of pomegranate molasses

Preheat the oven to 180°C.

Halve the plums, leaving the stones intact in some of the halves, and place in a close-fitting baking dish. With a swivel peeler, peel five strips of peel off the lemon and push it in around the plums. Scatter over the sugar and squeeze over the lemon juice. Wet a piece of parchment paper under the tap, then squeeze out the excess moisture. Spread the dampened paper over the dish and push down to cover the sides.

Bake in the preheated oven for about 25 minutes. Keep a close eye on the plums, as the cooking time will vary depending on the ripeness and the variety of plum being used. You want the plums to be perfectly soft but still holding their shape. There should be beautiful burgundy-coloured juices surrounding the cooked plums.

I like to serve the plums still slightly warm, though they are also delicious served chilled. If plating them individually, serve with plenty of the cooking juices, a dessertspoon of crème fraîche and a drizzle of pomegranate molasses. If serving family style, serve the crème fraîche and pomegranate molasses separately and ensure all diners also spoon lots of the cooking juices over the plums.

Cardamom Poached Pears with Dark Chocolate, Cocoa Nibs, Pistachio and Candied Orange

When teaching students about cooking pears, I like to remind them that as far as I am concerned, there was a good reason why it was an apple tree and not a pear tree that tempted the unfortunate Eve in that celestial garden. She knew a thing or two about her fruit, as clearly the pear (I speak of European and not Asian pears) would not have been ripe and delicious from the tree. Despite the terrible consequences of her choice, at least we know that from a gastronomic perspective, her decision to pluck the troublesome apple was a correct one. Yes, despite the beauty of the pear on the branch, there is no pleasure in a pear straight from the tree, as they don't ripen to perfect eating for a few days after leaving their natural home. So poor Eve – despite doing the right thing, she did the wrong thing, a miserable business indeed.

This is a classic combination of flavours with a few little twists. I have always loved chocolate with pears, and sometimes when a simple combination is so good and correct, it can be difficult to pluck up the courage to try something new or add another ingredient into the tried-and-tested equation. Cardamom is the new kid on the block here in terms of the upstart ingredient, and though cocoa nibs are of course related to chocolate, they don't often make such an unadulterated appearance. Little chunks of luscious homemade candied peel add a scented flavour to pull it all together.

Regardless of what flavour combinations you are using with pears, it is essential to poach them until they are tender. I usually buy my pears a few days ahead to ensure that they are in perfect condition for cooking. If they are hard and under-ripe they will probably be tough when cooked, and if too ripe before cooking they tend towards a softness that is just not pleasing.

There was a good reason why it was an apple tree and not a pear tree that tempted the unfortunate Eve in that celestial garden.

When these pears are arranged pinwheel style, glazed with the chocolate and scattered with the various other flavourings, they have a very pretty appearance. I usually add little bunches of small bay leaves or mint leaves as a final flourish and a little private homage to the hard-done-by Eve!

Serves 4–8

Pears
— 4 pears
— 1 lemon
— 70g caster sugar
— 3 cardamom pods, lightly crushed
— 100g dark chocolate (70% cocoa solids), roughly chopped
— 1 teaspoon sunflower or grapeseed oil
— 10g cocoa nibs, coarsely chopped
— 4 teaspoons pistachio nuts, coarsely chopped
— 4 teaspoons candied orange peel, finely diced (page 308)

To serve
— Softly whipped cream

Decoration
— Bunches of small fresh bay or mint leaves (optional)

Peel the pears with a swivel peeler and halve each one neatly from top to bottom to attain eight halves. Remove the cores and any tough fibres – I use a melon baller for this, though a sharp teaspoon also works. Place the pears in a heavy-based saucepan into which they fit quite snugly.

Peel four thin strips off the lemon and add to the pears along with all the juice from the lemon. Sprinkle on the caster sugar and the lightly crushed cardamom pods. Cover with a sheet of parchment paper and a tight-fitting lid and cook over a very low heat until the pears are tender. This takes about 30 minutes, but the time will vary according to the ripeness of the pears used. Allow the cooked pears to cool completely. The pears can be cooked a day ahead and refrigerated.

Place the chocolate in a small Pyrex bowl and sit the bowl over a saucepan of cold water. The bottom of the Pyrex bowl must not be touching the water in the saucepan. Turn on the heat and as soon as the water comes to the boil, turn off the heat. The chocolate will not be fully melted, but will continue to melt perfectly in the residual heat. Do not allow the chocolate to get cold.

Drain the pears from the cooking juices and pat dry. Place in a single layer in a flat serving dish. I arrange them in pinwheel or cartwheel fashion with the thinner tops of the pears pointing towards the centre of the plate.

Add the oil to the chocolate and mix well. Using a dessertspoon, spoon over the chocolate to cover each pear either completely or partially. Straight away sprinkle each pear with cocoa nibs, chopped pistachios and diced candied orange peel. Ideally you want the cocoa, pistachio and candied peel to hold their position on top of the chocolate-coated pears.

Put the pears in a cool place or in the fridge to allow the chocolate to set slightly. The pears will sit happily like this for several hours.

Serve the pears with a little of the cooking juices poured around them and some softly whipped cream. Finish the presentation with little bunches of bay or mint leaves between the pears at the edge of the serving dish if liked.

Roast Lamb Heart with Roast Red Onions, Black Garlic Aioli and Marjoram

There are a few recipes in this book that will definitely not appeal to a wide audience and I suspect that this is one of them, but for those among you who like animal innards, I think you will love this.

I grew up eating lots of offal and I adore it. As children we thought nothing of tucking in to liver, kidneys, sweetbreads and heart. My mother cooked these foods regularly with skill and finesse and we loved it. She did not go into any detail about the specific parts of the animal that we were eating – to us, it was just another delicious piece of meat. Her lack of information may have been important, but honestly we were not squeamish and in a household of nine children, we were all expected to (and indeed did) eat everything. She cooked both beef and lamb heart, often with a traditional breadcrumb stuffing. The cooked heart was then served thinly sliced with vegetables on the side. The lamb heart is considerably smaller and requires a shorter cooking time than the larger beef one.

Here the heart is gently spiced with cumin seeds and more robust flavour comes from the onions and black garlic. The sweetness of the garlic, with its flavour that nods in the direction of tamarind and balsamic vinegar, is perfect with the offal and I would happily pair it with kidney or liver on another occasion.

Serves 2
— 1 lamb heart, trimmed of excess fat
— 1 teaspoon roasted and roughly ground cumin seeds
— 2 medium red onions, peeled and each onion cut into eight wedges
— A few drops of extra virgin olive oil
— 100ml chicken stock (page 319)
— 1 tablespoon black garlic aioli (page 306)

The sweetness of the garlic, with its flavour that nods in the direction of tamarind and balsamic vinegar, is perfect with the offal and I would happily pair it with kidney or liver on another occasion.

Black garlic

Red Onion

— 2 generous sprigs of fresh marjoram
— Sea salt and freshly ground black pepper

To serve
— Rustic oven roast potato wedges (page 294)
— Green vegetable or salad

Preheat the oven to 180°C.

Heat a small ovenproof frying pan on a medium heat. Add the fat trimmings from the heart and allow to cook gently for a few minutes to render out a little liquid fat. Pop in the heart, roll it in the fat and allow it to colour gently. Turn the heart occasionally to seal and lightly colour its entire surface area. Pour off the fat and season the heart with salt and pepper, then sprinkle over the lightly crushed cumin seeds.

Place the onion wedges around the heart and season with salt and pepper and a few drops of olive oil. Cover with a piece of dampened parchment paper and put the pan into the preheated oven. Cook for about 45 minutes, until the heart is just cooked and the onions are completely tender. The heart will feel firm and springy to the touch.

Remove the heart and onions from the pan and keep warm in the oven reduced to 100°C. Add the chicken stock to the pan and stir with a wooden spoon to loosen any cooking juices. Bring to a gentle simmer, then taste and correct the seasoning. Remove from the heat. Add enough of the cooking juices to the aioli to achieve a coating consistency.

To serve, slice the heart into 12 slices, each 3mm thick, and place overlapping on a hot serving dish. Surround with the onions. Nap the heart and onions with the bubbling hot cooking juices, then drizzle over the aioli. Finally, sprinkle with marjoram leaves and serve immediately with crisp oven roast potatoes and a green vegetable or salad.

Eggs Stuffed with Mayonnaise and Nasturtium

The humble and undemanding nasturtium that scurries in its colourful way along the ground and happily clambers wherever it is allowed to go is the star of these retro stuffed eggs. The flowers and leaves are both used, and apart from the spicy flavour they lend an almost carnival appearance to the finished eggs.

I suppose this is a classic case of fashion in food, as for a period of time eggs stuffed like this were looked at as if they only had a place on the Arc and were way too old-fashioned to be taken seriously. What a mistake it is to think like that. Something is either delicious or it is not! We are all of course influenced by the changing trends in cooking, by the arrival of new ingredients on our shores from abroad or a new ingredient grown for the first time at home. We pick up ideas in magazines and books, at food markets, on TV shows, eating in restaurants and of course when we travel. That is all to be expected as we try to keep our tables interesting and ever-changing. All good and interested cooks are delighted with a new ingredient, a new flavour and a new recipe to bring it to life. But on the other hand, it is a pity to lose the confidence to be able to decide for ourselves what we like to eat.

Anyway, I have always loved a stuffed egg, partly, I suppose, because I love eggs, but mostly because they are quite delicious. These eggs can be served as a starter with a few salad leaves or as part of a selection of cold hors d'oeuvres. They are good with cold ham or chicken and also with smoked salmon.

Making your own mayonnaise to use here will make a world of difference and is a classic example of the value of knowing and being confident in a few key techniques and dishes that make a huge difference to the food that you cook and eat. Homemade mayonnaise is a keystone, or at least a building block, to great simple food at home.

I suppose this is a classic case of fashion in food, as for a period of time eggs stuffed like this were looked at as if they only had a place on the Arc and were way too old-fashioned to be taken seriously.

Serves 4
— 4 eggs
— 3 tablespoons homemade mayonnaise (page 306)
— 2 tablespoons finely chopped nasturtium leaves and flowers
— Sea salt and freshly ground black pepper

Garnish
— 8–16 small nasturtium leaves
— 8 nasturtium flowers
— 8 slivers of green olive (2 olives will easily yield this)

Bring a small saucepan of water to the boil and add a good pinch of salt. Drop in the eggs carefully and boil for exactly 10 minutes. Remove immediately and chill in cold water.

Peel the eggs and cut them in half lengthways. Remove the hard yolks and place in a fine-mesh sieve over a bowl. Push the yolks through the sieve, then scrape the bottom of the sieve to ensure you have not wasted any. Add the mayonnaise and chopped nasturtiums and mix well with a wooden spoon. Taste and correct the seasoning. I find it is easy to over-season stuffed eggs, as the eggs have been salted in the cooking and the mayonnaise will have been salted in the making, so proceed with caution.

Use a teaspoon to divide the egg yolk mixture into the hollowed-out egg whites. You could also use a piping bag fitted with a large plain or star nozzle. Garnish each egg with one or two small nasturtium leaves and a flower. Finally, place the sliver of green olive in a prominent place so that its sharp flavour does not come as a surprise to diners. By now the eggs embellished with flower and leaf should look like the smartest hat ready for the Chelsea Flower Show or a day at the races.

Pink Grapefruit, Cucumber, Pomegranate and Shiso Salad

Shiso is a plant I am intrigued by. Related to mint, this Asian leaf has a somewhat elusive flavour and it has taken me a while to find ingredients I really like with it. It grows brilliantly in this part of the world under glass or plastic. Gardeners will be thrilled by the shiso plant, as it lasts for months and has a rather lush and exotic appearance, adding great visual interest wherever it grows. It provides beautiful large green or bronze purple-hued leaves with serrated edges and a slightly hairy texture. It was the slightly coarse texture that I battled with, but here the leaf is chopped so any discomfort is lost. Combined as here with cucumber and grapefruit and a few pomegranate seeds for sweetness, its flavour comes into its own.

You could of course use a yellowed-skinned grapefruit here. The most common variety is Marsh, but these juice-filled fruits, which used to be the most widely available variety, now seem to have been replaced by the pink type. Surely this is a case of fashion in food – perhaps the pink one was regarded as being prettier and as demand for that grew, the more conventional yellow one withdrew from the market. I like a combination of both colours for the best effect.

This salad is wonderful paired with the cucumber and elderflower granita on page 99.

It was the slightly coarse texture that I battled with, but here the leaf is chopped so any discomfort is lost. Combined as here with cucumber and grapefruit and a few pomegranate seeds for sweetness, its flavour comes into its own.

Serves 4
— 2 pink or white grapefruit (or one of each)
— ½ cucumber
— 1 tablespoon pomegranate seeds
— 2 teaspoons honey
— 2 teaspoons finely chopped shiso leaves

Carefully remove the rind and pith of the grapefruits and cut into neat segments. Peel the cucumber, cut it in half lengthways and remove any excess seeds from the centre. Cut the flesh into neat 0.5cm dice and add to the grapefruit with the pomegranate seeds, honey and shiso. Stir very gently to encourage the honey to dissolve. Taste and add a little more honey if necessary. Serve chilled.

Citrus segments

Jerusalem Artichoke, Mussel and Saffron Soup

Jerusalem artichokes are a wonderful vegetable for the colder months of the year and their texture when cooked allows for a beautifully silky soup. Mussels pair particularly well with the tuber and the exotic saffron brings its own mysterious and smoky magic to the combination. The knobbly vegetable, which is a bit of a trial to peel, should be better known than it is. In the last few years, though, as people have concentrated on gut health and begun to understand the relationship between the gut and the rest of the body, the previously rarely seen artichoke is becoming more visible at farmers markets and good vegetable shops. It is regarded as one of the best possible foods to eat for gut health. It is not at all obvious when you look at them, as they are not conventionally pretty, that they are part of the sunflower family. This only becomes apparent if you see their tall foliage, which grows to a great height of 3 metres or so, and perched on top are small flowers of what could definitely be called a sunflower yellow. If you can manage to get the vegetables fresh from the ground, you can just scrub them thoroughly and not peel them, which will save a lot of time.

If I am making the soup ahead of time, which I normally would, I make it exactly according to the recipe but leave the addition of the prepared mussels until I am reheating the soup. I find that this way they retain their juicy texture in a more satisfactory way. Refer to the recipe for mussels with fennel and cannellini beans on page 12 for detailed instructions on how to cook the mussels.

Serves 6–8
— 50g butter
— 600g Jerusalem artichokes, peeled and chopped (weighed after peeling)
— 300g onions, peeled and chopped
— 300g potatoes, peeled and chopped (weighed after peeling)
— 800ml chicken stock (page 319)

It is not at all obvious when you look at them, as they are not conventionally pretty, that they are part of the sunflower family. This only becomes apparent if you see their tall foliage, which grows to a great height of 3 metres or so, and perched on top are small flowers of what could definitely be called a sunflower yellow.

— 300ml creamy milk (½ milk, ½ cream)
— 1.5kg mussels
— Pinch of saffron threads
— 2 tablespoons mixture of chopped fresh flat-leaf parsley and
  chives
— Sea salt and freshly ground black pepper

Melt the butter in a heavy-based saucepan and allow to gently
foam. Add the artichokes, onions and potatoes and season with
salt and pepper. Stir with a wooden spoon to coat the vegetables
in the butter and cover with a disc of greaseproof paper and a
tight-fitting saucepan lid. Cook over a very low heat for about
20 minutes to sweat the vegetables.

When the vegetables are starting to collapse at their edges,
add the chicken stock and bring to a simmer. Continue to cook,
covered, for about 20 minutes, until tender. It is worth noting
that these artichokes cook somewhat unevenly, so test several
pieces when determining whether they are all fully tender. If
they are not all soft, the texture of the soup will be gritty and
unpleasant.

Bring the creamy milk to a simmer in a separate saucepan
and add three-quarters of it to the vegetables. Using a
hand-held blender or liquidiser, purée the soup to a smooth,
silky consistency. If necessary, add the remaining milk. The
consistency of the soup should be similar to thin pouring cream.

Place the mussels in a low-sided pan and cover. Place over a
moderate heat and cook until the shells pop open. I use a clear
Pyrex plate as a lid, as that way I can be more in touch with what
is happening in the pan. The mussels cook unevenly and you
need to lift them out as they pop open, as if left cooking for too
long they will overcook and shrivel to a miserable size. It is also
important that you don't have the heat too high, as if you do
you will boil off the precious liquid that the mussels emit when
cooking. This 'mussel juice' is an essential part of the flavour of
the soup. Strain the juice through a fine-mesh sieve to remove
any grit or sand. Add the pinch of saffron to the juices and bring
to a simmer. Turn off the heat and allow the saffron to infuse.

Pick through the mussels, removing them from the shells and
also removing the beards that may or may not still be attached.

The beard is a tiny tuft of hair-like fibre that the mussels use to attach themselves to rocks, chains, ropes and so on when growing. It is harmless but somewhat unpleasant to eat.

Add the mussels and the cooking juices containing the saffron to the artichoke soup. Stir gently. Taste and correct the seasoning. It may be necessary to add a little more creamy milk if the soup is too thick.

Reheat the soup to a simmer when serving and ladle into hot bowls. Scatter the parsley and chives over each serving and serve immediately.

Grilled Panettone Chocolate Pudding

Panettone is a wonderful rich sweet Italian bread believed to have originated in Milan, but is now available all over Italy and indeed further afield. The quality of the breads varies enormously, so it pays to do some research and find ones made in the traditional way with a sourdough and flecked with the very best-quality dried and candied fruits. Once you have secured the bread, the rest is relatively easy. The combination with chocolate is not a new one, but the result here is so delicious and comforting that it definitely deserves inclusion.

This pudding needs to be assembled while the grilled bread is still hot and the custard is warm. This way the chocolate melts into a sauce-type consistency and blends gently with the custard.

I like to serve the pudding on the day it is made, though it is still great the day after. I prefer not to refrigerate the pudding if I am serving it on the same day, but if you are keeping it overnight, it is probably best to pop it in the fridge. In that case, remove it from the fridge 2 hours before serving to allow the wonderful textures to loosen up and become unctuous before eating.

The quality of the breads varies enormously, so it pays to do some research and find ones made in the traditional way with a sourdough and flecked with the very best-quality dried and candied fruits.

Serves 6–8
— 400ml milk
— 1/3 vanilla pod or 1 teaspoon vanilla extract
— 4 egg yolks
— 35g caster sugar
— 80g chocolate (62% cocoa solids)
— 350–400g panettone

To serve
— Softly whipped cream

Bring the milk almost to the boil with the vanilla pod (but not the extract, if using). Remove from the heat, allowing the vanilla pod to infuse the milk.

Beat the egg yolks with the sugar until thick and light. If you are using vanilla extract, add it now. Pour in the hot milk gradually, whisking all the time. Pour into a clean saucepan with the vanilla pod and cook on a low heat for 15–20 minutes, stirring constantly with a flat-bottomed wooden spoon. **The custard must not boil**, so keep a close eye on what is happening in the saucepan and the heat under it as well. Be patient and eventually the custard will thicken slightly, but not dramatically – just enough to leave a light trail along the back of the wooden spoon when a finger is drawn through it. Remember, this sauce is served with a thin consistency and also remember that it thickens a little as it cools, though here we are using it while still hot. Immediately remove the pan from the heat.

To maximise the flavour and appearance of the vanilla in the sauce, cut the vanilla pod in half and squeeze the oily-looking seeds into the sauce. When whisked this thick black liquid disperses into thousands of tiny little flecks of vanilla.

Chop the chocolate into coarse grit-sized pieces.

Heat a heavy-based cast iron grill pan or sauté pan. Cut the panettone into 1.5cm-thick slices. Grill the panettone on the dry pan until well coloured, then turn and repeat with the other sides. I like some of the panettone to become richly coloured as this greatly enhances the flavour of the finished dish.

Drizzle a little custard on the bottom of a pretty ceramic dish. I use one that is 25cm wide and 5cm deep, so something close to that will be fine. Cover with enough of the hot panettone to hide the custard and sprinkle on half of the chocolate. Spoon over about half of the remaining custard and repeat the process again with the rest of the panettone and chocolate, finishing with the remaining custard, being careful that there are no bits of dry panettone visible.

Allow the pudding to sit at room temperature for 1 hour before serving. Serve with softly whipped cream.

Elderflower and Lemon Syllabub

I have always loved the word 'syllabub'. There is something so pleasing about it. For me, the word conjures up images of the beautiful old glasses specifically blown for the serving of the pudding. I have four of these glasses – hardly a museum collection, but nonetheless precious to me. They come in a variety of shapes and sizes. Some are tall and slender, some are more rotund and solid, some have a single handle and some have none. Originally syllabub was a frothy milk and alcohol-based drink, but now we expect it to be a very gently whipped and flavoured cream.

It is a lovely thing, though, and simple to make. It was all the rage between the sixteenth and nineteenth centuries, but it slipped out of fashion and almost disappeared. I like my version here, with elderflower cordial and brandy combining to yield a flavour that is neither too strong in alcohol nor too sweet in sugar. The key to success is soaking the lemon rinds in cordial and brandy overnight, then keeping a watchful eye when whipping the cream to achieve barely set soft folds of the sweetened pudding. The final touches are fresh nutmeg that is grated directly onto the cream in the glasses and the finely sliced lemon rinds, which hold on to the flavour of the brandy and elderflower cordial they were soaked in. All these tiny details matter here to create a perfect balance of flavours.

If the elderflower is in season when I am making this, I sprinkle a few little elderflowers on the creams.

Serves 6–8
— 1 lemon
— 8 tablespoons elderflower cordial
— 2 tablespoons brandy
— 50g caster sugar
— 300ml cold cream
— Freshly grated nutmeg
— A few fresh elderflowers when in season

It is a lovely thing, though, and simple to make. It was all the rage between the sixteenth and nineteenth centuries, but it slipped out of fashion and almost disappeared. I like my version here, with elderflower cordial.

To serve
— Plain biscuits

The day before you plan to make and serve the syllabub, pare very thin strips off the rind of the lemon and add to the cordial and brandy. Place in a sealed container and allow to steep and infuse overnight. I use a clean jam jar with a tight-fitting lid.

The next day, strain the infused liquid into a large bowl, reserving the lemon strips for later. Add the sugar to the liquid and stir until completely dissolved.

Pour in the cream and whip to achieve soft folds rather than peaks. It is crucial not to overwhip the cream, as it will become grainy and the comforting and sophisticated texture will be lost. The cream is even thickened by the movement of it from the whisking bowl to the serving glasses, so do take care.

Divide between pretty little glasses and chill until ready to serve.

Slice the reserved lemon peels finely and neatly across the strips to achieve refined short pieces.

Just before bringing the syllabubs to the table, sprinkle a pinch of the lemon strips over each serving and finish each one with a scant grating of fresh nutmeg and a few fresh elderflowers if they are in season. Serve immediately with a fine plain biscuit.

Syllabub

The Wooden Spoon

When I was training how to cook, I had the good fortune
to spend a summer in the kitchen of a restaurant called
Chez Nico in London. Nico Ladenis and his wife, Diana,
ran their small operation in Battersea and at the time had
achieved two Michelin stars. In due course they went on to
gain the coveted third star after a move to the considerably
more fashionable Mayfair. For my summer sojourn, I
was to replace a member of kitchen staff who was leaving
to gain experience in restaurants in France. Nico had a
huge reputation both within and outside the industry as
being difficult and not taking any nonsense from anyone,
including his guests – he had famously asked a guest who
had requested salt to leave. He did not have salt on the tables
for fear of guests unbalancing the flavour of his carefully
seasoned food. Some of the red top press had lampooned
him by creating an illustration in classic cartoon fashion
of Nico chasing guests down the street waving a salt crock
threateningly at them. In reality he never chased anyone
anywhere, but I knew I was going into a kitchen where the
stakes were high and the tension might be at a similar level.

The first week proved to be tense, to say the least. There
were three of us other than Nico in the tiny kitchen. We
followed Nico's instructions to the letter. It was his way or
the highway, which I felt was entirely honest and fair. It was
all new to me and I needed to pick up all the details and
flavours of the dishes I was in charge of before the chap I
was replacing left for France.

During that first week, I travelled in every day from near
Gatwick on the outskirts of London. This meant getting up
at six in the morning and not arriving home until one a.m.
that night, up again at six and so on. We worked a split shift
with a few hours off in the afternoon. I plonked myself down
in an exhausted curl, vagrant style, on a bench in nearby
Battersea Park every afternoon and fell into a deep sleep,
shattered from the stress and lack of time in bed. As the
week wore on, my dearth of rest rendered me monosyllabic

and really not playing my best game. On Saturday night, as I bade farewell to the chef bound for France, I could tell that Nico was worried. His kitchen was too small for one weak link, his Michelin stars were precious and at that point it looked like I might snap. As luck would have it, over that first weekend I moved into a room that was within walking distance from the restaurant and arrived back to work on Tuesday rested, refreshed and enthusiastic. I could now have a proper rest every afternoon as my commute was literally minutes. I flourished and all went swimmingly.

In the kitchen, everything had its place. Each whisk, each bowl, each saucepan. I learned a great deal from Nico about food and also about being organised. The kitchen was always quiet. That was the way Nico liked it. I also learned that being as silent as Nico often did not mean that you were a brute or that you were rude – it just meant you were not saying anything unnecessary. It seemed to me that Nico felt the weight of those two stars heavily on his shoulders. One day we were working away, preparing for service. Nico was standing in his usual place beside the service hatch where all the food was passed through to the dining room – he handed every single plate for each guest to the waiting staff. Nothing escaped his attention. Suddenly, the wooden spoon I was using to beat something or other just snapped in my hand. I was somewhat amused by this unusual happening, thinking I was clearly putting my back into that particular exercise. However, I felt an unexplained chill descend. This was a different kind of silence to the silence we usually worked in.

Immediately I looked up from my bowl, as it was obvious that something that I had no knowledge of had just happened. The other two chefs and Nico had stopped what they were doing. Nico was looking at me and they at him, all three of them with their mouths somewhat ajar. Nico removed his spectacles, massaged the bridge of his nose and exclaimed gravely that I had just broken his 'lucky' wooden spoon. Well, had I previously known of the magic and talismanic powers of this simple spoon-shaped stick, I most certainly would never have picked it up in the first place.

Obviously I did not say that to Nico, but he continued to tell me in detail how far it had travelled with him and how he felt it was a part of his success. I of course pleaded ignorance and forgiveness. I cannot remember how we resolved the matter. I suppose diners started arriving and our minds were diverted back to the matter at hand: feeding the guests.

Nothing terrible happened in the following months of my stay. In fact, we all got on really well, Nico was delighted with my cooking and his shiny stars were to the best of his knowledge and mine still intact. As the stand-in for his travelling commis chef, I had been a success. We had a parting lunch on the day of my departure. All were in good spirits, as it coincided with the restaurant's annual holiday for the month of August. At the end of lunch, and to much hilarity, Nico presented me with an enormous wooden spoon which he had engraved with a message: 'Rory's lucky spoon'. We all laughed, me somewhat nervously. I think it was the first time in that long, hot, rewarding summer that I had seen Nico laugh with a wide and happy smile. He could now have a month off from the pressure of his own wooden spoon – his Michelin stars. This misunderstood, gentle, civilised, kind, quietly charming man had taught me a great deal about food and kitchens and how sometimes silence, once backed up by success, can be a lovely noise.

Rice Pilaf with Chicken, Courgettes and Coriander

This is what I would call a supper dish, but then I don't really differentiate between supper and dinner as long as the food is delicious. I suppose I connote it with a more informal meal as it arrives at the table in one single dish. This is the type of dish that we all need, as it is a brilliant vehicle for bits of leftover roast chicken, lamb, pheasant or bacon. I pick every scrap off a cooked carcass or bone and that becomes the meat addition to the pilaf. I love the skin, jellied cooking juices and those bits of meat that are hardest to get at. Invariably the hardest-fought-for morsels are the sweetest and it feels great to know you have extracted every bit of value and goodness from the remains of a previous meal.

Apart from the quick cooking of the courgettes in a sauté pan, the rest of the dish happens in just one saucepan. The quantity of the courgette could be increased to make a meat-free dish. In any event, it is a delicious and nutritious dish and I find it deeply satisfying and comforting.

This is the type of dish that we all need, as it is a brilliant vehicle for bits of leftover roast chicken, lamb, pheasant or bacon. I pick every scrap off a cooked carcass or bone and that becomes the meat addition to the pilaf.

Serves 4
— 20g butter
— 100g finely chopped onion
— 1 garlic clove, peeled and crushed to a paste
— 220g basmati rice
— 1 level teaspoon flaky sea salt
— 250g cooked chicken, cut into 2cm pieces
— 500ml chicken stock (page 319)
— 1 tablespoon extra virgin olive oil
— 300g coarsely grated courgette
— Pinch of chilli flakes
— 1 tablespoon chopped fresh coriander
— Sea salt and freshly ground black pepper

Melt the butter in a heavy-based saucepan or casserole. When the butter is foaming, add the onion and garlic and stir well.

Cover with a piece of greaseproof or parchment paper and the saucepan lid and cook on a very low heat for about 10 minutes. You want the onion to soften without getting any colour.

Add the rice and flaky salt and gently stir through the buttery onions. Cook for 1 minute before adding the chicken and giving that a gentle mix. Pour in the chicken stock and bring to a gentle simmer. Put the lid on the saucepan and cook over a very gentle heat for about 15 minutes.

While the rice is cooking, heat the olive oil in a sauté pan. Add the courgette and season with salt, pepper and a pinch of chilli flakes. Continue cooking over a moderately high heat while giving the occasional stir. Remove from the heat when the courgette is still slightly undercooked.

When the rice has absorbed all the stock, gently stir in the cooked courgette and chopped coriander. Taste and correct the seasoning and serve immediately.

Moroccan Harira Soup

Moroccan food is one of the great cuisines of the world, and in the hands of the skilled and knowledgeable cook strikes a beautiful balance between sweetness, saltiness, sourness and heady aromatic flavours.

In Morocco this soup is traditionally served to break the fast during the holy month of Ramadan. There are thousands of different recipes for the soup, with each household adding their own particular twist to suit tastes and preferences. Chickpeas, lentils and sometimes beans, meat (either beef or lamb), vegetables, herbs and spices are the basic ingredients. The smell of this soup cooking in the kitchen transports me back to exotic and mysterious Tangier. I prefer to use lamb rather than beef and find a more balanced flavour is achieved. This is a purely personal preference and I don't think there is a right or a wrong combination of ingredients. You may find the addition of the rice at the end of the cooking to be unusual, but it gives a velvety finish to the soup. Sometimes the rice is replaced with tiny bits of pasta, like orzo. In her wonderful book *Arabesque*, Claudia Roden mentions how in some cases a sourdough batter is added to give the velvety consistency or just a simple mixture of flour and water. In any event, this addition of starch needs to be very close to the time of eating, otherwise the rice or pasta can become soft and flabby.

This soup is substantial, as you can imagine it would need to be after fasting from sunrise to sundown. I like to serve it with lots of chopped fresh coriander and a lemon wedge on the side. The warmer the weather, the more inclined I am to squeeze a little juice into the soup too. I am not so sure that serving it with dates and honeyed pastries, as happens during Ramadan, is to our taste in this part of the world.

The smell of this soup cooking in the kitchen transports me back to exotic and mysterious Tangier.

Serves 8
— 100g dried chickpeas, soaked overnight in cold water
— 110g Puy lentils
— 450g lamb, trimmed of all fat and cut into 1cm cubes
— 1 large onion, peeled and finely chopped

HaRiRa

- — 1 teaspoon ground turmeric
- — ½ teaspoon ground cinnamon
- — ¼ teaspoon ground ginger
- — ¼ teaspoon saffron strands
- — ¼ teaspoon paprika
- — 50g butter
- — 100g long-grain basmati rice
- — 4 large ripe tomatoes, peeled, deseeded and chopped
- — Pinch of caster sugar
- — 4 tablespoons chopped fresh flat-leaf parsley
- — 2 tablespoons chopped fresh coriander
- — Sea salt and freshly ground black pepper

To serve
- — Lemon wedges

Soak the chickpeas in cold water overnight. The next day, discard the water and place the chickpeas in a saucepan with the lentils. Add the lamb, onion, turmeric, cinnamon, ginger, saffron and paprika. Cover with 1.5 litres of water and stir gently to mix. Season lightly with salt and pepper. Bring to the boil and skim off any froth that rises to the surface. Add half of the butter.

Turn the heat down and simmer the soup, covered, for 1–1½ hours, until the chickpeas are tender. Keep an eye on the level of liquid in the pan and add a little more water if necessary.

Towards the end of the cooking time, prepare the rice. Bring 850ml of water to the boil in a saucepan. Add the rice, stir gently and cook until tender. Drain the rice, reserving the cooking liquid.

Cook the chopped tomatoes in 3 tablespoons of the rice cooking water. Season with salt, pepper and a pinch of sugar. The tomatoes should have a 'melted' appearance.

Add the cooked rice, tomatoes and the rest of the butter to the soup and simmer for a further 5 minutes. Taste and correct the seasoning, adding some of the reserved rice cooking water to thin out the soup a little if necessary. Add the chopped herbs and serve with lemon wedges on the side.

Lime Pickle

I am somewhat addicted to the punchy flavour of these pickled limes and always have a jar of them in my fridge. In fact, there are usually two jars on the go – one for eating right now and another pickling away to ensure there won't be a gap and the horrible prospect of having to do without them for a while. You are going to need some patience here, though, before you get to taste these salty, spicy pickles, as once you have made them they need to rest for at least four weeks before eating. After that, the older they get, the more I like them.

There is one ingredient in this recipe that some cooks may not have used before and that is asafoetida. This highly flavoured seasoning is the dried sap from the roots and stem of a giant fennel-type plant. You can buy it in lump or ground form. I usually buy it already ground, though a strong spice grinder will render it to a powder easily. When you smell it for the first time it will seem very strong, and indeed it is, so it is generally used in small amounts to leave dishes with a faint and gentle garlic aroma.

I eat this pickle with all sorts of dishes. Indian foods are the classic accompaniment, but I enjoy it with grilled chicken or lamb, oily fish such as mackerel or grey or red mullet, and even just finely diced and scattered over the rice pilaf with chicken, courgettes and coriander on page 169.

Makes 500ml
— 10 limes
— 1 level teaspoon ground turmeric
— 60ml sesame oil
— 2 teaspoons black mustard seeds
— 4 rounded teaspoons chilli flakes
— 3 teaspoons flaky sea salt
— ¾ teaspoon ground fenugreek
— ⅓ teaspoon asafoetida

Give the limes a quick wash and place in a saucepan into which they fit quite snugly. Add the turmeric and cover with cold water. You may need to place a small plate or saucer over the

you are going to need some patience here, though, before you get to taste these salty, spicy pickles, as once you have made them they need to rest for at least four weeks before eating.

limes to ensure they are submerged. Bring the water to a simmer and cook the limes for 6 minutes. Remove from the heat and allow the limes to cool to room temperature in the cooking water.

When cooled, remove the limes from the saucepan and discard the water. Dry the limes gently, then use a sharp knife to cut in half, then into quartets and finally into eighths. I usually place the board I am chopping the limes on inside a shallow tray to catch any of the escaping lime juice.

Heat the sesame oil in a sauté pan. When it shimmers, add the mustard seeds and allow to pop. Remove the pan from the heat and immediately stir in the chilli flakes, salt, fenugreek and asafoetida. Stir to mix, then add the chopped limes and any juices that have gathered on the chopping board. If you taste the pickle now, it will be uncompromisingly bitter, salty and hot, and that is exactly how it should taste.

Allow to cool to room temperature, then pot into a sterilised jar and refrigerate. Wait for at least four weeks before use.

Lime Pickle

Almond and Orange Cake

This flourless almond and orange cake was inspired by a trip to the island of Majorca, where both oranges and almonds grow in abundance. The cake rises in the cooking and falls a little in the cooling to achieve a tender texture. The cake keeps well and I think it is appropriate served as an afternoon tea cake or after dinner.

I add a few drops of orange extract to the cake to elevate the flavour, but the cake will still be good without the addition of this intensely flavoured liquid. You can of course buy the extract, but making your own is rather easy, as you just soak thinly pared orange rinds in a flavourless alcohol such as vodka. After that you only need patience, as the rinds need at least a week to release their flavour into the alcohol.

The cake is iced with a simple butter and cream cheese icing into which I push candied orange slices. These crisp and deliciously flavoured thins are not difficult to make, but they do require plenty of time to dry out properly. Patience seems to be a recurring theme with this cake! Undoubtedly a dehydrator is the best piece of equipment for drying the oranges, but a conventional or fan oven will also produce a good result. I have a domestic version of the dehydrator in my kitchen and I find it very useful. I use it to dry some herbs, fruit, vegetables, flowers and so on. Of course it is one more piece of equipment taking up valuable countertop in kitchens that are already limited for space, but I would not be without my machine. I pop it in a cupboard when not in use (it is very light and easy to lift). If you look at the machine as a vehicle for preserving food, then making the decision to buy one might be easier.

Serves 8

Cake
— A little melted butter for preparing the cake tin
— 5 eggs
— 200g caster sugar
— 200g ground almonds
— Finely grated zest of 1 orange
— 1 teaspoon orange extract

The cake is iced with a simple butter and cream cheese icing into which I push candied orange slices. These crisp and deliciously flavoured thins are not difficult to make, but they do require plenty of time to dry out properly.

Icing
— 50g butter, at room temperature, but not oily and greasy
— 110g cream cheese, chilled
— 180g icing sugar, sieved
— Zest of 1 orange

Decoration
— 4 fresh mint leaves
— 16 candied orange slices (optional; see next page)

You will need
— 1 x 23cm cake tin

Preheat the oven to 170°C. Brush the sides and base of a 23cm cake tin with melted butter. Line the base of the tin with a disc of non-stick baking paper.

Separate the eggs, placing the whites in a spotlessly clean, dry bowl and the yolks in another bowl. Add the caster sugar to the yolks and use an electric hand whisk to beat to a pale, light and creamy consistency. Fold in the ground almonds, orange zest and extract. At this point the mixture will appear a little heavy.

Whisk the egg whites to soft yet firm peaks. Mix one-quarter of the egg whites into the yolks, then carefully but thoroughly fold in the remaining egg whites. The two mixtures will resist each other for a moment or two but will gradually become a single soft, light and air-filled consistency. Pour the mixture into the cake tin and gently smooth the top.

Bake in the preheated oven for 35–40 minutes. The cooked cake will be golden in colour and coming away slightly from the edge of the tin. You can also test to ensure the cake is cooked by inserting a skewer into the cake. Retract the skewer and if clean, then the cake is cooked.

Place the cake still in the tin on a wire rack to cool for 15 minutes. Gently run a table knife around the edge of the tin, then turn the cake out and allow to cool completely on the wire rack, paper side down.

For the icing, place the butter in a bowl and whisk to a creamy consistency. Add the cream cheese and whisk until smooth.

Gradually whisk in the icing sugar until it is all incorporated. Add the orange zest and stir briefly.

When the cake is completely cooled, remove the paper disc and spread the icing over the top of the cake. If using the candied orange slices, just stick them into the icing to create a random but lovely effect. Finally, tear the mint leaves and sprinkle all over the cake.

Candied Orange Slices
Makes approx. 30 slices
— 2 bright-skinned oranges
— 200ml elderflower cordial or simple syrup

Slice the oranges as thinly as possible into perfect slices. Place in a bowl with the cordial or simple syrup and allow to macerate for 2–4 hours.

Line oven or dehydrator trays with non-stick baking paper. Lift the orange slices out of the cordial or syrup one at a time and shake off any excess. Place the slices on the paper in neat rows. Place in a dehydrator or oven at 50°C and dry for 36–48 hours, until feeling crisp.

When dried, place on clean non-stick baking paper in an airtight box to store. Save the elderflower cordial for another use.

Frikadeller of Whiting with Horseradish Mayonnaise and a Salad of Foraged Wild Greens

I always associate frikadeller with Denmark, though they are also associated with German cuisine. More often than not these little patties or cakes are made with minced or ground meats such as beef, pork and veal, but when made with fish, as in this recipe, they are simple and lovely. A variety of fish can be used, such as cod, hake, ling and pollock, and I don't see why you could not have a mixture of fish, which might perhaps be a perfect way of using some bits of random fish in your freezer. The cakes are formed by hand, and though this is not a dish that requires a perfect and pristine presentation, it will be prettier and easier to cook if all are of a similar size.

I like to serve a salad with the cakes and the contents of that can vary throughout the year. The suggestion with this version is a salad of foraged leaves, but if that is not possible, mixed leaves would be perfect. In late summer, when I might make the cakes from mackerel, I would serve a tomato or courgette salad. Pickled beetroot would also be good and a perfect match with the horseradish mayonnaise.

A variety of fish can be used, such as cod, hake, ling and pollock, and I don't see why you could not have a mixture of fish, which might perhaps be a perfect way of using some bits of random fish in your freezer.

Serves 4–6
— 650g whiting fillet, free of skin and bones and cut into 2cm dice
— 60g plain flour, plus a little extra for dusting
— 100ml cream
— 1 egg, beaten
— 4 tablespoons finely chopped wild garlic leaves or chives
— 1 tablespoon capers, coarsely chopped
— 25g butter
— 1 dessertspoon extra virgin olive oil
— Freshly ground black pepper

To serve
— Lemon wedges
— A salad of foraged wild leaves
— Horseradish mayonnaise (see below)

Place the fish, flour, cream, egg and wild garlic or chives in a
food processor. Season with salt and pepper and using the pulse
button, process briefly to barely combine the ingredients. Be
careful not to over-mix or the texture will be too smooth and
lose its charm. Add the capers and mix in very briefly.

Divide the mixture into 12 little patties. With lightly floured
hands, shape into neat round cakes. Chill until ready to use.

To cook the fish cakes, divide the butter and oil between two
medium-sized frying pans or one large one. When the fat sizzles,
add the cakes, leaving a little space between them. Cook the
cakes over a medium heat for 4–5 minutes on each side, until
golden brown and cooked through.

Serve the cakes on hot plates with lemon wedges, a salad of
foraged wild leaves and horseradish mayonnaise.

Horseradish Mayonnaise

This is so easy and so good. The sauce will keep in your fridge
for a week and is delicious served with fish cakes and smoked
fish and I also love it with grilled or roast beef. The sauce needs
all the sugar and mustard as suggested to balance the flavours
beautifully.

— 2 egg yolks
— 2 tablespoons Dijon mustard
— 2 tablespoons white wine vinegar
— 1 tablespoon caster sugar
— 150ml sunflower or olive oil (or a mixture)
— 1 heaped tablespoon finely grated fresh horseradish
— 1 teaspoon chopped fresh tarragon
— Freshly ground black pepper

Put the egg yolks, mustard, vinegar and sugar in a bowl. Whisk
well and add the oil gradually in a slow, steady stream while
whisking all the time. The sauce will emulsify and thicken quite

easily. Add the horseradish and chopped tarragon. Taste and correct the seasoning. It is unlikely to need salt because of the large quantity of mustard. Chill until needed.

Sprouting Kale Tops with Anchovy, Parmesan and Lemon

This works well served as a starter salad with some grilled bread to accompany. It is also terrific as an accompaniment to grilled meats, poultry and fish. The kale shoots themselves are not nearly as well-known as they should be. Essentially they are new shoots that grow on overwintered kale. If left unpicked these shoots would eventually become the flowers, which are also good to eat, but by the time they flower, the stalk can be unpleasantly tough. I am just thrilled by the fact that the kale throws up this second crop, which in my opinion is superior to the actual leaf kale that we all know and love. I see no reason why these shoots could not be elevated onto a piece of buttered toast in the way that the frightfully grand asparagus is and cloaked with a hollandaise sauce with a soft poached egg popped on top as well.

As with all green vegetables, I like to cook the kale shoots in plenty of boiling salted water with no lid and then dress the cooked shoots while still warm but not hot. This is a subtle point, as if the oil and other seasonings land on the hot kale, they will take on a cooked flavour and lose their vibrancy from the heat of the vegetable. I actually want the flavour of the seasonings to be a little more aggressive and undiminished, and by waiting until the kale is warm rather than hot, that is what is achieved.

The small amount of anchovy adds a deep savoury note to the dish and the egg a delicious richness.

It is also worth saying that the Parmesan here (as in any situation) is best grated straight from the piece of cheese onto the kale. It will never be more vibrant in taste than those moments immediately after it is grated. I prefer to use an old-fashioned grater when rendering this cheese to a coarse powder rather than using the (undeniably brilliant) Microplane. The coarse grater tears the cheese in a different way from the airy, super-light shreds one gets from the Microplane, yielding a fine, gritty texture with an astonishingly superior flavour.

I am just thrilled by the fact that the kale throws up this second crop, which in my opinion is superior to the actual leaf kale that we all know and love.

Broccoli Shoots

Serves 4
— 2 eggs
— 450g sprouting kale tops or purple or white sprouting broccoli
— 4–6 anchovy fillets, finely chopped
— 1 lemon
— 8 tablespoons extra virgin olive oil
— Parmesan cheese, for grating
— Sea salt and freshly ground black pepper

Lower the eggs into a saucepan of boiling salted water and cook for exactly 10 minutes. Remove immediately and cool in cold water. Remove the shells and chop the whole eggs coarsely to about 0.5cm pieces. Keep the eggs covered until ready to use.

Bring a large wide saucepan of water to the boil and add a good pinch of salt. Taste the water – it should taste well salted. Add the kale tops or broccoli and cook, uncovered, until tender. Strain the kale tops or broccoli and lay on a rack or in a colander to cool slightly and drain off any cooking water.

Lay the cooled but still warm to the touch kale tops or broccoli on a flat dish in a single layer. Scatter over the anchovies as evenly as possible, followed by the zest of half the lemon. Drizzle over the olive oil and 2 tablespoons of lemon juice. Tease the oil and lemon juice through the kale tops or broccoli with your fingers to coat the vegetable. Taste a little of the kale or broccoli and season with salt and pepper if necessary.

Even though I like to serve this dish straight away, it will sit happily like this for a couple of hours, but avoid the temptation to refrigerate it, as it dulls the flavour.

When ready to serve, scatter the chopped eggs all over the kale or broccoli, followed by a coarse grating of Parmesan, and serve as soon as possible.

Ricotta with Smashed Cherries, Olive Oil, Lemon and Mint

This is quick, easy and delicious, but a good result is dependent on really fresh ricotta, very ripe cherries and excellent olive oil. There is no cooking as such in this recipe, but even so there are specifics that need to be noted – it is all about careful and timely shopping. This is what charms me about a dish like this, where a few perfectly chosen ingredients in pristine condition can produce a memorable dish with great ease. I am sure that the importance of ripe cherries goes without saying, but perhaps the freshness of the ricotta is not so obvious to all. Ricotta, whether made from cow, sheep or buffalo milk, is a subtle, delicate cheese both in taste and structure, but it loses that freshness of taste and softness of texture quite quickly. I always try to find out from my shopkeeper what day the cheese will be delivered and then I plan this dish based around that information.

You will need to stone and macerate the cherries 30 minutes in advance, but the final assembly of the dish, which is only a matter of minutes, should happen just before you take it to the table. Chopping or tearing the scattering of mint is also a last-minute task, as they oxidise when the leaves are broken for any length of time and as a result they develop a bitter and tired flavour with none of the perfume that we associate with that herb.

This is what charms me about a dish like this, where a few perfectly chosen ingredients in pristine condition can produce a memorable dish with great ease.

Serves 4
— 24 ripe cherries
— 1–2 tablespoons caster sugar
— 320g ricotta cheese
— 4 tablespoons cream
— 2 tablespoons extra virgin olive oil, such as Fontodi or Capezzana
— Zest of 1 lemon
— 16 small fresh mint leaves, torn or chopped just before serving

Remove the stones from the cherries and smash the cherries slightly. You can do this using a cherry stoner or else place the cherries on a chopping board and press them with the flat blade of a knife to squash them and loosen the stone. You can then pick out the stones by hand. Place in a small bowl and sweeten them to taste with some of the caster sugar. Allow to sit and macerate for at least 30 minutes to draw out some of the juice and to allow the sugar to dissolve.

Divide the ricotta between four plates. Try to make a loosely domed shape with a hollow in the centre. Sweeten lightly with a sprinkling of caster sugar. Spoon the cherries and juices into the hollow in the cheese. Drizzle over the cream and olive oil. Finally, zest the lemon over each serving, sprinkle on the mint and serve immediately.

Smoked Mackerel, Tomato and Chive Custard

These are elegant little savoury custards and suitable for serving as a first course. They would also make a lovely lunch or supper accompanied by lots of hot crisp or grilled bread and a simple leaf salad.

The mackerel in the recipe can be replaced with smoked salmon or eel cut into 1cm dice. The various elements of the recipe can all be prepared ahead and the custards assembled close to the time of cooking. I serve this in small portions, as the custards are rich. Almost any kind of heatproof receptacle is suitable, such as small coffee cups, dariole moulds or heatproof glasses.

The mackerel in the recipe can be replaced with smoked salmon or eel cut into 1cm dice. The various elements of the recipe can all be prepared ahead and the custards assembled close to the time of cooking.

Serves 6
— 6 tablespoons tomato stew (page 328)
— 110g smoked mackerel, skinned and gently pulled into small pieces
— 2 eggs
— 1 egg yolk
— 300ml cream
— 50g finely grated Parmesan cheese
— 1 tablespoon finely chopped fresh chives, plus extra to garnish
— Sea salt and freshly ground black pepper

To serve
— Hot crisp or grilled bread

Preheat the oven to 180°C.

Place 1 tablespoon of tomato stew in each of six little ovenproof dishes (see the introduction). Divide the mackerel between the dishes.

Beat the eggs, egg yolk and cream well. Add the Parmesan and chives and season to taste with salt and pepper.

Divide the custard between the six dishes and place in a bain-marie in the oven. I use a small roasting tray half-filled with boiling water. You want the water to come halfway up the sides of the dishes when placed in the tray. Cover the dishes with a butter wrapper or a piece of dampened greaseproof paper. This prevents a skin forming during the cooking.

Cook in the preheated oven for 20–30 minutes, until the custards are just set. The custards are best if allowed to cool slightly before serving or they will sit quite happily for up to 1 hour with the oven temperature reduced to 100°C.

Serve warm with plenty of the bread of choice and a little extra chopped chives to garnish. I usually give my guests teaspoons to eat the custard with.

Homemade Stem Ginger and Chocolate and Ginger Mendiants

I fully accept that this may seem a little – or maybe a great deal! – eccentric. I suppose it is one of those 'life is too short' type of questions. Is life too short to preserve your own ginger? For many people the answer will be an absolute yes and that is a response I can fully understand. The thing is, I had bought too much ginger and could not bear to see it go to waste or at best lose its fat, juicy freshness, so I decided to candy it to preserve it. It is pretty wonderful and actually really easy to do. This is the ginger that I sprinkle over a lemon geranium ice (page 202) and ginger, lemon and turmeric cake (page 239) or as below, onto discs of melted chocolate for mendiants.

The thing is, I had bought too much ginger and could not bear to see it go to waste or at best lose its fat, juicy freshness, so I decided to candy it to preserve it.

Makes approx. 500g
— 325g fresh ginger
— 300g caster or granulated sugar

Place the ginger in the freezer overnight. This helps to soften the fibres and as a result the preserved ginger will be lovely and tender.

The next day, peel the ginger and cut into 0.5cm-thick slices. Cover with cold water and bring to a simmer. Cook, covered, for about 1 hour, until the ginger is tender. Strain the ginger from the water and **reserve 150ml of the cooking water**.

Add the sugar to the reserved cooking water, bring to a simmer and cook for 5 minutes. Add the ginger and continue cooking at a bare simmer until the ginger looks translucent and the syrup has thickened to a thread. This takes about 40 minutes. To check the 'thread' stage, dip a spoon in the syrup – the final drops that fall off the spoon should form thin little threads.

Decant the ginger and syrup into a sterilised container. I reuse a spotlessly clean jam jar and lid that I have put through the dishwasher. Allow to cool completely and store in the fridge, where in my experience it keeps for at least six months.

Chocolate and Ginger Mendiants

These charming little chocolates are simple to make. A mendiant is a traditional French confection composed of a chocolate disc studded with nuts and dried or candied fruit representing the four mendicant or monastic orders of the Dominicans, Augustinians, Franciscans and Carmelites. Each of the nuts and fruits used to refer to the colour of the monastic robes, with tradition dictating raisins for the Dominicans, hazelnuts for the Augustinians, dried figs for the Franciscans and almonds for the Carmelites. Nowadays various other ingredients, such as candied citrus fruit, pistachio nuts and crystallised or stem ginger, have become popular.

Makes 20–30, depending on size
— 225g dark chocolate (62% cocoa solids), roughly chopped
— 50g stem ginger

Place the chocolate in a Pyrex bowl and sit it over a saucepan of cold water. The bottom of the bowl must not be touching the water. Heat the water to a simmer and turn off the heat immediately. The chocolate will not be fully melted at this stage, but the residual heat in the saucepan will melt the chocolate perfectly. Stir the chocolate with a rubber spatula.

Remove the ginger from its syrup and dry well on kitchen paper. Cut into 3mm dice.

Lay a sheet of non-stick baking paper or a silicone mat on a baking tray. Spoon small blobs of the melted chocolate onto the paper – about the size of a €2 coin. Leave a little space between the chocolate blobs, as they will spread slightly. Carefully scatter little dice of the stem ginger onto the chocolate. Allow to chill and set.

Peel the mendiants off the paper and serve.

beets

Elderflower Pickled Beetroot

This is a perfect combination of flavours – the elderflower makes the beetroot sing brightly. The elderflower has seen its position in the plant world rise from being a hedgerow 'weed' to being gentrified to a now highly collected prize. The tree has few redeeming visual features for most of the year, but in full bloom in early summer it is a gorgeous sight, with white flowers the size of side plates adorning the entire tree. The less well-known pink elderflower is perhaps an even more pleasing sight, with lacy blooms of that colour and stalks of deep burgundy. Any flowers that have not been harvested from the tress (usually out of reach) will bear beautiful berries in the autumn – another prize for us lucky cooks and another moment of beauty for the tree itself. Orchards of the trees are now being planted to keep up with the seemingly endless demand for the cordial that is scented with its muscat flavour. For so long there were only a few cooks who understood the marvellous exotic flavour that this pretty flower has to offer, but the flavour and scent are now mainstream and are to be found in cocktail bars, kitchens and spas.

Makes approx. 1 litre
— 700g beetroot, weighed after leaves have been removed (leaving 2cm of stalks attached)
— Pinch of sea salt
— 450ml water
— 225g caster or granulated sugar
— 225ml white wine vinegar
— 4 elderflower heads

Wash the beetroot gently with your hands under a running tap. Place the beets into a small saucepan. It should be a snug fit but with enough space to cover them in water. Add a pinch of salt and bring to a simmer. Cover and cook until the skin of the beets rubs off easily or if tested with a skewer, they offer no resistance. If the water evaporates, top it up to keep the beetroot covered at

The elderflower has seen its position in the plant world rise from being a hedgerow 'weed' to being gentrified to a now highly collected prize. The tree has few redeeming visual features for most of the year, but in full bloom in early summer it is a gorgeous sight.

all times. The cooking time will depend on the age and size of the beets. Younger beets about the size of a golf ball can cook in 20 minutes, whereas larger ones can take up to 2 hours.

While the beets are cooking, combine the 450ml of water with the sugar, vinegar and elderflower in a saucepan and bring to a simmer. It may be necessary to stir occasionally to encourage the sugar to dissolve. Continue simmering for 3 minutes.

When the beetroot are cooked, remove the skins, which should slide off easily, and cut into slices 4–5mm thick. Place in a bowl and pour over the hot pickling syrup.

The beets are now ready to eat or once cold can be refrigerated, where they will keep, covered, for six months.

Caramel Labneh

This is simplicity itself. The labneh is tightly packed into a receptacle, the surface scattered with the rich dark sugar and placed in the fridge overnight. The sugar dissolves to create a treacly sauce that both sits on top of the labneh and melts down through it. The finished dish can simply be eaten as it is, but I like to serve a fruit of some description with it. Roast plums (page 145) would be perfect.

The sugar dissolves to create a treacly sauce that both sits on top of the labneh and melts down through it.

Serves 4–6
— 270g labneh (dripped from 650g thick Greek-style yoghurt – see the method on page 321)
— 3 rounded teaspoons Barbados soft dark brown sugar

Pack the labneh into a small receptacle and smooth the surface to compact it in the dish. I use a bowl that is 12cm wide at its mouth and 7cm deep with sides tapering inwards, in other words, not straight sided. Scatter over the sugar, covering the entire surface in an even layer. Cover and place in the fridge overnight or for at least 12 hours.

When serving the labneh, dip your spoon right down to the bottom of the receptacle to get a proper cross-section of the flavour from the sugary top to the unsweetened bottom.

Grilled Cucumber Salad with Tahini Sauce and Dukkah

I love cucumber, a vegetable that perhaps we take for granted and maybe does not get the credit it deserves as a vehicle for all manner of flavour additions. Many will think of it as a vegetable that is only to be eaten raw, but it can be terrific when carefully cooked. It is delicious with chicken and guinea fowl and also with lamb. Its association with smoked and pickled fish is well known, particularly in its raw state, but when peeled, finely diced and lightly cooked in butter, it is a revelation with cooked fish such as turbot, brill and plaice.

If you ever get a chance to pick a cucumber straight from the plant, break or cut it open, taste it and smell it there and then – it is quite a different experience from a chilled, plastic-wrapped one from the supermarket shelf. Yes, cucumber does have a lovely smell, and for a cook to truly understand the possibilities of an ingredient, nothing beats the experience and knowledge gained when you see, feel, smell and taste an ingredient when it is at its most perfect.

If you ever get a chance to pick a cucumber straight from the plant, break or cut it open, taste it and smell it there and then – it is quite a different experience from a chilled, plastic-wrapped one from the supermarket shelf.

Serves 6–8

Grilled cucumbers
— 2 cucumbers, about 345g each
— 1 tablespoon sesame oil
— Sea salt and freshly ground black pepper

Dressing
— 1 tablespoon rice vinegar
— 1 tablespoon sesame oil
— 2 teaspoons soy sauce
— 2 teaspoons honey
— 1 rounded teaspoon toasted sesame seeds

To finish
— Tahini sauce (see below)
— 1–2 tablespoons dukkah (page 310)
— Fresh coriander leaves
— Fresh mint leaves

Cut the cucumbers in half lengthways, then cut each half lengthways again to attain four long pieces. Remove any of the excess seeds, then cut the strips of cucumbers at an angle into 4cm pieces. Toss the pieces of cucumber in the oil and season.

Heat a heavy-based cast iron pan grill and as soon as it is hot and just about to smoke, place the cucumbers on the pan in a single layer. Allow to colour really well before turning to the other side and repeating the process. This will take 15–20 minutes.

Mix all the dressing ingredients and whisk well. Taste and add a few more grains of salt if necessary.

Remove the well-coloured cucumbers from the grill pan and allow to cool to tepid before adding to the dressing and giving a good mix. Taste and correct the seasoning.

To assemble the salad, spread the tahini sauce on the base of individual plates or a large flat serving dish. Arrange the cucumbers on the sauce. Finish each salad with a sprinkling of dukkah, followed by coriander and mint leaves.

Tahini Sauce
— 125g tahini
— 1 garlic clove, peeled and crushed to a paste
— Juice of 1 lemon (approx.)
— Pinch of salt
— 120ml water (approx.)

Place the tahini, garlic, lemon juice and a pinch of salt in the bowl of a food processor and add half of the water. Blend to a thick consistency and **cautiously** add the remaining water while blending until it loosens up to a creamy texture. Be careful not to make the sauce too thin, but if this does happen, correct the consistency by adding a little more tahini. The consistency should be just softer than softly whipped cream. Taste again, adding salt and lemon juice as necessary. Store chilled.

Good Things, My Mother, Sponge Cake and Jane Grigson

When I first started cooking professionally, or at least started to learn my trade in the kitchen at Ballymaloe House, one of the first cookery books I became aware of was a book called *Good Things* by Jane Grigson. Up till that point of my life, when I had been helping my mother in our own kitchen at home, the books referred to were for the most part oilcloth-covered notebooks that my mother had transcribed recipes into in her beautiful, neat handwriting. There were also scrapbooks with recipes carefully cut out of magazines and newspapers and pasted onto the pages. These home-compiled records were very important and my mother referred to them regularly and followed them assiduously. Though she was a natural and instinctive cook, capable of creating lovely food by eye, experience and imagination, there were particular dishes that definitely required a recorded list of ingredients, a scale and a measuring jug to comply with the directions.

Unlike *Good Things*, where Grigson wrote precise and lovely words of introduction, creating little mental pictures for the cook (there are also simple line drawings in *Good Things*), there were no colourful stories in my mother's handwritten books. Occasionally a recipe was credited to a particular person who had shared the treasure, such as Mrs Dillon's Sponge. I always wanted to know who so-and-so was to have deserved a particular mention and to try to create my own imagined picture, though it was the cooking that brought these dishes to life rather than the prose preamble in *Good Things*.

I adore my mother's books, but find that nowadays I have to be in the correct frame of mind before I open them. Any little chink in the emotional armour can be chiselled into a larger fissure of loss when I see her perfect script.

Somehow, print just does not affect me in the same way. I suppose it is the difference between the physical appearance of the printed word on the page and the meaning of the same words. The meaning can move me, of course, but the look, shape and colour of the print does not. Print can be beautiful, classical, floral and elegant, but I don't find its appearance emotional – aesthetically pleasing, definitely, just not heart-wrenching. The word laid down by the hand is a different matter. In the rising and falling of the letters and words formed by hand, with I's dotted and T's crossed, there is another story rather than just the one being recorded – the story of the hand that held the pen, the relationship between the reader and those hands.

The title of a recipe that I had forgotten is enough to take me back to that happy kitchen and a flood of memories ensues. The memories are not just of the food, the meals and the thrice-daily gatherings, but of my siblings and, of course, of her – my mother. I can see her with her hair gathered into a neatly plaited bun and covered with a little headscarf tied at the nape of her neck, looking industrious rather than fashionable. However, she almost always wore a scarf leaving the house, different ones for different events, but in that instance tied below the chin, which was fashionable then. This is what happens when I open those recipe books – my mind wanders off and I become lost in a mist of memories that are mostly far removed from, but nonetheless prompted by, the handmade copy.

The sponge cake recipe will have transported me to the bank of the river where we would swim in the summer. We would walk the couple of miles there and back, down the road past the village pump where most local houses got their drinking water and then over the stone stile on the wall beside the chapel and through the chapel meadows.

Of course not all those days were warm and sunny, but those are the ones I remember. The silence of the single-file walk on the single-file path broken by the deafening hum of bees and the fizz of flies, twittering of birds, squawking of crows, purring of pigeons, protestations of thirsty cows and cattle – this country landscape was a kind of 'wilding' long before we knew what wilding now means. Cattle and cows were wary of you then, not like now, when many seem angry, aggressive, threatening, pumped – back then, we walked among them without fear. Our minds wandered, with no smartphone to distract or with which to capture or share the scene. Somehow these images have been carefully filed in glorious Technicolor in my mind, ready to be pulled out when prompted or needed. I can see there and be there. I can move the vista around in my head in full 360-degree imaging – hazelnut-brown and stick-thin limbs, a single puffy cloud, shriekingly white tan lines, a horsefly screechingly batted away, little fields that had never been turned by the plough, dry summer grasses shaking a dusty haze through the air, summer shorts and sandals, handed-down T-shirts, towels over shoulders or rolled up like a Swiss roll, swimming things and a basket with a flask, cups and a sponge cake.

Neat and efficient, my mother fed us beautifully, the food made more delicious by the love that went into preparing it. Feeding nine hungry mouths, she must have felt like a mother sparrow relentlessly returning to the nest to chirping hungry beaks. The table was always set with a little bunch of flowers. It wasn't grand, but it was civilised.

Getting back to *Good Things* and Jane Grigson, the book was first published in 1971 and was full of treasures. When I pick it up today, it is still fresh and relevant. Over the years I have cooked many dishes from this book, some unchanged from the original recipe, others tweaked to suit how we like to eat nowadays. What I am trying to get to here in a rather roundabout fashion is how over the years we have come to use the words 'good thing' to describe a particular type of dish. Did this come from the connection to the title of this classic book and what does 'good thing' really mean in the context of a dish? It is certainly not an expression I would use to describe a fantastic and complicated dish in a contemporary restaurant. I might call such a dish sublime or sensational, but not a good thing. It is reserved for dishes that are less involved, though nonetheless require skill. There is more of a suggestion of comfort, timelessness, endurance, intelligence, a friend impervious to fashion and shifting trends, though of course sophistication and elegance are inherent in the title too. It could be a dish with just a few ingredients or one with a long list of additions. I suppose it is a title that describes much of the food that I like to cook – that is, dishes that are delicious, possible, relevant, seasonal and stylish but not faddy. My mother cooked many good things. Where possible, I like to cook good things.

So there are no foams, froths, skids or slicks in this book. Those are for kitchens with time, space and manpower, where many hands make light work of those clever tricks. That is not to say that I will not suggest a foamy consistency to a soup or a frothy drizzle of cream whipped softly with a little milk to make it lighter and, yes, frothy. But I draw the line at skidding or slicking.

Lemon Geranium Ice with Stem Ginger and Candied Rose Petals

This recipe calls for my beloved scented geranium leaves. These delicious-smelling plants are relatively easy to find at good garden centres and can be grown year round as a houseplant. They will benefit from being moved outside to a sunny sheltered spot in late spring, after the last of the frosts, and being brought in again in autumn before the frosty nights resume. In some gardens with unusually warm and protected corners they may survive outside all year, but keep an eye on them and if they appear to be suffering as a result of the cold, bring them inside.

The variety I particularly like is *Pelargonium graveolens*, which is lemon scented, but there are also rose-scented ones. You may not want cola-flavoured geraniums, which indeed exists, and like the mint family, some of the scented geranium are really unpleasant, so be specific when buying or ordering your first plant. Once established, it is very easy to propagate further plants and then you can happily become the purveyor of scented geraniums to all and sundry, in which case you will truly be spreading great joy!

If you want to candy your own ginger and sugar your own rose petals, the recipes for both are in this book. I take great pleasure in doing both of those tasks, whereas some will regard the prospect as akin to torture. Fresh (unsprayed) rose petals can be used instead of the candied ones. The effect will not be the same, but they will look lovely and you can of course buy the ginger already sugared.

Serves 4–8
— 250ml milk
— 130g caster sugar
— 5g lemon-scented geranium leaves, chopped
— Zest and juice of 1 lemon
— 1 egg
— 1 dessertspoon very finely chopped lemon-scented geranium leaves

You may not want cola-flavoured geranium, which indeed exists, and like the mint family, some of the scented geraniums are really unpleasant, so be specific when buying or ordering your first plant.

To serve
— 1 tablespoon finely diced stem ginger (page 190)
— 8–16 candied or fresh rose petals (page 332)

Place the milk, sugar and 5 grams of geranium in a bowl and stir well. Cover and refrigerate for 4 hours or overnight.

Strain the geranium out of the milk through a fine-mesh sieve, pushing firmly on the leaves to extract as much flavour and liquid as possible. Zest the lemon with a Microplane grater and add to the milk, then stir in the lemon juice.

Separate the egg, placing the white in a spotlessly clean, dry bowl. Whisk the yolk into the milk. Whip the egg white stiffly, then gently whisk it into the milk with the dessertspoon of finely chopped geranium. Freeze in an ice cream machine, then decant into a chilled bowl. Store in the freezer.

If you don't have an ice cream machine, you can simply freeze the mixture in an airtight freezerproof container, then as it begins to freeze, break it up vigorously with a fork. Repeat this five times and you will end up with a lovely ice. The texture will not be as smooth as one churned in a machine, but it will still be worthwhile and delicious to eat. Its texture will be akin to a cross between a sorbet and a granita, so your scooped shapes will be somewhat abstract.

When ready to serve, scoop the ice cream into neat balls and sprinkle the stem ginger and rose petals over the top. Serve immediately.

Grilled Pork with Roast Almond and Sage Leaf Salsa and Yellow Apple Sauce

A juicy pork chop from the loin or belly is a treat. Often the most difficult part of the cooking process is the shopping, because finding good-quality meat can be a challenge. I insist on free-range or ideally organic pork meat, which I get from my local craft butcher. I try to give my butcher advance notice when I want a specific piece of meat. You can justify the extra cost of this slowly and carefully reared meat by eating less of it and increasing the quantity or variety of vegetables being served alongside. You will need a generous coating of fat on a loin chop and a generous streaking of fat through the belly pieces. The fat keeps the meat succulent in the cooking and adds lip-smacking flavour. I always ask my butcher to remove the rind, as I find it is never cooked to my satisfaction when left attached to the meat for grilling. I cook it in the same pan alongside the chops, sometimes cut into 1cm dice or 5cm pieces. That way, all the liquid fat will be rendered out and the rind will become shatteringly crisp, which is the way I want it.

Whereas previously I might have served a pork chop to each person, I now tend to divide a chop between two people, or if I know my guests are especially big eaters, I might divide three chops between four people. I carve the meat into 0.75cm angled slices before it goes to the table, in which case I think it looks nicer than the rather more robust chops.

you will need a generous coating of fat on a loin chop and a generous streaking of fat through the belly pieces. The fat keeps the meat succulent in the cooking and adds lip-smacking flavour.

Serves 4
— 2–3 x 150g pork chops from the loin or belly
— Pork rinds from the chops, cut into 1cm dice or 5cm pieces
— Sea salt and freshly ground black pepper

To serve
— Roast almond and sage leaf salsa (see below)
— Yellow apple sauce (see below)
— Apple-glazed carrots (page 208)

Season the chops on both sides with salt and pepper.

Heat a heavy-based cast iron grill pan or frying pan until moderately hot. Scatter on the pieces of pork rind and cook over a moderate heat until the liquid fat begins to render out.

Turn up the heat and when the pan is hot, push the rinds to the edges and pop in the chops. Allow to cook until golden in colour before turning to cook on the other side. The cooked chops will feel gently firm to the touch, but beware of overcooking them, as they will become dry and hard. I like my pork cooked through and not pink, though this is personal.

Serve the pork on hot plates cut into 0.75cm angled slices with your sauces of choice. My suggestion here is to serve the pork with roast almond and sage leaf salsa and yellow apple sauce. I also like to serve the pork with apple-glazed carrots.

Roast Almond and Sage Leaf Salsa

This is a crisp and piquant salsa that I serve with grilled pork chops or piece of grilled beef. If serving with pork, a traditional apple sauce or my yellow apple sauce is a lovely addition to the flavours. With beef, I serve a salad of rocket leaves and a blob of mayonnaise.

Serves 4–6
— 50g unskinned almonds
— 20g fresh sage leaves (approx. 30 leaves)
— 4 tablespoons extra virgin olive oil
— 1 tablespoon freshly squeezed lemon juice
— 1 tablespoon balsamic vinegar
— Sea salt and freshly ground black pepper

Preheat the oven to 180°C.

Place the almonds and sage leaves on an oven tray. Roast in the preheated oven until the nuts are crisp and golden all the way through and the sage leaves are also crisp. This takes about 10 minutes in my oven. Remove from the oven and allow to cool completely.

Chop the nuts and leaves together until a gritty texture is achieved. Add the olive oil, lemon juice and balsamic vinegar and season with salt and pepper. Mix to emulsify the oil and vinegar. Taste and correct the seasoning.

Yellow Apple Sauce

This is simple and really a lovely surprise. The combination of apple and fresh turmeric is quite perfect. My regime of adding a little fresh turmeric to my morning drink of lemon, ginger and honey has yielded a few surprisingly good results as I become more familiar with the wonderful flavour of the fresh rhizome rather than the dried powder. The powder has its place, of course, and I continue to use it, but the scented, sweet flesh of the freshly grated root is something of a revelation to me.

It is worth noting that when you are cooking bitter Bramley apples, the smaller you cut up the raw apple, the longer it takes to collapse to a frothy purée. Yes, this seems entirely illogical, but that is my experience. The fluffiness of the cooked froth is lighter and airier from the collapsed larger pieces than smaller ones.

We tend to take lovely bitter cooking apples such as the Bramley for granted in this part of the world, but in France, which has given us so many of the great apple tarts, such as tarte au tatin, Normandy apple tart, tarte fines au pommes and so on, all those creations are made with sweet dessert apples. They do not grow or really know the bitter apples that we love and are using in this recipe. I wonder if they grew them, would they have ended up in some of the classic pork and apple dishes or with pheasant and cream, as in sauce Vallée d'Auge?

Serves 6–8

— 375g Bramley cooking apple, peeled, cored and coarsely grated (weighed after peeling and coring)
— 25–30g caster sugar
— 1–2 tablespoons water
— 1 tablespoon peeled fresh turmeric root, grated on a Microplane grater
— A few drops of freshly squeezed lemon juice

Place the apples in a small saucepan with the caster sugar and water. Cover with a tight-fitting lid and cook over a low heat until the apples collapse to a lovely froth. Stir in the turmeric and add a few drops of lemon juice to brighten up the flavour.

Apple-Glazed Carrots

Carrots are an extremely versatile vegetable that will happily take all kinds of flavours and I enjoy cooking them in many different ways. Sometimes, however, when carrots are an accompaniment to other dishes such as a roast or a grill, they need a more restrained approach and this recipe is definitely that. The ingredients list is short and the cooking technique is specific. Care is needed so that by the time the carrots are cooked, the apple juice will have reduced completely to form a rich, shiny glaze. This concentrated liquid that coats the cooked carrots is the key to a delicious result. Carrots cooked or 'drowned' in too much liquid are hopeless, as most of the flavour is lost and thrown down the drain in the superfluous cooking water. I feel very strongly about this type of recipe, as all it takes is a little care and vigilance to make what might have previously been regarded as ordinary into extraordinary.

It is worth noting that the quantity of apple juice is small and that at the beginning, the carrots appear to be sitting in a scant pool of liquid rather than being covered. This is one of the keys to success with this dish, as covering them with too much liquid dilutes the flavour and means that by the time the liquid has reduced to a glaze, the carrots will be soggy and overcooked.

The size of the carrots being used will determine whether you cook them whole or cut them into smaller pieces. New season baby carrots are best left whole and scrubbed rather than peeled. The larger thick-skinned main season carrots are best thinly peeled and cut into neat, even-sized pieces. Taking the time when preparing an ingredient such as the carrots in this recipe will stand to you at the end of cooking. The more evenly sized the pieces are, the more evenly they will cook and the nicer they will look in the serving dish.

There is increasingly a selection of different coloured and shaped carrots available rather than the classic tapered orange ones that we associate with the vegetable's name. Purple and yellow varieties looking rotund and jolly are a lovely addition to the pot and will amuse and hopefully help to allay the notion that carrots are just a predictable and boring vegetable.

Care is needed so that by the time the carrots are cooked, the apple juice will have reduced completely to form a rich, shiny glaze.

Serves 4
— 450g carrots, peeled or scrubbed clean
— 30g butter
— 200ml apple juice
— Zest of ½ lemon and a few drops of juice
— Sea salt and freshly ground black pepper

Place the carrots, butter and apple juice in a small low-sided saucepan. Season with salt and pepper and bring to a simmer. Cover with a tight-fitting lid. I usually use a Pyrex plate, as that way I can see the level of liquid in the saucepan and react if it gets alarmingly low or remains too high. The object of the exercise here is perfectly cooked vegetables at the same time as the liquid has evaporated to form the shiny coating glaze. You may need to turn the heat up or down depending on how the cooking is going.

You may also need to remove the lid to allow the liquid to evaporate more quickly if the carrots are nearly cooked. This recipe needs you to be vigilant, and if you are, you may end up with carrots tasting more 'carroty' than ever before. Add the lemon zest and juice to the cooked glazed carrots and serve as soon as possible.

Smoked Eel with Fennel, Apple and Crème Fraîche

This is an elegant dish suitable to serve as a starter. It combines smoked eel, a favourite ingredient of mine, with thinly sliced apple and fennel. The surprising ingredient here is a very small amount of elderflower cordial, which brings the apple and fennel together in a most lovely way. Smoked eel has become easier to source and I get mine from Lough Neagh in Northern Ireland. It freezes very well and I find it to be a useful store cupboard ingredient. The meaty, oily flesh is rich and succulent and if one was to simply slice it onto buttered brown bread with a lick of mayonnaise, well, that would be a simple feast.

Serves 4
— 135g fennel bulb
— 100g eating apple, weighed after peeling and coring (about ½ a standard-sized apple)
— 2 tablespoons crème fraîche
— 100g filleted and skinned smoked eel
— 2 teaspoons finely chopped fresh chives
— 1 tablespoon extra virgin olive oil
— Sea salt and freshly ground black pepper

Dressing
— 3 tablespoons extra virgin olive oil
— 1 tablespoon freshly squeezed lemon juice
— 2 teaspoons elderflower cordial

To make the dressing, place the olive oil, lemon juice and elderflower cordial in a bowl and season with salt and pepper. Whisk gently to emulsify. Taste and correct the seasoning.

Slice the fennel and apple very thinly. I generally slice the fennel lengthways from top to bottom. If the little stalks protruding from the top of the fennel are longer than usual, I slice some of them crossways. Season with salt and pepper and mix gently but thoroughly through the dressing.

Smoked eel has become easier to source and I get mine from Lough Neagh in Northern Ireland. It freezes very well and I find it to be a useful store cupboard ingredient.

Spread the crème fraîche in a 15cm disc on a large flat plate.
Place the dressed fennel and apple on top, leaving a 1cm rim
visible around the edge. This rim is purely for aesthetics, so don't
be too worried if the fennel and apple go over the edge.

Cut the eel into 0.5cm-thick slices at an angle and arrange
them in slightly overlapping slices on the fennel and apple.
Drizzle any dressing remaining in the bowl over the ingredients.

Finish the salad with a sprinkling of chopped chives, a few
grains of sea salt and the tablespoon of olive oil. Serve as soon as
possible.

Sweet Marjoram Flatbread

I love the flavour of sweet marjoram, *Origanum majorana*
from the oregano family. Its sweet, smoky flavour reminds me
somewhat of Middle Eastern flatbreads, such as this one here.
There is another variety of oregano, *Origanum syriacum*, that
is particularly used in these breads in the Middle East. This is
confusing on two fronts, as it is sometimes called hyssop, but it
is not the same herb that we know in this part of the world as
hyssop, *Hyssopus officinalis*. It is also sometimes called za'atar,
which can cause confusion as many people will know za'atar
as a blend of dried herbs, seeds and spices used in the Middle
East. None of the above is crucial information, but it goes to
show how complex pinning down a correct ingredient can be.
Having said all that, the sweet marjoram that I like to use is a
trouble-free plant in my garden and I use both the leaves and
flowers fresh before harvesting them at the end of the summer
for drying. As it dries, its aroma seems to me to be more
evocative of faraway places, just a bit more mysterious and from
somewhere dustier, with bustling souks, a hidden oasis and a
hotter climate than ours.

The dough for the flatbread is relatively straightforward
to make and most of the work can be done by machine if you
wish. After mixing, rising and knocking back, the dough is
rolled and folded like a letter, layering fragrant marjoram leaves
within. The bread can be cooked on cast iron pans or grills or
on a barbecue directly over the hot coals. It is delicious just as
it is with a few drops of olive oil, but I love it with the grilled
cucumber salad with tahini sauce and dukkah on page 196. It is
easy to imagine how warm shredded shoulder of lamb would be
great here also.

If you leave the herb out altogether you have plain flatbread.
One of my favourite ways to eat this is at breakfast time, hot off
the pan, buttered and with local honey – wonderful.

The dough for the flatbread is relatively straightforward to make and most of the work can be done by machine if you wish. After mixing, rising and knocking back, the dough is rolled and folded like a letter, layering fragrant marjoram leaves within.

Serves 8–10
— 450g strong white flour, plus extra for dusting
— 350ml tepid water
— 2 teaspoons caster sugar
— 1 level teaspoon dried yeast or 1 rounded teaspoon fresh yeast
— 1 tablespoon extra virgin olive oil, plus extra for brushing
— 1 rounded teaspoon fine sea salt
— 30g fresh or dried marjoram or hyssop leaves
— Coarse sea salt, for sprinkling

Combine the flour, water, sugar and yeast in a large bowl for hand mixing or the bowl of a stand mixer if you would like the machine to do the work. Mix for about 3 minutes using the dough hook in the stand mixer to achieve a coarse but amalgamated dough. Add the oil and the teaspoon of salt and continue mixing on a medium speed for 5 minutes. If you are mixing and kneading by hand, it will probably take 8–10 minutes before you achieve the required smooth, homogenous dough.

Place the dough in a large lightly oiled bowl and cover with a light kitchen towel. Allow to sit and rise at room temperature until doubled in size. The rising time will vary depending on the heat of your kitchen.

When the dough has sufficiently risen, just gently push your fist into it to expel some of the air. Divide the dough into four equal pieces and roll each piece into a ball. Allow to rest for 15 minutes or refrigerate overnight. At this point you could freeze some of the dough balls if you don't want to use them all. When you next want to use them, remove from the freezer the night before using and defrost in the fridge overnight.

On a well-floured work surface, roll out one piece of dough at a time to achieve a square about 20cm in size. Brush the dough with olive oil and scatter on the herbs. Fold in three as if folding a letter and allow to rest for a further 15 minutes. Repeat with the remaining three pieces of dough. (At this point, the pieces of dough can be refrigerated until later.)

When ready to cook the bread, heat a heavy-based cast iron frying or grill pan. Cut each piece of folded dough into three pieces that will look vaguely like squares. Drizzle a wooden chopping board with olive oil and use your fingers, a rolling pin or a combination of both to stretch the square-ish pieces of dough until they are very thin and about 20cm square. I turn the dough over so there is oil on the top and bottom of the dough, as this facilitates easier stretching. If the dough tears a little, don't worry, just patch it up.

Slap a piece of stretched dough on the hot dry pan and cook for about 3 minutes on each side, until well coloured and slightly blistered. Drizzle on a few drops of olive oil and sprinkle with a few grains of coarse sea salt.

Serve immediately while hot or stack the cooked flatbreads and wrap in a clean kitchen towel. Keep warm until ready to serve.

Dried Fig, Date, Almond, Pistachio and Chocolate Cake

The dried fruit and nuts in this cake lend a rich flavour and a pleasingly chewy texture. The cake is not without its surprises, though, as the fruit and nuts sink to the bottom of the tin in the cooking. Normally this would be considered to be a disaster, but in this case the cake is turned upside down after cooling to achieve a layer of fruit and nuts floating magically on the top of the finished cake. Delight. The glossy chocolate icing turns the cake into a rich confection suitable for serving as a dessert cake as much as a tea cake.

I think this might be a nice alternative at Christmas for cooks who want some of the dried fruit flavours of the season but not the full-on traditional cake with all its bells and whistles. The cake, which is rich and should be served in small slices, keeps well. I have happily been eating this cake a week after I baked and iced it.

I think this might be a nice alternative at Christmas for cooks who want some of the dried fruit flavours of the season but not the full-on traditional cake with all its bells and whistles.

Serves 8–12

Cake
— 4 eggs
— 170g caster sugar
— 200g butter, melted and cooled, plus extra for greasing the tin
— 200g ground almonds
— 150g Medjool dates, stoned and chopped into 0.5cm dice
— 150g dried figs, chopped into 0.5cm dice
— 100g pistachios, coarsely chopped
— 1 teaspoon orange flower water
— 1 teaspoon orange or vanilla extract

Icing
— 80g chocolate (62% cocoa solids), roughly chopped
— 80g butter, chilled and diced

To serve
— Softly whipped cream or crème fraîche

You will need
— 1 x 24cm springform or regular cake tin

Preheat the oven to 170°C. Paint the sides of a 24cm springform or cake tin with a little melted butter and line the base of the tin with a disc of non-stick baking paper.

Place the eggs and sugar in the bowl of a stand mixer and whisk until the mixture is pale and light. This will take about 5 minutes to achieve. The mixture should be firm enough to hold a figure of eight if lifted up with the whisk.

Using a long-handled flexible spatula, fold in the melted butter followed by the ground almonds, dates, figs, pistachios, orange flower water and orange or vanilla extract. Pour the batter into the prepared tin and smooth the surface.

Bake in the preheated oven for 50 minutes, by which time the cake should be well coloured and beginning to come away from the sides of the tin.

Remove from the oven and place the cake, still in the tin, on a wire rack to cool. After 30 minutes, run a blunt table knife around the inside of the tin and turn out the cake. You will notice that the fruit and nuts have fallen to the bottom of the cake, which is perfect as you will be serving the cake upside down. I like to leave the disc of baking paper on the cake until it is completely cool.

To make the icing, place the chocolate in a Pyrex bowl and sit the bowl over a saucepan of cold water. The water must not be touching the bottom of the bowl. Bring the water to a simmer and immediately turn off the heat. The chocolate will not be fully melted, but will continue to melt over the residual heat in the saucepan.

When the chocolate is melted, remove the bowl from the saucepan and allow to cool until barely tepid. This is very important, as if the chocolate is too warm as you beat in the butter, you may end up with a sauce rather than a spreadable icing. Using an electric hand whisk, whisk the butter into the chocolate a few pieces at a time until all the butter is incorporated to yield a glossy, spreadable icing. If you have whisked in the butter too quickly or if the chocolate was too hot as you added the butter, the icing may become runny and more like a sauce. If this happens, place the bowl in the fridge and allow it to become cold. When cold, whisk it again and it should firm up to a spreadable consistency.

Remove the disc of baking paper from the cake and place it fruit side up on a large flat plate. Using a spatula or flexible palate knife, spread the icing over the top and sides of the cake.

The cake is now ready to serve with softly whipped cream or crème fraîche.

Pistachio Cake with Raspberries, Lemon or Lime Basil and Rosewater Cream

I love this combination of flavours and this moist little cake has the added advantage of keeping beautifully for several days. I generally serve it as a dessert cake, but have also enjoyed it a few days later with a cup of tea or coffee. The raspberries and basil are great, but if you can't find the herb, little sprigs of mint would be a good addition. Don't replace the citrus-flavoured basil with the more widely available sweet basil, as the flavours don't work. The other alternative to the herb would be a last-minute grating of lime zest over the cake. Pomegranate seeds rolled on a tea towel to dry them would also make a sparkling addition.

I add a few drops of rosewater to the cream when whipping. Be careful, though, as too much rosewater will yield a flavour that is too strong and overpowering. The flavour of the rosewater cream should be akin to catching the scent of a rose while walking about the garden – there, but almost elusive.

The raspberries and basil are great, but if you can't find the herb, little sprigs of mint would be a good addition. Don't replace the citrus-flavoured basil with the more widely available sweet basil, as the flavours don't work.

Serves 8–12
Cake
— 5 eggs
— 150g caster sugar
— 200g butter, melted and cooled, plus extra for greasing the tin
— 50g cream flour
— 1 level teaspoon baking powder
— 200g pistachios, ground to a fine but slightly gritty powder
— Zest of 1 lemon
— 2 drops of almond extract

Icing
— 150g icing sugar
— Zest of 1 lemon
— 1 tablespoon freshly squeezed lemon juice (approx.)

Decoration
— 150g fresh raspberries
— 24 small fresh lemon or lime basil leaves or 24 whole pistachios

To serve
— Softly whipped cream with a few drops of rosewater (see the recipe introduction)

You will need
— 1 X 24cm springform tin

Preheat the oven to 170°C. Paint the sides of a 24cm springform tin with melted butter and line the base with a disc of non-stick baking paper.

Place the eggs in a large bowl and whisk until foamy. Add the sugar and continue to whisk well to mix. The volume of the mixture will not increase, but the sugar will be dissolved.

Add the butter gradually while continuing to whisk. Sieve in the flour and baking powder and fold in gently. With a light hand, fold in the pistachios, lemon zest and almond extract and continue to mix thoroughly.

Pour the batter into the tin and smooth the surface. Bake in the preheated oven for 35 minutes, until the cake is nicely coloured and barely coming away from the sides of the tin.

Place the cake, still in the tin, on a wire rack and allow to cool for 30 minutes. Run a blunt table knife around the inside of the tin and remove the cake. Replace on the wire rack, baking paper side down, and allow to become completely cold.

To make the icing, sieve the icing sugar into a bowl. Add the lemon zest and using a wooden spoon, add the lemon juice to make a barely spreadable icing. Be cautious with the addition of the lemon juice, as even a few too many drops of juice can create a thin, liquid icing. If this happens, sieve in a little more icing sugar in small increments.

Remove the disc of baking paper from the cooled cake and place the cake on a large flat plate. Spread the icing over the top of the cake just to the edge. Some of the icing will drizzle down the sides in pleasing drips.

Cut the raspberries in half lengthways or in cross-section slices to reveal their shiny interiors. Place on the icing in no particular order but at the same time distributing them as evenly as possible. Scatter on the basil leaves or whole pistachios.

Serve with softly whipped rosewater cream.

Raspberries

Sandwiches and Tartines

I have always loved the French word 'tartine', which describes an open-faced sandwich. It just sounds so much better than, well, an open-faced sandwich. It is worth thinking a little about sandwiches and what makes a perfect one. Strictly speaking, I suppose a tartine is not a sandwich, as the filling sits on top rather than in the middle of two slices of bread. Oh dear, what a dilemma.

Apart from the quality of ingredients, proportion is everything in a sandwich. If you think of a perfectly executed cucumber sandwich made with crustless bread buttered to the edges, it is both a joy to behold and a joy to eat. The correct amount of bread in relation to the filling is key.

I also need to speak about butter for a moment. The butter should be spread thinly, but not meanly, to the very edge of the bread. Coming across a bit of unbuttered bread is, in my experience, most disappointing. It is unfortunate that the word 'spread' can correctly be used to describe things other than butter that increasingly find their way into a sandwich. These blends of ingredients, sometimes containing up to and above 20 ingredients, are not even a pale imitation of butter. Butter, by the way, has two ingredients: cream and salt. That's it. And can we please stop using the expression 'real butter'? That is like calling something a tofu sausage. I love good tofu, but you can't make sausages from it. You can make something sausage-shaped, perhaps, even sausage-coloured, but it is not a sausage. Sausages are made of pork.

I drifted off the topic there slightly, so getting back to the cucumber sandwich, it was a morsel that you could get to your mouth with one hand while carrying on a lovely chat and occasionally taking a sip of tea, all the time looking fabulous and in control. There was a time when the word 'sandwich' conjured up such a surrounding as the cucumber sandwich might have been served in, all high ceilings made of glass, as in a conservatory, with potted palms, wicker tables and chairs and properly starched linen with embroidered appliqués or lace edges. This was when a sandwich was part of a repast to tide you over from one of the main meals of the day to the next. A delicate, savoury hunger suppressor bolstered by equally refined sweet treats rather than a meal in itself, which is precisely what most sandwiches have become. As far as I can see, I doubt anyone ever eats a little crustless sambo on the way to work or on the bus. No, those sandwiches are generally great whopping portable meals that require immense concentration while eating them to avoid having half the contents strewn all over oneself, like a waterfall of excess. Honestly, I believe the best place to eat the modern iteration, if you choose to do so, is in a corner with your back to a wall, on your own, seated or standing, because this has become a pursuit, an exercise, a mission. Mission impossible, mostly, if you ask me. There is none of the genteel precision of the nibbled finger sandwich. Eaters will be noticed sizing up the brute of a thing that requires two white-knuckled hands and a good deal of concentration to line it up, ready for the 'I'm going in' moment. Really, what has happened to us? Can we not just have two smaller sandwiches so that we can resume the hitherto straight back rather than the hunched-shoulders approach of today? I really don't think it can be good for one's digestion.

Ricotta Gnocchi with Chanterelle Mushrooms and Parmesan

There are several types of gnocchi, but the ones made with ricotta are my favourite. Other versions are made with potatoes, cornmeal, breadcrumbs, semolina and so on, all with varying textures and methods of cooking. These are tender and require a fairly light hand when mixing the dough, as the ricotta in the recipe makes for delicate little dumplings.

It is always important to remember with ricotta that freshness is the key. The delicate cheese loses some of its sweet charm when a few days old and you will note that in this recipe most of the flavours are fairly gentle to allow this lightness of taste to shine.

These tender little gnocchi pair beautifully with the mushrooms. When the mushrooms are not in season I replace them with other seasonal ingredients, such as squash, finely chopped and roasted until tender, or cooked and shelled broad beans. If I have broad bean leaves, I wilt those into the sauce at the last minute. Purple or white sprouting broccoli cooked and then chopped into 2cm pieces is also great, as are sprouting kale tops. Asparagus cooked and chopped to a similar size as the gnocchi would also be lovely.

Serves 8 as a starter
Gnocchi
— 300g ricotta cheese
— 50g fine semolina, sieved, plus extra for rolling and shaping the gnocchi
— 30g grated Parmesan cheese
— 3 large egg yolks
— Pinch of freshly grated nutmeg
— Sea salt and freshly ground black pepper

Freshness is the key. The delicate cheese loses some of its sweet charm when a few days old and you will note that in this recipe most of the flavours are fairly gentle to allow this lightness of taste to shine.

Mushrooms
— 20g butter
— 150g chanterelle mushrooms

Sauce
— 50g butter
— 4 tablespoons cream
— 50g grated Parmesan cheese, plus extra for the final sprinkling

With a wooden spoon, mix the ricotta, sieved semolina, Parmesan and egg yolks in a bowl, adding nutmeg, salt and pepper to taste. The ingredients will come together in a soft but manageable mass.

Lightly dust a chopping board with sieved semolina. Divide the mixture into five pieces and gently roll each piece into a sausage shape about 1.5cm in diameter. Cut each piece into 2cm pieces and place on a tray lined with non-stick baking paper and dusted with sieved semolina. Refrigerate until needed.

When ready to cook, bring a large, wide, low-sided saucepan of water to the boil.

While the water is coming to the boil, prepare the mushrooms and sauce. Heat a heavy-based cast iron sauté pan and melt the butter. Add the chanterelles and season with salt and pepper. Cook over a gentle heat until the mushrooms have tenderised and somewhat collapsed. Keep warm.

Place the butter and cream in a small saucepan and bring to a simmer. Allow to cook for 1 minute, then add the Parmesan. Mix and simmer for a further minute. Season to taste with salt and pepper.

Gently drop the gnocchi into the boiling water and simmer for a couple of minutes, until the gnocchi float to the surface.

Lift the gnocchi out of the water with a slotted spoon and place in a warmed serving dish. Sprinkle over the warm chanterelles and drizzle over the hot sauce. Give the serving dish a shake or a gentle stir to blend the gnocchi, mushrooms and sauce. Sprinkle with extra Parmesan and serve immediately.

Aubergine Soup with Coriander

I have tried many different approaches when making an aubergine soup, ranging from heavily spiced Indian versions to chilli-laden South East Asian ones, but this rather mundane-sounding list of ingredients always comes up trumps. It may seem unusual to include potato with the aubergine, but I think that is part of the secret here, as the humble tuber adds a silkiness to the soup consistency that the aubergine lacks.

There are many garnishes that will be delicious to serve with the soup. A simple dollop of softly whipped cream or crème fraîche, a drizzle of fruity olive oil or a roasted red pepper, peeled and finely diced, are all easy last-minute additions.

Serves 8–10
— 40g butter
— 285g onion, peeled and finely diced
— 285g potato, peeled and finely diced
— 4 garlic cloves, peeled and finely chopped
— 2 teaspoons roasted and coarsely ground cumin seeds
— 1kg aubergines, diced into 2cm cubes
— 1 litre chicken stock (page 319)
— 125ml cream
— 125ml milk
— 4 tablespoons finely chopped fresh coriander leaves
— Sea salt and freshly ground black pepper

Melt the butter in a heavy-based saucepan and allow to foam. Add the onion, potato, garlic and cumin. Toss the vegetables to coat them in the butter and season with salt and pepper. Cover with a disc of greaseproof paper and the saucepan lid and allow to sweat over a very gentle heat until the potatoes are just starting to soften. This takes about 15 minutes.

Add the aubergines and stock and stir well. Cover again with the saucepan lid and bring to a simmer. Cook until the aubergines are tender – this will take about 20 minutes.

It may seem unusual to include potato with the aubergine, but I think that is part of the secret here, as the humble tuber adds a silkiness to the soup consistency that the aubergine lacks.

Purée the soup to a silky-smooth consistency using a liquidiser or hand-held blender. Return to the saucepan and add the cream and milk. Bring back to a simmer, then taste and correct the seasoning. Add the coriander just before serving.

AUbERyiNes

Aubergine and Ginger Pickle

This is a spiky, well-flavoured pickle with a vegetable I love, the aubergine. The recipe has its roots in India, but another day I might treat the vegetable with Mediterranean flavours such as olive oil, tomatoes, garlic and basil. It will simmer just as happily with a South East Asian combination of ingredients.

The pickle probably falls into that unusual category of dishes that taste great with a million things. It works on a Cheddar cheese sandwich, with a grilled pork chop and apple sauce, with lamb cooked quickly or slowly, alongside a bowl of pilaf rice or couscous, with a fried or hard-boiled egg, a burger of beef, pork or chicken, or grilled oily fish such a mackerel or mullet. The list goes on and on.

Asafoetida, a strong and somewhat foul-smelling spice, is the sap, resin or gum extracted from a species of *Ferula asafoetida*, a member of the same family as celery and fennel. Widely used in Indian cooking, it is sometimes referred to as a savoury flavour enhancer. In the diets of some Jains and Brahmins, the spice is used to flavour food where onions and garlic are regarded as unclean and hence are forbidden. It adds a tremendous kick and depth of flavour in certain dishes. It is now widely available and can be purchased in a powdered form ready for adding to dishes as it is or in little dried chunks that will need grinding or fine grating depending on size. When it is called for in a recipe, it is vital and there is no substitute that I know of that delivers the same flavour.

Another ingredient that you would expect to find in a recipe such as this in India is jaggery. Jaggery is a traditional sugar made from cane and I had the good fortune to see it being made from start to finish on a small farm in Maheshwar in Central India. The process, which involved four generations of the same family, started with a large trailer of the freshly harvested cane, which was then juiced by an ear-splittingly loud machine that looked as if its origins might have been rooted in Victorian engineering. The rest of the effort involved was manual and seemed to be a process that had changed little over the centuries. The fresh

The pickle probably falls into that unusual category of dishes that taste great with a million things. It works on a Cheddar cheese sandwich, with a grilled pork chop and apple sauce, with lamb cooked quickly or slowly, alongside a bowl of pilaf rice or couscous, with a fried or hard-boiled egg, a burger of beef, pork or chicken, or grilled oily fish such a mackerel or mullet. The list goes on and on.

juice, which we were encouraged to taste straight from the juicer, was decanted straight into huge cast iron frying pans that were heated by fires made from the superfluous cane trimmings.

The rest of the process was curiously similar to making fudge, as the sugar-rich juice was furiously boiled down while being stirred all the time to prevent it from sticking. The more fudge-like the mixture became, the more beautiful it looked. It cooked from a pale, murky liquid through shades of straw, gold, caramel and toffee before the most alarming part of the process happened. The now thick, boiling, molten liquid had to be quickly moved from the pan into a tray, where it would cool and thicken. An air of urgency prevailed as the older male members of the family deftly placed iron bars through the handles of the great pans, while the smallest members of the family were gathered up and firmly tucked behind the sari-draped legs and bracelet-decorated ankles of elder sisters, mother, grandmother and great-grandmother, with only faces and wide expectant eyes visible. In a couple of swift movements, the pan was upended and the most treacherous part of the process was complete. Now a more relaxed stirring of the mixture began to cool and set the sugar. Finally, the sugar was decanted for the last time into age-old moulds, where it would set into solid blocks of deeply and intriguingly flavoured sugar. What an experience that was. I buzzed for days after at the skill, the pride, the family effort, the sheer beauty of the event. To the farming family this was their norm, but to me this was 'the exquisiteness of the ordinary'.

When jaggery is not available to me, I replace it in this recipe with Barbados soft dark brown sugar with excellent results.

Serves 10
Roasting the aubergines
— 650g aubergines, cut into 2cm dice
— 50ml sesame oil
— Pinch of sea salt

Pickling ingredients
— 70ml sesame oil
— 1 level tablespoon black mustard seeds
— 70g fresh ginger, peeled and cut into fine julienne

— 70g garlic, peeled and cut into fine julienne
— 2 fresh green chillies, slit open and deseeded
— 2 tablespoons jaggery or Barbados soft dark brown sugar
— 1 level teaspoon sea salt
— 1 rounded teaspoon ground turmeric
— 1 level teaspoon chilli powder
— 1 level teaspoon asafoetida
— 70ml apple cider or white wine vinegar

Preheat the oven to 200°C. Line a baking tray with non-stick baking paper.

Place the aubergines in a large bowl and drizzle over the oil and a pinch of salt. Toss the aubergines with your hands, encouraging the scant amount of oil to coat the vegetable. Scatter the aubergines on the lined tray, spreading them out to allow a little space between the pieces. Roast in the preheated oven for about 20 minutes, until well coloured.

Heat the sesame oil in a heavy-based low-sided saucepan. When the oil shimmers, add the mustard seeds and allow them to crackle and burst. Immediately add the ginger, garlic, chillies, jaggery or sugar and the salt and stir well to mix. Cook gently for 3 minutes, then add the turmeric, chilli powder and asafoetida and stir and cook for a further 3 minutes. Add the vinegar, bring to a bare simmer and cook for 5 minutes. Add the aubergines and stir in well. Cook for a further 5 minutes at the merest simmer. This gentle simmering is important to allow the flavours to mix properly without the mixture scorching. Taste and correct the seasoning.

The pickle keeps for two months in a covered sterilised jar in the fridge.

Red Onion, Kale, Marjoram and Bacon Broth with Grilled Parmesan Crouton

This is a robust broth that is almost a meal in a bowl. There is something about a broth made with a good bone stock (in this case, chicken) that seems to immediately nourish and comfort. The quality of your stock is of paramount importance to ensure a deep, sweet flavour. I would happily use a stock made with turkey or duck bones in place of the chicken.

For most of the cooking time, I like the broth to simmer gently so as not to concentrate the flavour of the stock too much, which would throw off the balance of flavours. The kale should be torn into small bite-sized pieces so that they are comfortable to eat and the marjoram needs last-minute chopping, as if chopped in advance it will quickly oxidise and lose its sweet taste. I sometimes replace the kale in the recipe with green cabbage leaves or florets of broccoli or Romanesco.

Broths should arrive at the table steaming hot, as they are not great when somewhat tepid. I like having to wait for a moment for the broth to cool just a little or the rather old-fashioned habit of genteelly blowing on your spoon before eating. In the past, it seems our recent forebears generally liked most hot foods to be steaming hot, though this was certainly to the detriment of some dishes such as roast meats, whose charm perished when introduced to red-hot plates and boiling gravy. Mind you, there are many stories of the occupants of very grand houses where the kitchen was often a good jog from the dining room being surprised when eating their first 'hot' meal in less elevated surroundings. The journey along freezing corridors rather sucked the heat from many a smart dish. There was a hopeful practicality to the grand silver cloches of yore designed not just as a highly polished piece of dining room bling, but an often vain attempt to simply keep the food hot. In our contemporary homes of a rather more compact nature and improved insulation, it is easier to achieve perfect temperatures.

Broths should arrive at the table steaming hot, as they are not great when somewhat tepid. I like having to wait for a moment for the broth to cool just a little or the rather old-fashioned habit of genteelly blowing on your spoon before eating.

I ♥ love Cabbage!

Even though the appearance of this, and indeed other broths, is rather rustic, I still find that with the last-minute additions of freshly grated Parmesan and a grassy olive oil, it is elevated to a rather sophisticated level.

Serves 4–6
— 1 tablespoon extra virgin olive oil, plus extra for drizzling
— 175g rindless streaky bacon, cut into neat lardons
— 420g red onions, peeled and cut into neat wedges
— 4 garlic cloves, peeled and thinly sliced
— 1.5 litres chicken stock (page 319)
— 150g kale leaves, weighed after destalking, torn into bite-sized pieces
— 4–6 slices of sourdough bread or baguette
— 2 tablespoons fresh marjoram or 1 teaspoon fresh thyme leaves
— 4 tablespoons grated Parmesan cheese
— Sea salt and freshly ground black pepper

Heat the olive oil in a heavy-based saucepan and add the bacon lardons. Cook over a moderate heat, allowing the fat to render out and the bacon to turn golden brown. Stir every now and then to ensure even colouring. Remove the bacon pieces from the rendered fat and reserve.

Add the onions and garlic and toss in the fat. Season with salt and pepper and cover with a disc of greaseproof paper and the saucepan lid. The combination of paper and lid will create the steamy atmosphere the onions need to cook in. Cook on a very gentle heat, allowing the onions to sweat for about 30 minutes, until nearly softened.

Remove the saucepan and paper lid and increase the heat to high for just 2 minutes. I find this brief cooking over high heat adds a little caramel flavour to the onions. Add the stock and bring to a simmer. Cover and continue cooking again very gently until the onions are completely tender. All the time you are trying to keep the onion wedges intact, though it is by no means a disaster if they come apart. The broth can be put aside now until later.

Bring a large saucepan of water to a boil and season with salt. Drop in the kale and cook briefly until wilted and just tender. Strain and press off the excess water, though there is no need to be too heavy handed, as a little kale cooking water will not impact adversely on the broth. Add the kale and reserved bacon lardons to the broth, stir well and bring to a simmer. Taste and correct the seasoning.

When ready to serve, grill or toast the bread, allowing it to gain plenty of colour. Place one piece of bread in deep, hot soup bowls. Chop the marjoram or thyme and sprinkle it over the bread.

Pour over the broth and finish each bowl with a scattering of Parmesan and a drizzle of olive oil. Serve immediately.

yoghurt dripping

Labneh

Whey

Labneh Ice Cream

I like to serve this ice cream with roast, baked or poached fruit of some description. Rhubarb, gooseberry, apple and blackberry are all good, but roast plums, pomegranate molasses and a little crème fraîche (page 145) is a particular favourite. The labneh gives a depth to the flavour of the ice – sharp though not bitter.

Making your own labneh as directed on page 321 is simplicity itself and I strongly suggest you use a thick, full-fat, Greek-style yoghurt when doing this. By dripping the yoghurt to achieve the labneh, you are removing the watery whey, hence there will be fewer icy crystals in the finished ice cream.

The dark, soft and almost sticky Barbados sugar adds a deep flavour and colour to the ice cream. The texture of the ice is definitely smoother and superior when the mixture is churned and frozen in an ice cream machine or sorbetiere, though just freezing it in a normal freezer gives a tolerable, if somewhat more icy, result.

The dark, soft and almost sticky Barbados sugar adds a deep flavour and colour to the ice cream.

Serves 8–10
— 150g honey
— 540g labneh (page 321)
— 225ml cream
— 80g Barbados soft dark brown sugar

Place the honey in a small saucepan and warm a little to liquefy. Add the honey to the labneh with the cream and sugar and beat or whisk well to dissolve the sugar grains.

Freeze in an ice cream machine according to the manufacturer's instructions.

Store in the freezer until ready to serve. Remove from the freezer and keep at room temperature for 15 minutes before serving in neat scoops with the fruit of your choice.

Turmeric + ginger cake

Ginger, Lemon and Turmeric Cake

The defining ingredients at the heart of this cake sound like a combination of what you might be ingesting from a glass in the form of a tincture first thing in the morning. Well, if it makes you wince at that early hour, I think in this case the reaction will be more pleasant. The cake itself is very straightforward and brightened up with lemon and fresh ginger, while the turmeric arrives in a blaze of deep primrose yellow on top in the icing. A sprinkling of finely diced stem ginger is the final gesture in what is an easy but delightful cake. Keeping up with the current fashion in cake decoration, you could sprinkle a few bright orange marigold or deep golden dahlia petals over the cake for added pizzazz.

This is a cake to be eaten at any time of the day with tea or coffee or also as a dessert cake after lunch or dinner. It is definitely best eaten on the day it is made, when it still retains that just-baked fresh charm.

The cake itself is very straightforward and brightened up with lemon and fresh ginger, while the turmeric arrives in a blaze of deep primrose yellow on top in the icing.

Serves 6–8

Cake
— 175g butter, at room temperature, plus extra melted butter for greasing the cake tin
— 175g self-raising flour, plus extra for dusting
— 150g caster sugar
— 30g fresh ginger, peeled and finely grated
— 3 eggs
— Zest of 1 lemon

Icing
— 80g icing sugar, sieved
— 55g cream cheese
— 45g butter, at room temperature
— 2 teaspoons freshly squeezed lemon juice
— 1 teaspoon finely grated peeled fresh turmeric

— 50g stem ginger (page 190), chopped into 0.3cm dice

To serve
— Crème fraîche or softly whipped cream

You will need
— 1 X 22cm cake tin

Preheat the oven to 180°C. Brush a 22cm cake tin with a little melted butter and line the bottom with a disc of non-stick baking paper. Dust the sides of the tins with a little flour, then tap the tins to remove any excess.

Place the butter, flour, sugar, ginger, eggs and lemon zest in a food processor. Using the pulse button, process the ingredients very briefly to achieve a creamy consistency. This may take as little as 20 seconds. Ensure that all the flour from the base and sides of the processor is amalgamated evenly into the batter. Spread the batter into the lined tin as evenly as possible.

Bake in the preheated oven for about 25 minutes, until the cake is risen, richly coloured and just barely starting to come away from the edges of the tin. Test that the cake is cooked by inserting a skewer into the cake and retracting it. The skewer should come out of the cake clean.

Place the cake, still in the tin, on a wire rack and allow to cool for 15 minutes before carefully removing from the tin and replacing on the wire rack, leaving the baking paper on top.

To make the icing, place the sieved icing sugar, cream cheese and butter in a bowl. Beat with a wooden spoon until a creamy, fluffy consistency is achieved. Add the lemon juice and turmeric and mix in gently. Chill the icing until you are ready to ice the cake.

When the cake has completely cooled, remove the baking paper and place on a flat serving plate. Spread the icing over the top of the cake, achieving a gentle, swirling finish. Scatter the diced stem ginger over the icing as evenly as possible.

Serve the cake with crème fraîche or softly whipped cream.

Marshmallow, Raspberry and Rose Cake

This cake is quite the confection, but when the separate elements are broken down, it is perhaps not quite as complicated as it at first sounds. The cake consists of a classic Victoria sponge, raspberries, both frozen and in the form of jam, and a big cushion of marshmallow to cover the whole thing. I like to decorate the cake with either fresh or crystallised rose petals, which make it look ridiculously pretty. This is not a cake to make on a whim – it is definitely a party cake for a celebration. It would make a glorious birthday cake and would also be suitably romantic for a small wedding.

You would expect this combination of ingredients to taste delicious, but what was a surprise to me is how well this cake keeps. Normally I find a Victoria sponge starts to stale on the second day and by the third day I am thinking trifle might be its best future. However, in this case it seems that the cloak of marshmallow keeps the cake fresher in texture and in flavour than I would normally expect. I have tasted the cake after four days and found it to still be remarkably good.

Because the berries in the cake are essentially preserved and not fresh, it means this cake can be made at any time of the year. The frozen berries have a sharp tartness, and when combined with the sweet and intensely flavoured raspberry jam they cut through the sweetness of the other ingredients. The other curious advantage of using frozen berries is that they melt somewhat in the cake, giving an almost trifle-type texture to the part of the slice they are sitting in.

Fresh floral decorations (edible, of course) can be added according to the season in which you are making the cake. For many months of the year, roses will be available. Yellow primroses and deep purple violets could herald the arrival of spring. Some lilac flowers would be gorgeous, as would a light scattering of cherry blossoms. Apple blossoms and pink or white elderflowers would be equally pretty. In summer, dahlia flowers will provide a myriad of colour possibilities. In autumn, there

The cake consists of a classic Victoria sponge, raspberries, both frozen and in the form of jam, and a big cushion of marshmallow to cover the whole thing. I like to decorate the cake with either fresh or crystallised rose petals, which make it look ridiculously pretty.

will be fresh raspberries for an appropriate decoration. Watch out for the variety known as Autumn Bliss, which sometimes is still providing a few berries in a mild November. In the winter months, myrtle berries would be charming.

Serves 12–20

Cake
— 125g butter, at room temperature, plus extra melted butter for greasing the cake tins
— 175g caster sugar
— 3 eggs
— 175g cream flour, plus extra for dusting the cake tins
— 1 teaspoon baking powder
— 1 tablespoon milk

Marshmallow
— 25g powdered gelatine
— 500g granulated sugar
— 50g egg whites

Filling
— 6–8 tablespoons raspberry jam
— 225g frozen raspberries
— 3 teaspoons rosewater

Decoration
— Fresh or candied organic rose petals (page 332)

To serve
— Softly whipped cream

You will need
— 2 x 20cm cake tins

Preheat the oven to 180°C. Brush 2 x 20cm cake tins with a little melted butter and line the bottom of each tin with a disc of non-stick baking paper. Dust the lined tins with a little flour and tap the bottom to remove the excess.

Place the butter in a large heavy bowl, such as Pyrex or ceramic, and beat with a wooden spoon until it has paled somewhat in colour. Add the caster sugar and continue to beat until light and fluffy. Beat in the eggs one at a time, beating well between each addition. Sieve the flour and baking powder together and mix well, then fold with the milk into the egg and butter mixture gently but thoroughly. Divide the batter between the prepared tins.

Bake in the preheated oven for 20–25 minutes, until the cakes are well risen, a rich golden colour and feel somewhat spongy to the touch. The cakes will have shrunk very slightly from the edge of the tins and a skewer inserted into the cake should be completely clean when withdrawn.

Remove from the oven and place on a wire rack, still in the tins. Allow to cool for 15 minutes, then gently remove from the tins and place paper side down on a wire rack to cool completely.

To make the marshmallow, place the gelatine in a small heatproof bowl such as Pyrex or ceramic. Do not use plastic or light metal or the gelatine will stick to it. Pour 125ml of water over the gelatine, being careful not to splash it. Allow to sit and sponge for 10 minutes. The gelatine will swell and literally take on a sponge-like appearance. Place the bowl directly in a saucepan of simmering water and cook gently until the gelatine had dissolved into a clear liquid. I prefer not to stir the gelatine but allow it to melt in its own time. There should be no undissolved grains of gelatine still visible in the mixture. Turn the heat off under the saucepan and allow the gelatine to sit.

Place the sugar and 250ml of water in a saucepan and stir over a low heat until the sugar has dissolved. You don't have to stir continuously, just occasionally. Increase the heat and continue to boil until it reaches 122°C on a sugar thermometer. Remove from the heat and stir in the melted gelatine with a wooden spoon.

Place the egg whites in the clean, dry bowl of a stand mixer and whisk to stiff but not dry peaks. With the machine still running, pour the syrup down the side of the bowl onto the egg whites. The mixture will liquefy somewhat at this stage, but that's fine. Continue whisking at a high speed until the mixture becomes really thick but still pourable. In my machine this takes 10–15 minutes.

To assemble the cake, remove the baking paper from the cakes and split each one in half horizontally. Place the first half on a wide flat plate and spoon on 2 generous tablespoons of the jam, not pushing the jam right out to the very edge, but rather leaving a 1cm rim around the edge of the cake. Scatter on one-third of the frozen raspberries. I tend to squash the berries between my fingers to get them to sit flat.

Drizzle 1 teaspoon of rosewater over the berries and smear with 2 generous tablespoons of the marshmallow, again not going quite out to the edge. Place the next layer of cake on top, firming it gently into place.

Continue as previously and place the final layer of cake on top. You will now have four layers of cake and three layers of jam, berries, rosewater and marshmallow. Spoon some of the marshmallow on top of the cake and spread it down over the edges. Continue using the marshmallow until the sides and top of the cake are generously iced. If you have a little marshmallow left over, pop it into a tin lined with oiled non-stick baking paper and dusted with a teaspoon each of icing sugar and cornflour, sieved and mixed, and allow to firm up.

Place the cake in a cool place to allow the marshmallow to set, but do not refrigerate.

When ready to serve, decorate the cake with fresh or candied organic rose petals. Serve softly whipped cream to accompany the cake.

Radishes with Smoked Eel Butter

The butter here, flavoured with smoked eel, is tremendously useful, and though this is not a substantial dish, in its simplicity lies its elegance.

Recipes don't get any easier than this one. The butter here, flavoured with smoked eel, is tremendously useful, and though this is not a substantial dish, in its simplicity lies its elegance. I serve this as a little bite before dinner with a glass of wine or place it on the table at the same time as the bread and allow guests to draw the crisp radishes through the butter and pop them straight into the mouth, thereby creating a build-up to the dishes that will follow.

In a way this dish is a good example of the fashion for food in restaurants, where sharing plates or small plates are featuring and the informality associated with this way of eating is making for a more relaxed, less uptight dining experience. Many diners no longer want to sit rigid in their chairs and restaurateurs understand it is possible to serve food of the highest order in an atmosphere conducive to having a relaxed time rather than in a tension-filled temple, which surely cannot have been good for digestion.

Serves 4–6 as a starter
— 100g smoked eel
— 50g butter, cold but not rock hard
— A few drops of freshly squeezed lemon juice
— Sea salt and freshly ground pepper

To serve
— 16–24 chilled radishes, with leaves attached

Blend the eel and butter in a food processor until just blended. Season with a few drops of lemon juice, a little pepper and if necessary a little salt.

Place the butter in a bowl and serve alongside the radishes sprinkled with a little sea salt.

If plating the dish individually, spread a little of the butter on each plate and simply but artfully lay the radishes alongside with a sprinkling of sea salt. Serve immediately.

Pan-fried Plaice with Roast Chicken Sauce, Grapes, Cucumber and Chervil

I am sure that the title of this recipe may seem a bit unusual. This sauce, made with a leftover roast chicken carcass, is as good with a firm-textured fish as it is with the chicken itself. Bone stocks made with meat were not an unusual addition to sauces for fish in classical French cooking, but the practice has gone out of fashion. I also serve this sauce with grilled young beef and guinea fowl and of course a roast chicken. The grapes and cucumber, both of which are as good with fish as they are with chicken, lighten the sauce and are little bursts of freshness when eating the dish. I sometimes freeze a chicken carcass after a roast if I am not immediately making it into a stock or to use in a sauce such as this. The notion of not getting value out of the cooked carcass is anathema to me – it seems like such a waste of food, flavour and goodness.

This is quite a grown-up sauce that demands a bit of concentration to allow the sauce to bubble at a gentle pace and to whisk in the butter to emulsify the sauce. If you have difficulty finding chervil, you can replace it with a pinch of French tarragon.

Serves 4
— 100ml roast chicken sauce (see below)
— 150g cucumber, peeled, deseeded and cut into 0.5cm dice
— 600g fat fillets of skinned plaice, brill or turbot
— Plain flour seasoned with salt and pepper
— 25g butter, at room temperature
— 24 grapes, peeled and deseeded
— 50–70g cold diced butter
— 1 tablespoon chopped fresh chervil or 1 teaspoon chopped fresh French tarragon
— Sea salt and freshly ground black pepper

This is quite a grown-up sauce that demands a bit of concentration to allow the sauce to bubble at a gentle pace and to whisk in the butter to emulsify the sauce.

Reheat the chicken sauce to a simmer. Add the cucumber to the sauce and allow to bubble very gently while you cook the fish. Do not allow the sauce to reduce – you are just warming the cucumber through at this stage.

Heat a heavy-based cast iron frying pan over a moderate heat. Dip the plaice fillets in the seasoned flour and shake well to remove the excess flour. Spread each side of the fillets lightly but thoroughly with the 25g of soft butter and add to the hot pan in a single layer. The fish should sizzle lightly on contact with the heat of the pan. Cook the fish until richly coloured, then turn over and cook briefly on the other side. Remove the fish to hot serving plates.

Add the grapes to the sauce and allow to heat through. At the same time, using a wooden spoon, add the cold diced butter to the simmering sauce a few pieces at a time. The butter will emulsify to slightly thicken the sauce and give it a more luscious appearance. Add the chervil or tarragon and swirl it through the sauce. Taste the sauce and correct the seasoning.

Spoon the simmering sauce, cucumber and grapes over and around the fish. Serve immediately.

Roast Chicken Sauce

This is a versatile sauce and in many ways is like making a double stock. If you have any jellied chicken juices in the chicken roasting tray, no matter how small the amount is, save it for adding sensational flavour to the sauce. I keep any meat jellies in little covered jam jars in the fridge and regard them as highly important magical flavour bombs for perking up a sauce, gravy, pie, broth, soup and so on.

Serves 6
— 1 carcass left over from a roast chicken
— 100ml white wine
— 500ml chicken stock (page 319)
— Sea salt and freshly ground black pepper

Preheat the oven to 200°C.

Break up the chicken carcass as much as you can and place in a small roasting tray. Roast in the preheated oven for about 20 minutes, until richly coloured.

Transfer the bones into a saucepan they fit into snugly. Pour the wine into the roasting tray, place over a medium heat and allow the wine to reduce by two-thirds.

Add the chicken stock and bring to a simmer. Pour the liquid over the bones and simmer for about 1 hour. At this point you want the liquid to have reduced to approx. 200ml.

Strain the sauce through a fine-mesh sieve and discard the bones. Taste and correct the seasoning. This is the basic sauce, which can be put aside for finishing later or can be stored in the fridge for several days. It will also freeze successfully.

Heavenly Hens

Heavenly Hens

In a world gone crazy, I sometimes need to stop and try to find my bearings. We all do. The place I go to recalibrate my thoughts and find a bit of calm is not a spa, not a deserted palm-fringed beach, not an abstract notion, not a thoughtful journey, but a visit to observe a living creature, and a rather nervous little creature at that. It is the daily doings of the laying hen that provides me with my mindless middle distance.

Shivering, shaking, scratching, bathing in sunshine and dust, perching and clucking, these harmless birds have a way of easing my brain, calming my mind, allowing me to just be as I regard their busy or calm practice. One eye focusing on the observer, the other on the ground, I can lose myself while watching them searching for a bug, a seed, a grain, a blade of grass. One foot on searching duty, the other performing the balancing act, I find them hypnotic.

Sometimes plain, sturdy and unruffled, sometimes elegant, shining and frizzled, they exhibit themselves in a catwalk of variety that in a mixed flock can be manna and visual titillation for the jaundiced eye. Then there is the outrageously haughty cockerel – Jack the lad, grandly overseeing the goings-on, stretching to his full height to emphasise his authority, howling loudly to broadcast to all his proximity. Extravagantly plumed, a dandy in the yard, all he seems to be missing is a drum to beat. Somehow his gentle lady friends seem to render his noisy banter irrelevant.

I adore the feathered fowl as they go about their business demanding little and at the same time gifting us with one of the most beautiful foods known to man. The eggs they produce are a sight to behold, one of nature's beautiful shapes, ovoid, perfect. Though many will only think of hens' eggs as either white or brown in colour, there are also blues, creams, greens, pinks, light and dark browns and variously speckled.

I love the fact that they don't bark, they don't need to be walked, they don't need leather leads or tartan coats, tinkling bells or booties or accessories of any kind, for that matter. They are self-sufficient as long as shelter and a little space to run and graze are allotted and water and a little food are provided. They are a beacon of sustainability with their capacity to consume our leftovers, produce a delightful and important food and manure so rich that it needs to be tempered because of its potency.

I think that they are perhaps the most underappreciated creature on the planet. For the most part, these humble character-filled food machines have been treated with utter disdain, and apart from the few lucky ones whose owners care about the welfare of the birds, they have generally been housed in the most appalling conditions. I find it astonishing that in a world where cats and dogs are treated with such care and pampered to the point of spoiling that the welfare of the undemanding hen has been almost completely forgotten. If household pets were mistreated in the way battery hens are, caged in frightful conditions, I suspect there would be uproar and marches on the street.

Gardeners will label them as terrorists, as they can wreak havoc in the shortest time if allowed to forage unguarded. There is nothing they prefer more than a freshly seeded bed or lawn for a root, hence the reason that an old gardener I knew likened them hysterically to a 'stallion horse in the garden'. I can forgive them for that, even though I, too, have been frustrated by their ferocious rootling, but when they look me in the eye with that trembling guilty nervousness, I melt and generally just break into a smile over my whole body.

Scrambled Eggs with Chanterelle Mushrooms on Grilled Sourdough Bread

Chanterelle mushrooms, which some people will also know as girolles, are one of the best wild mushrooms of the year. Yellow in colour, delicate in flavour and easy to prepare and cook, they are a true joy and I look forward to their arrival every year. The foragers who hunt for them keep their knowledge of where they grow a secret, and so they should as this is precious bounty. I won't list all the things they are delicious with because that would fill an entire page, but if only pan-fried with a little parsley and a faint hint of garlic and mounted on a buttered slice of toast, that simple repast would be a feast fit for a king.

Here the mushrooms are combined with scrambled eggs. Generally speaking, when you think of making scrambled eggs it is with a view to eating them straight away, as if held for any length of time they become hard and dull. In this recipe I add the creamy cooked chanterelle mushrooms to the just-cooked eggs still in the saucepan, which prevents the eggs from becoming solid. The resulting consistency is lovely and it can be prepared ahead of time and kept warm enough to retain the flavour of the eggs and the mushrooms.

The bread for grilling should be a good chewy sourdough and it should be cooked on a hot pan quite quickly so that the outside is crackling and richly coloured but before the bread becomes hard and crisp all the way through. The bread could also be toasted in a more conventional way.

I make scrambled eggs by starting to cook the beaten eggs and butter in a cold saucepan. I find this slow process gently cooks the eggs to give the softest and creamiest set. I prefer not to use a non-stick saucepan, as I find the texture of eggs cooked in this way is more like an omelette than a soft scramble. The downside of that choice is washing the saucepan, but hey-ho, some things in life are worth the extra effort. In fact, you could say the dilemma of the scrambled egg saucepan choice – the easy

I make scrambled eggs by starting to cook the beaten eggs and butter in a cold saucepan. I find this slow process gently cooks the eggs to give the softest and creamiest set. I prefer not to use a non-stick saucepan, as I find the texture of eggs cooked in this way is more like an omelette than a soft scramble.

non-stick route versus the more challenging, definitely stick route – is similar to many choices we face in life. Who knew that the choice of a saucepan for a scrambled egg could spark a philosophical discussion?

Serves 4
Mushrooms
— 25g butter
— 1 garlic clove, peeled and finely chopped
— 225g chanterelle mushrooms
— 4 tablespoons cream

Scrambled eggs
— 25g butter
— 8 free-range eggs, beaten
— Sea salt and freshly ground black pepper

To serve
— 4 slices of sourdough bread
— Extra virgin olive oil
— 2 tablespoons chopped fresh chives
— 2 tablespoons finely grated Parmesan cheese

Start by cooking the mushrooms. Melt the butter in a sauté pan and allow the butter to foam. Add the garlic and cook gently for a few minutes to temper its harshness. Add the mushrooms and season with salt and pepper. Sauté over a gentle heat until the mushrooms are tender. If the mushrooms have exuded a lot of water during the cooking, I like to remove them from the pan and reduce the liquid down to a syrupy consistency before adding them back in. Add the cream and allow to bubble up once, then immediately draw the pan off the heat and set aside.

To make the scrambled eggs, add the butter to a heavy-based low-sided saucepan. Add the beaten eggs, season with salt and pepper and cook over a low to moderate heat, gently stirring regularly until you have a softly scrambled mixture. This process cannot be rushed. If you cook the eggs over too high a heat, the curds of egg will be hard and not the soft, creamy consistency desired.

Draw off the heat, immediately add the mushroom mixture and stir to mix. Transfer into a bowl and keep in a warm place. Reserve until you are ready to serve.

Heat a heavy-based grill pan. Place the slices of sourdough bread on the dry pan and grill on both sides until well coloured. Drizzle each slice with a little olive oil.

Divide the bread between hot plates and top each slice with the egg and mushroom mixture. Finish each serving with a sprinkle of chives and Parmesan and serve immediately.

Kumquats
thinly sliced

Caramelised Kumquat and Vanilla Cake

The finished appearance of this cake is beautiful. Burnished kumquats, the smallest members of the citrus family, are studded into the top of the shiny caramelised and rust-coloured cake, giving it an almost jewelled appearance. It is a relatively easy cake to make, though the rub here is the preparation of the little kumquats. They need to be thinly sliced and deseeded and there is no denying that it is a slow and tedious task. The tiny little underdeveloped white seeds don't need to be removed, as they dissolve and disappear in the cooking. The kumquats can be prepared the previous day and stored in the fridge, making the job of assembling the cake considerably quicker.

The vanilla pod should be very finely chopped so that when you taste a little in the cake, it is not too strong. I use vanilla pods that I have previously used in custard and then gently washed, dried and stored in a jar of sugar. It is great to get a second use out of this expensive ingredient, plus you will have the scented sugar that can be used in biscuits, cakes and so on, so I suppose that is a third use. I love that sort of thrifty housekeeping.

This task definitely demands commitment, but if you have a willing pair of helping hands, it is certainly easier, so think like an Italian mama and enlist the help of little hands, which are perfect for removing the pesky seeds.

Serves 8–12
Kumquats
— 325g kumquats, thinly sliced and seeds removed
— 200g caster sugar
— 4 tablespoons water

Cake
— 150g butter, at room temperature
— 150g caster sugar
— 150g self-raising flour
— 50g ground almonds
— 3 eggs
— Zest of 1 lemon
— ½ vanilla pod, very finely chopped

To serve
— Softly whipped cream or crème fraîche

You will also need
— 1 x 25cm ovenproof sauté pan

Preheat the oven to 180°C.

Place a shallow oven tray close to your hob and add 1cm of water. You will need this ready to stop the caramel from overcooking and burning in the first stage of the recipe.

Place the kumquats, sugar and water in a low-sided ovenproof sauté pan 25cm in diameter. Bring to a simmer and cook gently until the water has evaporated and the sugar has caramelised to a pale chestnut colour. The kumquats will have taken on a sticky appearance. This will take about 10 minutes, but do allow enough time for the sugar to caramelise. Immediately place the pan in the tray of water to stop the caramel cooking. Do this carefully, as when the bottom of the pan hits the water, it will spit and splutter. You don't want any of the water in the tray to get into the pan with the kumquats.

Place the butter, sugar, flour and ground almonds in a food processor. Pulse for a few seconds. Add the eggs and process again very briefly until a smooth consistency is achieved. Finally, add the lemon zest and chopped vanilla and pulse again to combine. It may be necessary to run a spatula around the edge of the food processor bowl to draw in any unmixed batter.

Remove the kumquat pan from the tray of water and spread the cake batter evenly over the fruit.

Transfer the pan to the preheated oven and bake for about 30 minutes. The cake is cooked when richly coloured and feeling slightly firm to touch. The cooked cake will also have shrunk very slightly from the edge of the pan.

Place a large flat plate over the top on the cake pan. Using a dry kitchen cloth to protect your hands from the heat and to prevent anything from slipping, very carefully flip over the cake onto the plate.

Serve the cake warm with softly whipped cream or crème fraîche.

Caramel Citrus Sauce

This is a rather obvious combination of flavours, but nonetheless it is a useful sweet sauce. It will keep at its best in the fridge for up to five days, but after that the flavour gets a little stronger with a hint of marmalade to the taste. It is very good served with labneh ice cream (page 237) or with the caramelised kumquat and vanilla cake on page 257.

This is a rather obvious combination of flavours, but nonetheless it is a useful sweet sauce.

Serves 8
— 225g caster sugar
— 125ml water
— 8 thin strips of orange zest (use a swivel peeler)
— 165ml freshly squeezed orange juice
— 2 tablespoons freshly squeezed lemon juice
— 1 teaspoon finely grated orange zest

Place the sugar, water and orange strips in a low-sided saucepan and place on a gentle heat. Stir occasionally before the water comes to a simmer. When the water does simmer, do not stir again and allow the sugar and water to cook to a light caramel. If the caramel is cooking unevenly, tilt the saucepan to and fro but do not be tempted to use a spoon to stir it. It will eventually come to a single caramel colour.

While this is happening, heat the orange juice in a separate small saucepan, also to a simmer. Remove the saucepan of caramel from the heat and immediately add the orange juice. The caramel will spit and splutter and you will have a thick caramel and a thinner liquid in the saucepan. Replace on a gentle heat and cook until the caramel has dissolved into the rest of the liquid. Do not be tempted to stir during this stage – if all the thick caramel does not dissolve, that's fine.

Allow the caramel to cool completely and it will thicken as this happens. Sieve out the strips of orange peel and stir in the lemon juice and finely grated orange zest. The sauce is now ready to serve or can be stored in the fridge for several weeks.

Saffron Mashed Potatoes

Few dishes are more comforting than a bowl of mashed potatoes, but I know that some cooks are not always happy with their efforts. There are a few simple rules to follow for that bowl of perfectly fluffy, smooth potatoes. I buy local potatoes with the earth still on rather than the prewashed ones, as I find the flavour to be far superior. Scrubbing them clean seems like a small sacrifice for the improved taste. Peel and mash the piping hot potatoes immediately after they are cooked and always make sure the milk that you add is boiling. Keeping everything really hot is the key to fluffiness rather than a sticky result. Passing the hot peeled cooked potatoes through a vegetable mouli (or mouli légumes, as it is sometimes called) undoubtedly improves the texture, but an old-fashioned hand masher also works well. Use a floury variety of potato, such as Golden Wonder or Kerr's Pink, and definitely do not try to make mashed potatoes with new potatoes, as they will be gluey and dull.

I serve the mash with mackerel cakes with spiced tomato oil (page 45), rustic turkey or chicken pie (page 131) or chicken braised with wild garlic and lemon (page 81).

Serves 4
— 900g floury potatoes
— 120ml milk (approx.)
— 1 teaspoon saffron threads
— 50g butter
— 1 egg (optional)
— Sea salt and freshly ground black pepper

Scrub the potatoes well. Cover with cold water and salt generously. Cover the saucepan with a tight-fitting lid and bring to a boil, then turn the heat down to a simmer. The variety of potato and the time of year will determine how careful you will need to be when cooking the potatoes. The more floury the potatoes are, the more they are likely to split in the cooking, hence the more you need to steam them. In that case, pour off

Peel and mash the piping hot potatoes immediately after they are cooked and always make sure the milk that you add is boiling. Keeping everything really hot is the key to fluffiness rather than a sticky result.

most of the water after about 10 minutes of cooking, just leaving 2cm of water to steam the potatoes for the remaining time, which takes about a further 20 minutes. The potatoes need to be completely tender.

When the potatoes are nearly cooked, put the milk and saffron on to boil.

As soon as the potatoes are cooked, immediately peel them and pass through a vegetable mouli or potato ricer if you wish. This will give a smoother consistency to the finished dish. If you don't have a mouli or potato ricer, use an old-fashioned hand masher. It is essential, however, to deal with the potatoes the minute they are cooked, as if they are allowed to cool at all before mashing, they may become gluey.

If your milk has gone off the boil, bring it back to a boil and add the boiling milk slowly. It may not take all the milk, so be careful not to make soup, but do scrape all the saffron into the potatoes. Beat the potatoes vigorously with a wooden spoon or in a food mixer. Add the butter and egg (if using) and season well with salt and pepper. Beat again, then taste and correct the seasoning.

Serve the potatoes steaming hot.

Yellow Rice

This pilaf rice dish is richly flavoured and beautifully coloured. The technique captures the flavour of the rice, spices and chicken stock brilliantly. I sometimes stir a generous amount of chopped coriander leaves into the rice just before serving.

I am often happy to eat a bowl of this rice on its own as a supper dish as it is so satisfying. It is also delicious with roasted chicken legs or with the casserole roast pheasant with Jerusalem artichokes and Indian spices on page 84. The mackerel cakes with spiced tomato oil (page 45) are also good with this rice. A few mussels steamed open in a dry covered pan, then removed from the shell and debearded, are also a delicious addition to the cooked rice along with the mussel cooking pan juices.

I am often happy to eat a bowl of this rice on its own as a supper dish as it is so satisfying.

Serves 4–6
— 15g butter
— 1 tablespoon finely chopped onion or shallot
— 1 level teaspoon saffron strands
— 1 level teaspoon ground turmeric
— 250g basmati rice
— 500ml light chicken or vegetable stock
— 1 level teaspoon fine sea salt
— 1 tablespoon chopped fresh coriander leaves (optional)

Melt the butter in a heavy-based saucepan and allow to foam. Add the onion or shallot and coat in the butter. Cover and cook on a very gentle heat for 5 minutes. You want the onion or shallot to soften slightly without colouring. The aim here is that it will disappear into the rice.

Add the saffron and turmeric and cook on the same gentle heat for 1 minute. Add the rice and turn the grains gently in the buttery onions and spices. Make sure not to break the grains of rice by being too heavy handed while stirring. Add the stock and salt and again stir gently to mix. Bring to a simmer and cover tightly. If you think the lid of your saucepan is not a tight fit, place a layer of non-stick baking paper under the lid. Cook very gently on a low heat on the stove or place in a moderate oven (180°C) for about 15 minutes.

By this time the rice should be perfectly cooked and have absorbed all the liquid. Avoid the temptation to take the lid off the saucepan before the 15 minutes have elapsed, as this would allow the precious steam to escape. When the rice is cooked it will remain hot in the covered saucepan for at least 30 minutes (or for longer in an oven with the temperature reduced to 110°C). Add the chopped coriander leaves (if using) just before serving.

Rhubarb Collapsed in Blood Orange Juice

Many people have unpleasant memories of rhubarb cooked to threads and shreds as a result of overcooking. In this recipe, which combines two seasonal ingredients, the aim is perfectly cooked pieces of fruit that still holds its shape. When cooked this way, rhubarb can be a revelation in terms of texture and flavour. The combination of tart blood orange and tart rhubarb is lovely and the scent added by the small amount of vanilla is perfect. Serve with labneh ice cream (page 237).

Serves 4 as a compote or 6 as a sauce
— 350g rhubarb, cut into 2cm pieces
— 200ml blood orange juice
— 100g caster sugar
— ¼ vanilla pod

Place all the ingredients in a small low-sided saucepan that fits the rhubarb in a snug single layer. Bring to a bare simmer and cover. I use a glass saucepan lid or Pyrex plate so that I can see what is happening inside the saucepan. Maintain the heat at a bare simmer for 10 minutes, then remove the pan from the heat. Give the rhubarb a gentle turn and replace the lid. All the fruit may not be tender and cooked, but it will continue to tenderise in the residual heat. I like the pieces of rhubarb to be perfectly soft but still holding their shape, so be very gentle when stirring.

Serve the fruit warm or chilled.

When cooked this way, rhubarb can be a revelation in terms of texture and flavour. The combination of tart blood orange and tart rhubarb is lovely and the scent added by the small amount of vanilla is perfect.

golden Beets

Pickled Beetroot Tacos with Smoked Eel Butter and Radishes

This is a little bite that can be served as a starter or to accompany a drink. A soft goats' cheese can be used instead of the smoked eel butter with good results. If you can't find the tiny little radishes with soft leaves that I suggest, the bulb of larger radishes can be thinly sliced or diced and pushed into the smoked eel. The advantage of the tiny radishes is that the leaves are soft and lovely to eat as well as the peppery nature of the radish itself. The leaves of larger radishes are coarser with an unpleasant texture when eaten raw, though they are good when cooked. In any event, the peppery heat of the radish works beautifully with the rich meaty eel. A fine grating of horseradish added to the eel butter would also be good here.

Serves 6 as a starter or makes 24 individual bites

Beetroot tacos
— 2 medium beetroot, topped, tailed and peeled
— 60g caster sugar
— 100ml white wine vinegar
— 100ml water
— 24 tiny radishes with leaves attached, washed and dried
— 4 sprigs of fresh dill
— Sea salt and freshly ground black pepper

Smoked eel butter
— 45g smoked eel
— 25g butter
— A few drops of freshly squeezed lemon juice

Use a mandolin or very sharp knife to cut very thin slices of beetroot. You need 24 slices. The top and bottom of the beetroot, which are not big enough to achieve slices of the required size, may be reserved for another recipe.

The peppery heat of the radish works beautifully with the rich meaty eel. A fine grating of horseradish added to the eel butter would also be good here.

Place the sugar, vinegar and water in a small saucepan and bring to a simmer, ensuring the sugar dissolves completely. Immediately pour the simmering liquid over the sliced beetroot. Season with a little salt and pepper and allow to cool completely. Chill until ready to use.

Place the eel and butter in a small food processor and season with salt and pepper and a few drops of lemon juice. Blend briefly until smooth.

Drain the beet slices and dry on kitchen paper. Spoon or pipe a little of the smoked eel butter on the middle of the dried beet slices. Place a tiny radish sitting on top of the butter. The leaves will overhang the top of the slices. Fold over the beetroot to hide the radish and butter. Press the edges to ensure a secure seal and a neat finish. You are relying on the smoked eel butter to glue the beet together.

Garnish with small sprigs of dill and serve as soon as possible.

Beetroot Tacos with Goats' Cheese and Mint

Serves 6 as a starter or makes 24 individual bites
Beetroot tacos
— 2 medium beetroot, topped, tailed and peeled
— 60g caster sugar
— 100ml white wine vinegar
— 100ml water
— Sea salt and freshly ground black pepper

Goats' cheese
— 70g soft fresh goats' cheese
— 1 tablespoon extra virgin olive oil
— 1 tablespoon finely chopped walnuts, plus extra for sprinkling
— 2 teaspoons finely chopped mint
— 1 teaspoon honey

If serving as a starter
— 24 fine mustard greens
— 1 tablespoon pomegranate seeds
— Extra virgin olive oil

Prepare the beetroot as outlined in the main recipe. Chill until ready to use.

Mix the goats' cheese, olive oil, walnuts, mint and honey and season with salt and pepper.

Drain the beet slices and dry on kitchen paper. Spoon or pipe a little of the goats' cheese on the middle of the dried beet slices. Sprinkle a little extra chopped walnut on the goats' cheese, keeping it in from the edge of the beetroot slices. Fold over the beetroot to hide the goats' cheese. Press the edges to ensure a secure seal and a neat finish.

If I am serving these as a starter, I serve four tacos per person and garnish each plate with fine mustard leaves, a few pomegranate seeds and a drizzle of extra virgin oil. Serve as soon as possible.

Carrot, Halloumi and Dill Cakes with Tahini Sauce, Mint and Pomegranate Yoghurt and Sumac

These are light and fresh-tasting little cakes suitable to serve with a drink or as a starter or they would make a lovely accompaniment with their sauces to a platter of grilled lamb chops. The cakes and sauces can be made ahead of time and kept chilled, but I like to serve the cakes as soon after they come off the pan as possible. The different textures here add to the pleasure of eating the dish. The cakes are somewhat firm, that firmness coming mainly from the halloumi. The tahini sauce has the consistency of softly whipped cream and the pomegranate seeds in the minted yoghurt add a little crunch.

Try to find the best halloumi, as it varies a bit in quality. The cheese originated in Cyprus and was an artisan product traditionally made from either goats' or sheep's milk or a mixture of both milks. Now much of what is for sale outside of Cyprus is made from cow's milk and a lot of it is highly processed and has suffered in the same way that highly processed mozzarella has.

The lemony-tasting sumac that is sprinkled on the cakes at the last moment is a marvellous spice that comes from the seeds of the deciduous Staghorn sumac shrub. Many people will have this relatively common garden shrub, *Rhus typhina*, growing without realising that the red fuzzy 'flowers' are actually the source of this spice. Its leaves turn to shades of orange, gold and red in the autumn. In some parts of the world the tree is known as the lemonade tree, as refreshing syrup for adding to lemonade is made from the beautiful tart, tangy flowers.

Try to find the best halloumi, as it varies a bit in quality. The cheese originated in Cyprus and was an artisan product traditionally made from either goats' and sheep's milk or a mixture of both milks. Now much of what is for sale outside of Cyprus is made from cow's milk and a lot of it is highly processed.

Serves 6 as a starter or makes 30 bite-sized pieces
Carrot, halloumi and dill cakes
— 250g carrots, peeled and coarsely grated (weight after peeling and grating)
— 250g halloumi, coarsely grated
— 60g plain flour
— 1 egg, beaten
— 4 tablespoons chopped fresh dill
— 1 heaped teaspoon roasted and coarsely ground cumin seeds
— 1 teaspoon paprika
— Extra virgin olive oil, for frying
— Sea salt and freshly ground pepper

Mint and pomegranate yoghurt
— 250ml natural yoghurt
— 2 tablespoons chopped fresh mint
— 1 tablespoon pomegranate seeds
— ½ teaspoon roasted and ground cumin seeds

To serve
— Tahini sauce (page 197)
— Pinch of sumac

To make the mint and pomegranate yoghurt, mix all the ingredients together. Taste and correct the seasoning. Set aside.

Place the carrot, halloumi, flour, egg, dill, cumin and paprika in a bowl. Season with salt and pepper and mix well. Taste to ensure the seasoning is correct. Measure out 20g pieces of the mixture and form into little cakes. Place on a tray lined with non-stick baking paper and chill until ready to cook.

Heat a little oil in a sauté pan and fry the cakes until golden brown on both sides. Keep warm if necessary for a short time in an oven preheated to 100°C.

To serve, place the cakes on a heated flat plate and top each cake with a little dollop of tahini sauce and a light sprinkling of sumac. Serve as soon as possible, passing the mint and pomegranate yoghurt separately with a little spoon for guests to serve themselves.

Purple gArlic

Quail Scotch Eggs with Spiced Tomato Oil

I love quail eggs and their miniature size always suggests a party to me. The speckled shells are a joy to behold and the preparation, though somewhat tedious, is a matter of attitude, as whenever you are preparing them, it is generally for a somewhat special event. I love that element of cooking when the cook is making an extra-special effort preparing delightful dishes for loved ones. I can't imagine myself preparing these for a meal alone on a damp winter evening. These are for sharing, ideally to be accompanied by a drink. Let's face it, if you go to the effort to boil, peel, wrap and fry a little egg such as these, I think it undoubtedly sends a message of great care at least and quite possibly love. This sums up for me part of the joy of food, a joy to be enjoyed alone sometimes, but more rewardingly a joy to be shared.

The eggs are not as fiddly as they sound to assemble and they make a perfect bite. Once prepared they will sit happily in the fridge for cooking at a later time. The spiced tomato oil will keep in the fridge for several weeks.

The season in which I am serving these determines what the final little garnish will be. Wild garlic flowers would be lovely, as would the later-arriving chive flowers. A pinch of finely chopped chives or coriander is perfect and in summer a fried small basil leaf would be shiny, brittle and glamorous.

I love that element of cooking when the cook is making an extra-special effort preparing delightful dishes for loved ones.

Makes 24 pieces
Quail Scotch eggs
— 12 quail eggs
— 250g minced belly or shoulder of pork
— Pinch of chilli flakes
— Pinch of English mustard powder
— Plain flour seasoned with salt and pepper
— 1 egg, beaten
— 200g fresh crustless white breadcrumbs
— Sunflower oil, for deep frying

— Sea salt and freshly ground black pepper

To serve
— Spiced tomato oil (page 8)

Garnish
— Finely chopped fresh chives

Place the quail eggs in a saucepan of boiling salted water and cook for 6 minutes. Remove immediately and immerse in cold water.

Mix the pork, chilli flakes, mustard powder and some salt and pepper in a bowl and mix well. Fry a tiny piece of the mixture in a little pan, then taste and correct the seasoning.

Place the seasoned flour, beaten egg and breadcrumbs in three separate wide, shallow bowls. Roll each egg in a little seasoned flour, then wrap each egg in a 20g piece of the pork mince. Roll the wrapped eggs in the palms of your hands to ensure a perfect ovoid shape. Dip in the beaten egg, shaking off any excess, then roll in the breadcrumbs to coat. Place on a tray lined with non-stick baking paper and chill in the fridge until needed.

Heat the oil in a deep fat fryer to 170°C.

Carefully place the eggs in the fryer basket and drop into the oil. Cook no more than six eggs at a time. Fry until they achieve a rich hazelnut colour. Keep warm on a piece of kitchen paper until ready to serve.

When ready to serve, cut the eggs in half lengthways and place on a pretty serving dish. Place a little spoonful of the spiced tomato oil on top of each egg and garnish with a pinch of finely chopped chives. Serve immediately.

HORseRadish

Potato Crisps with Venison Tartare, Juniper and Horseradish and Walnut Sauce

These delicate bites need to be served immediately after assembling. I often serve them with drinks, but large plates served family style would make an amusing starter. All the elements of the dish can be prepared ahead of time, so the last-minute nature of the assembly should not be too worrisome. If serving as a starter, all parts of the dish could be served in bowls placed on the table, allowing you to take the lead and show your guests exactly how it is done. Eating like this is sometimes more fun and also demands that diners concentrate a little more on what they are eating rather than swallowing the morsels as if they just appeared by magic.

The venison in the recipe could be replaced with beef, but I think we don't eat enough of this wild food, which has marvellous flavour. It is no more expensive than good-quality beef and in many ways is more interesting and complex in taste. Not every butcher will have it in stock, but a little advance warning should guarantee you get it.

All parts of the dish could be served in bowls placed on the table, allowing you to take the lead and show your guests exactly how it is done.

Makes 30 pieces
— 150g venison loin or fillet, trimmed of all fat or gristle and finely chopped
— 1 tablespoon extra virgin olive oil
— 1–2 teaspoons very finely ground juniper berries, or to taste
— 30 homemade potato crisps (page 278)
— 4 tablespoons horseradish and walnut sauce (page 279)
— Zest and juice of 1 lemon
— 2 tablespoons finely chopped fresh flat-leaf parsley
— Sea salt and freshly ground black pepper

Mix the venison, olive oil and juniper and season to taste with salt and pepper. Place 1 teaspoon of the venison mixture on one end of each crisp. Place ½ teaspoon of horseradish and walnut sauce beside the venison. Grate a little lemon zest and squeeze a few drops of lemon juice over the venison, then finish each crisp with a few grains of sea salt and a tiny pinch of parsley. Serve immediately.

Homemade Potato Crisps

Making potato crisps at home is definitely worthwhile – a few potatoes produce a lot of wafers and nothing beats the fresh flavour of crisps cooked at home. A mandolin is well worth buying for making the crisps (and for so many other slicing jobs in the kitchen), but mind your fingers by fastidiously using the safety guard that these invaluable tools are sold with.

— 450g large, even-sized potatoes
— Sunflower oil, extra virgin olive oil or beef dripping, for deep frying
— Sea salt

Wash the potatoes with a vegetable brush. You can peel the potatoes if you prefer, but I like the appearance of the little line of skin on their edges, so I leave the skins on. For even-sized crisps, trim each potato with a swivel peeler until smooth. Slice them very finely, preferably with a mandolin. If you hold one up to the light you will see the light coming through, so they should be thinner than a coin but not quite paper thin. Soak in cold water for about 30 minutes to remove the excess starch. The starch will fall to the bottom of the bowl, then you can carefully lift out the potato slices and give them another rinse under cold water.

Heat the oil or beef dripping in a deep fat fryer to 180°C. Preheat the oven to 80°C.

Lay a clean cloth or towel on your work surface and lift out some of the crisps. Dry them really well before dropping a few slices at a time into the hot oil. Give them a gentle stir. Do not overfill the fryer as it will bring down the temperature of the oil, resulting in greasy crisps, and also because it could cause the oil to dangerously overflow. Drain the golden cooked crisps on kitchen paper, season with a pinch of salt and keep warm, but not hot, in the oven. They will happily sit like this for 2 hours.

Horseradish and Walnut Sauce
As unlikely as this combination may sound, it is delicious. I serve it with warm poached salmon and smoked fish and can also easily envisage a meal where it would happily accompany grilled or roast beef or lamb.

It is worth searching out fresh horseradish root whenever it is called for, as the pre-grated and pickled product is invariably too vinegary and the sweet, fiercely hot charm of the fresh root is lost. The root itself is easy to grow, though it is best to leave it for a couple of years to get established before enjoying it in your kitchen. It also has a spreading habit, so bear that in mind when planting. The fresh horseradish that is sold in shops and greengrocers is almost all imported, which is a pity, as it seems to thrive in this part of the world. It does grow wild in some parts of the country, but you will need to know your horseradish leaves from your dock leaves to make an accurate identification. However, in the event of confusion over the leaves, once dug up, cracked open and smelled, the aroma of the root is instantly recognisable by its sinus-cleansing vapour and sweet scent. It is truly an ingredient that I would be lost without.

It is worth searching out fresh horseradish root whenever it is called for, as the pre-grated and pickled product is invariably too vinegary and the sweet, fiercely hot charm of the fresh root is lost.

Serves 6
— 50g shelled walnuts
— 30–50g grated peeled fresh horseradish
— 75ml cream
— 75ml crème fraîche
— 1 tablespoon fresh white breadcrumbs
— 1 level teaspoon caster sugar
— Sea salt and freshly ground black pepper

Chop the walnuts finely and combine with the rest of the ingredients. Mix gently to combine and taste to correct the seasoning. The sauce will keep in the fridge for two days in a covered container.

Smoked Black Pudding and Cheddar Croquettes with Bramley Apple and Blackberry Sauce

I use smoked black pudding from Hugh Maguire in County Meath for this recipe. Hugh is known as 'the Smokin' Butcher' and his pudding is excellent. His pudding is made using fresh pigs' blood and natural pork casings, yielding both great flavour and texture.

These flavoursome bites are perfect as a hot nibble with drinks or served with a salad of leaves as a lunch or starter dish. The croquettes can be prepared ahead of time and refrigerated for frying later. Like most foods that are deep-fried, they are at their best as soon as they are cooked, when the filling is hot and loose and the outside is crisp.

Like most foods that are deep-fried, they are at their best as soon as they are cooked, when the filling is hot and loose and the outside is crisp.

Makes 40 little croquettes
Croquettes
— 400g potatoes
— 130g smoked black pudding, very finely diced
— 100g Cheddar cheese, finely grated
— 2 tablespoons cream
— Seasoned plain flour
— 3 eggs, beaten
— 150g crustless fresh white breadcrumbs
— Sunflower oil, olive oil or beef dripping, for deep frying
— Sea salt and freshly ground black pepper

Bramley apple and blackberry sauce
— 450g Bramley apples
— 2 tablespoons caster sugar
— 2 tablespoons water
— 100g fresh or frozen blackberries

BERRY
confused

To make the sauce, peel, quarter and core the apples, then cut each quarter in half. Place in a small saucepan with the sugar and water. Cover tightly and cook on a very low heat. The apples will gradually collapse to a frothy snow. Add the blackberries and cook for a further 2 minutes. Stir lightly, taste and add a little more sugar if necessary. Set aside.

Place the potatoes in a saucepan and season with a pinch of salt. Bring to a boil, cover and simmer for 10 minutes. Pour off all except 2cm of water, cover and replace on the heat to cook for a further 20 minutes or so, until completely tender.

Immediately peel the skins off the potatoes – you want 300g of peeled cooked potatoes. Place in a bowl and mash to a smooth fluff. Add the black pudding, Cheddar cheese and cream and season with salt and pepper. Gently mix everything together. Chill the mixture until completely cold.

Roll the mixture into 15g balls. Place the flour, beaten eggs and breadcrumbs in separate bowls. Roll the balls in the flour first, followed by the beaten egg and finally the breadcrumbs. Place on a tray lined with non-stick baking paper and chill for at least 15 minutes.

Heat the frying fat of choice to 170°C in a deep fat fryer. Preheat the oven to 100°C.

Fry the croquettes a few at a time until well coloured and crisp. Drain on kitchen paper and keep warm in the oven.

Serve the croquettes with bamboo skewers to hold and the Bramley apple and blackberry sauce on the side.

Carpaccio of Scallops with Chilli, Lemon and Coriander

This dish is simple to make, but the key to the success is the quality of all the ingredients used. The scallops for this dish are served raw and need to be spanking fresh so that the sweet, untainted flavour of the fish shines through and the olive oil needs to be the best you can get. I use the best new season olive oil from Tuscany in Italy for this dish, and when the scallops are as fresh as suggested and the oil is as good as suggested, this simple dish is one of the best of the year. You need to season the scallops with a delicate hand, so go carefully, watching where the seasonings land. When available the flowers of the coriander plant are a pretty addition to the dish. The scallop coral is not used in this dish, as their texture is not entirely suitable for eating raw, but save them for a chowder or a scallop mousse.

When the scallops are as fresh as suggested and the oil is as good as suggested, this simple dish is one of the best of the year.

Serves 4
— 8 large scallops, trimmed of their coral
— 4 pinches of chilli flakes
— Zest and juice of 1 lemon
— 1 tablespoon fresh coriander leaves and flowers (if available)
— 2 tablespoons extra virgin olive oil, the best-quality olive oil you can find, such as Capezzana, Fontodi or Selvapiana
— Sea salt and freshly ground black pepper

Cut the scallops horizontally into slices 3–4mm thick and divide in a single layer between four cold but not chilled plates, allowing two scallops per serving. Season the scallops with a small pinch of chilli flakes, sea salt and freshly ground black pepper. Finely grate some lemon zest over the scallops and squeeze a little lemon juice over each serving. Sprinkle on the coriander leaves and flowers (if available). Finally, drizzle the olive oil over. Serve immediately.

Mussels with Indian Spiced Mayonnaise, Apple and Coriander

I generally serve these mussels with drinks, to be eaten straight from the shell, though they will also make a lovely first course to be eaten at the table. If I am serving them as a starter, I serve thinly sliced brown bread and butter to accompany.

The key element in this dish that is not listed in the ingredients list is the juice that the mussels expel as they cook. This wonderful sweet-tasting, mild juice is used to thin the mayonnaise to a coating sauce and is the making of the dish. To ensure that you don't lose this sometimes scant amount of juice, you need to cover the shellfish and cook them over a moderate heat. If the heat is too high, the juices just evaporate during the cooking and are lost. I am a big fan of the juices that shells such as mussels, cockles and clams emit when cooking and I often freeze surplus juices for use another day, when they can be a marvellous addition to a soup or a sauce.

If you would like to get very organised with the preparation of this dish, you could cook the shellfish ahead of time and also prepare the sauce. The shells can then be coated with the mayonnaise at a later stage. In that case, both the mussels and sauce should be chilled until ready for assembly. Having said that, the silky texture of the unchilled cooked fish, still warm from the pan, is superior to that of the firmer, chillier ones.

I always use a Pyrex plate or glass saucepan lid when cooking shellfish so as to be more visibly aware as to when they are cooked. The shellfish cook unevenly, so you need to be removing cooked ones from the pan as soon as they pop open. Refer to the recipe for mussels with fennel and cannellini beans on page 12 for detailed instructions on how to cook the mussels.

The key element in this dish that is not listed in the ingredients list is the juice that the mussels expel as they cook. This wonderful sweet-tasting, mild juice is used to thin the mayonnaise to a coating sauce and is the making of the dish.

Serves 4–6 as an accompaniment to a drink or serves 2 as a starter

— 20 mussels, rinsed in cold water
— 2 tablespoons homemade mayonnaise (page 306)
— 2 tablespoons finely diced peeled eating apple
— 1 teaspoon curry powder
— Pinch of sea salt
— A few drops of freshly squeezed lemon juice
— 20 fresh coriander leaves

Place the cleaned mussels in a small low-sided saucepan or sauté pan and cover with a Pyrex plate. Place on a low heat and allow the mussels to cook and pop open. As soon as the flesh in the shells looks plump and cooked, immediately remove them from the pan. Continue cooking until all the mussels are cooked.

While the mussels are cooling, strain 1 tablespoon of the mussel cooking juices into the mayonnaise. Add the diced apple and curry powder and mix well. You want a coating consistency that will cover the mussels in a light cloak, so if it is looking a little thick, add a little more of the mussel liquid. Taste and correct the seasoning, as a pinch of salt or a few drops of lemon juice may be required.

Carefully remove the mussel meat from the shells and remove the little tuft of hair known as the beard. Sometimes the beard will have fallen out during the cooking, so if it is not obviously visible it may not be there, so don't worry about it. You are trying to keep the mussels intact, so be gentle when handling them as they are easy to tear, in which case they are not as lovely to look at or to eat. Replace one mussel in each half shell. Discard the rest of the shells.

Coat each refilled shell with a little of the spiced mayonnaise and garnish with a coriander leaf. Serve immediately or keep chilled for no longer than 1 hour.

Biscotti

I played around with several biscotti recipes before I came up
with this version, which I really like. This recipe makes a large
quantity of the biscuits, but they will keep well in a sealed
container. The classic way to eat them is dipped into a glass
of Vin Santo, an Italian dessert wine primarily produced in
Tuscany. When the biscotti and wine are paired in this famous
Italian tradition of welcome, the combination is then known as
'Cantucci e Vin Santo'. The wine is produced all over Italy, with
other notable producers in both Veneto and Trentino. I also like
the biscotti dipped into a cup of coffee or tea – a practice deeply
frowned upon by my Italian friends. Dipping half of the biscuit
into great-quality melted chocolate and allowing them to set
would also raise a perfectly plucked Italian eyebrow or two, but
it is actually quite delicious.

The notable spice in the recipe is anise, with its pungent
liquorice flavour. It is related to the more easily available fennel
seeds both in family and in flavour, but the anise is sweeter, more
intense and better here.

The vanilla pod does not especially need to be a new unused
one, but could easily be one retrieved from a previous custard
outing, washed gently and allowed to dry completely before
saving for a recipe such as this.

Makes 100 **biscuits**
— 6 eggs
— 560g caster sugar
— 225g unsalted butter, melted and cooled
— 250g mixture of unskinned almonds, walnuts and hazelnuts,
   coarsely chopped
— 175g raisins
— Finely grated zest of 3 oranges
— 1 vanilla pod, split in half lengthways and chopped to a fine
   dust
— 1 teaspoon anise seeds (optional)
— 1kg plain flour, sieved, plus extra for dusting
— 1½ teaspoons baking powder, sieved

The notable spice in the recipe is anise, with its pungent liquorice flavour. It is related to the more easily available fennel seeds both in family and in flavour, but the anise is sweeter, more intense and better here.

Preheat the oven to 180°C. Line two oven trays with non-stick baking paper.

Separate the eggs, placing the yolks in one mixing bowl and the whites in another spotlessly clean, dry bowl. Using a food mixer, whisk the yolks with **half of the sugar** until pale in colour and creamy in consistency.

Whisk the egg whites using a mixer to achieve a stiff peak, then gently fold in the remaining sugar. With a heavy flexible rubber spatula, gently fold the egg white mixture into the egg yolks.

Now add the melted butter, again using a light and delicate hand. Add the chopped nuts, raisins, orange zest, chopped vanilla and anise seeds (if using). Fold the sieved flour and baking powder into the egg mixture one-quarter at a time. You will need to use a wooden spoon as you add in more of the flour, as the mixture will become heavier to handle.

When everything is properly combined, divide the dough into six pieces. Roll the pieces into cylinders about 20cm long. You may need to lightly flour your worktop for this process. Divide the logs between the two lined trays, leaving 5cm between each cylinder and at the outer edge of the trays.

Bake in the preheated oven for about 30 minutes, until the cylinders are golden brown on top. Remove from the oven and allow to cool for 5 minutes. Remove them one at a time to a chopping board and with a sharp serrated knife (I use my bread knife), cut them into 1.5cm-thick slices at a 45 degree angle. Place the cut biscuits, lying down, back on the lined sheets and bake again in the oven for a further 15 minutes or so, until golden brown at the edges and starting to feel crisp. Remove from the oven and allow to cool on the trays. The biscuits will continue to crisp as they cool.

Store the cooled biscuits in sealed containers using layers of kitchen paper to act as shock and moisture absorbers.

Pestle and Mortar

Picture the scene: in my imagination, we are definitely either in a cave or at least at its entrance, where better light is guaranteed. We are dressed in rather stinky animal hides and we are pretty smelly, hairy and unkempt ourselves. Wild nuts have been gathered and are having their shells cracked by a stone – all very easy-to-conjure-up mental images of that scenario. However, the nut cracker, he or she, is enthusiastic, and rather than a single tap on the nut to crack the shell to yield the meat inside, multiple taps are administered and we end up with nut and shell meal in crushed form rather than a meal of nuts. This is how I imagine the early stages in the evolution of what we know as the pestle and mortar. A bit more concentration on the selection of the stones being used could easily have yielded one of the boulders with a bowl shape or in due course the depression could have been hacked into the stone using another tool. So there you have it, that is my view of the discovery of the pestle and mortar, one my most-loved pieces of kitchen equipment. Where this scene might have taken place is a matter for conjecture, most likely in many caves over many hundreds of years on many different parts of the planet.

Many, many years later, a slightly modified version of these two stones sits on kitchen counters all over the world. In the history of the evolution of practical objects, the pestle and mortar must be one of the few items that has changed so little. I can imagine the residents of the aforementioned cave dwelling being totally comfortable with the present day iteration of their two stones. Is that not just marvellous? I am tickled pink that something I use on a daily basis in my kitchen has largely remained unchanged for 10,000 years.

It is perhaps this timeless and unchanged presentation of the tool that causes some cooks to shy away from using it. I can imagine myself clad in a bear skin (definitely better than my bare skin!), grinding away merrily with the two stones with a view to that evening's supper. It is this easily pictured proximity of the leap from now to then that can

Pestle & Mortar

mentally and emotionally deter some from wielding the pestle. We have moved on, after all, to a place where most of our kitchen tools are propelled by a power that is not created by our own bodies. There is no on/off switch on the pestle. You are the power behind this tool. You are the on button. The words 'carbon neutral' and 'zero emissions' do not even begin to do justice to the benign impression it has left on the planet's resources.

There is a larger message involved here, but before I become too philosophical and preachy, even though there are machines that will approximate the results of the pestle and mortar, there is no machine that I know of that comes anywhere close to replicating the particular consistency and texture achieved by stone on stone. It is elemental. It is quite simply a different result that not only changes the texture of ingredients, but also the appearance and taste. You are so close to and involved with what is happening. There is no lid to shield or inhibit your view – you are up close and in control. Unless you take the grinding and pounding to Olympian levels of speed and force, you can react to the subtleties of the change in the ingredients to catch them at exactly the stage you want. Fine, gritty, coarse, creamy, silky – all can be achieved and by the sweat of your own brow. How lovely.

Beetroot with Yoghurt, Honey and Mint

This is a very simple Middle Eastern dish that may be eaten as a starter or as part of a selection of salads. It would make a good side dish to serve with ham or bacon, smoked fish or just hard-boiled free-range eggs. Search out the best-quality yoghurt for this dish. One cannot be definitive about the cooking time of beetroots, as it depends on the size and freshness of the beets.

Search out the best-quality yoghurt for this dish.

Serves 6–8
— 900g beetroot
— 2 garlic cloves, peeled and finely chopped
— 425ml natural, unsweetened yoghurt
— 6 tablespoons extra virgin olive oil
— 2 tablespoons freshly squeezed lemon juice
— 2–4 tablespoons chopped fresh mint
— 1 teaspoon honey
— Sea salt and freshly ground black pepper

Remove the leaves from the beets, leaving 2cm of stalk attached to the beets. Do not pinch off the little tail. Rub under a cold running tap to clean. Do not pierce with a knife.

Place in a saucepan, cover with cold water and add a pinch of salt. Cover and cook at a simmer until tender. The beets can take anything from 30 minutes to 2 hours to cook. The cooking time depends on the size and freshness of the beets. Test whether the beets are cooked by rubbing the skin with your thumb – the skin should offer no resistance. If the skin does not rub off easily, cook for a further 10 minutes or so and try again. As soon as the beets are cooked, strain off the cooking water and peel them.

Stir the garlic into the yoghurt. Spread the yoghurt over the base of a large shallow serving dish. Slice the beets thinly and arrange in overlapping slices over the yoghurt.

Mix the olive oil, lemon juice, mint, honey and some salt and pepper together thoroughly, then drizzle over the beets.

Juniper Salted Roast Venison with Horseradish and Walnut Sauce

Venison is the leanest of all meats and requires very careful timing when cooking. Traditional methods of cooking this fine meat were very heavy handed indeed and have left many people with less-than-pleasant memories of eating it. Red wine marinades, full of strong spices and seasonings, were considered de rigueur and as a result the meat was strong and quite often seriously overcooked. Venison has such a low fat content that cooking it more than medium tends to produce a dry, flavourless result. Because we are using loin of venison here, which is a slender cut of the meat, the cooking time may seem short but in my experience it is absolutely accurate.

The juniper is a berry that most people will have ingested or at least enjoyed the flavour of while drinking a gin and tonic – in fact, a gin cannot be called a gin unless it has some of the berry infused in the making of the spirit. It has certainly come under pressure over the past few years as a dizzying array of flavourings have been flung into the previously minimal concoction, thereby challenging the berry's position as the spice that for most people determined the taste of a gin. Interestingly, it is not a true berry but rather a seed cone that has the appearance of a berry with a dusty deep blue colour.

Its flavour is reflected in its scent, which is quite aromatic and somewhat antiseptic. There is also fruitiness and a hint of pepper going on too. I also love it with pigeon and wild duck.

In this recipe, the fiery horseradish sauce, walnuts and pink venison combine brilliantly. I serve a simple green vegetable such as kale or sprouting broccoli alongside.

Serves 6–8
— 1kg loin of venison, trimmed of all grizzle
— 1 tablespoon extra virgin olive oil
— 1–2 tablespoons juniper berries
— 4 tablespoons brandy

Venison has such a low fat content that cooking it more than medium tends to produce a dry, flavourless result.

— 300ml red wine
— 300ml beef or chicken stock (page 319)
— 55g cold butter
— Horseradish and walnut sauce (page 279)
— 1 tablespoon chopped fresh chives
— Sea salt and freshly ground black pepper

Preheat the oven to 200°C.

Rub the venison with olive oil. Place the juniper berries in a pestle and mortar or spice grinder and grind to a coarse powder, then add a good pinch of salt and pepper. Rub the oiled venison in the spice mixture.

Heat a heavy-based sauté pan until quite hot. Add the venison to seal and colour on all sides, then place in a roasting tray that it fits into snugly and roast in the preheated oven for about 10 minutes.

When the meat is cooked, remove it from the tray. Place on an upturned plate sitting inside a larger one to capture any escaping juices and allow to rest in a warm oven.

Place the roasting tray on a medium heat and add the brandy. Let the brandy bubble up and evaporate almost completely, then add the wine. Allow the wine to boil and stir the bottom of the pan to loosen any caramelised meat juices. Allow the wine to reduce by three-quarters. Add the stock and allow to boil. Strain into a small saucepan, bring to the boil again and reduce until the sauce thickens very lightly.

Taste and if you are not happy with the intensity of the flavour, keep reducing. Otherwise, turn the heat down so that the sauce barely simmers and add the cold butter. Shake the pan to and fro to create a gently swirling liquid or little waves. The butter will gradually melt and thicken the sauce a little more. The sauce should now be glossy and lightly thickened and taste flavoursome and rich.

To serve, carve the rested meat (adding any meat juices to the sauce) into slices 1cm thick. Arrange on hot plates. Place a blob of very cold horseradish and walnut sauce carefully on the edge of the meat or pass separately if preferred.

Sprinkle the plates with a little finely chopped chives and serve immediately.

Rustic Oven Roast Potato Wedges with Chorizo and Burnt Spring Onion Sauce

For those among you who don't own a deep fat fryer but long for chips, these wedges are perfect. The scrubbed potatoes are left unpeeled and cut into large wedge-shaped chips, with each wedge having some of the skin attached. The skin on each piece of potato is important, as it prevents them from sticking to the roasting tray and of course it also has a good flavour.

When buying potatoes, if possible buy them unwashed, as the soil will keep in the flavour and nutrients before scrubbing and cooking. Serve these potatoes with roast and grilled meat, poultry or fish. They are a great accompaniment to a warm salad and you can ring the changes with the use of different herbs. The burnt spring onion sauce is deliciously savoury and the chorizo adds depth and a little spice to the dish.

The spring onion sauce can be prepared ahead of time and will keep in the fridge for a couple of days. Once you taste it, you will realise that it would be good served with many other things, such as grilled beef or lamb, oily fish such as salmon or mackerel, or on a simpler note with raw radishes and baby carrots as a crudités-type salad.

The onion sauce can be prepared ahead of time and will keep in the fridge for a couple of days. Once you taste it, you will realise that it would be good served with many other things, such as grilled beef or lamb, oily fish such as salmon or mackerel.

Serves 6
— 900g potatoes
— 4 tablespoons extra virgin olive oil or duck or goose fat (approx.)
— 4 branches of fresh rosemary or sprigs of thyme
— 2 garlic cloves
— 100–150g thinly sliced ready-to-eat deli-style chorizo
— Flaky sea salt and freshly ground black pepper

Preheat the oven to 220°C.

Scrub the potatoes well – there is no need to peel them. Dry them in a clean kitchen towel and cut lengthways into thick chip-like wedges (or for a quicker cooking time, cut into smaller pieces). Put in a bowl and drizzle on a little olive oil or your fat of choice. Turn in the fat to coat lightly. There should not be a pool of fat in the bottom of the bowl, but the potatoes should be covered with a thin sheen. Do not season the potatoes until they are cooked, as it tends to cause the potatoes to stick to the cooking tray, hence you may lose the crispy skins.

Place on a roasting tray, spreading them out in a single layer, skin side down. Add the herb of choice and the unpeeled, uncrushed garlic cloves. Roast in the preheated oven for about 35 minutes, until the skins are crispy and the centres are tender. Avoid the temptation to move them on the tray halfway through the cooking, as this will only break up the potato skins. The potatoes will eventually crisp up and loosen from the bottom of the tray. Season with salt and pepper and serve in a hot serving dish.

Scatter the sliced chorizo through the hot potatoes and serve the burnt onion sauce on the side.

Burnt Spring Onion Sauce
Serves 6
— 1 bulb of garlic
— 4 tablespoons extra virgin olive oil
— 150g spring onions (about 12)
— 150g cream cheese
— 110g sour cream
— Sea salt and freshly ground black pepper

Preheat the oven to 220°C.

Slice through the top of the bulb of garlic, leaving it hinged at the edge. Sprinkle a pinch of salt on the cut surface and drizzle on 1 tablespoon of the oil. Replace the garlic lid and place the whole bulb on a square of non-stick baking paper large enough to wrap up and tightly seal the garlic. Place on a tray and roast in the preheated oven for 30–40 minutes, until the garlic is completely tender and soft. Allow to cool, then squeeze the soft garlic flesh out of the skin.

Slice the spring onions lengthways, place in a bowl and mix with 2 tablespoons of the olive oil. Season with salt and pepper. Grill on a heavy-based cast iron sauté pan or grill pan or roast in a hot oven until they are tender and partly blackened. Allow to cool, then chop finely.

Mix the cooled spring onions with the cream cheese, sour cream, roast garlic purée, 1 tablespoon of the olive oil and a pinch of salt and pepper. Beat vigorously to mix all the ingredients well. Taste and correct the seasoning.

Keep chilled until ready to serve.

Nougatine

I love these lacy, hole-filled biscuits. They are delicate and brittle and melt in the mouth. It is the sort of recipe that produces a result that some home cooks feel is perhaps beyond them. In other words, if you ate these in a smart restaurant, you might think they are frightfully difficult to make, but in fact they are really easy. We all need recipes like this in our arsenal, something a little bit clever and glamorous but actually an easy dream to make.

I generally serve the biscuits as flat thins, but with care the slightly cooled cooked mixture can be moulded over upturned cups or glasses to create receptacles for mousses, ices and so on. Equally, you can wrap the cooked but still malleable dough around wooden spoons to create a little biscuit tube or what might previously have been known as a cigarette russe. Draping the cooked dough over a rolling pin or bottle will yield the classic tuile biscuit shape. All in all, there is scope here for creativity in terms of the possible shapes you might wish to achieve.

The cooked biscuits keep perfectly for several days stored in an airtight container. The uncooked mixture is quite safe once refrigerated for up to a month and behaves perfectly when cooked at a later time. I serve them with ice creams, sorbets, granitas, mousses, soufflés and anything to do with chocolate. During the summer I will deliver a plate of them alongside a platter of figs or a bowl of peaches. When the pears start to ripen later on in the autumn, I will serve them with those and a wedge of mature Coolea cheese from West Cork.

The apple pectin may be a new ingredient to some cooks, but this is easily found nowadays in health food shops. Glucose syrup has also become widely available as the continuing obsession with celebration cakes of gargantuan proportions and multiple shades, hues and flavours continues unabated.

Makes approx. 30
— 175g nuts, either a mixture or the entire quantity of a single nut such as almonds, walnuts, pecan nuts and Brazil nuts (hazelnuts may also be used, but should be roasted and peeled before chopping)

If you ate these in a smart restaurant, you might think they are frightfully difficult to make, but in fact they are really easy.

- 150g caster or granulated sugar
- 125g butter
- 50g glucose syrup
- 2 teaspoons water
- ¾ teaspoon apple pectin

Preheat the oven to 190°C.

Chop the nuts in a food processor using the pulse button to render them to a semi-coarse texture. It is important that you don't render the nuts to a powder, but equally if the texture is too coarse, the mixture will not knit together well. Think grit rather than gravel.

Combine the remaining ingredients in a small saucepan and cook on a very low heat just until the mixture is melted and smooth. Add the nuts and stir to mix.

Using a silicone baking mat or an oven tray lined with non-stick baking paper, drop on scant teaspoons of the mixture, allowing plenty of room for the mixture to spread as it cooks. A standard oven tray, about 40cm x 35cm, will accommodate about four biscuits this size. You can of course make smaller biscuits by reducing the amount of mixture.

Bake in the preheated oven for about 10 minutes, until the biscuits have spread into lacy and lightly caramelised flat crisps. They will be the colour of toasted hazelnuts.

The cooked biscuits will be soft and molten when removing them from the oven, so allow the biscuits to cool until set on the tray before removing to a wire rack to cool completely.

Any remaining uncooked mixture will store perfectly in the fridge for up to one month. It will solidify but you simply prise off bits and cook as above.

Mini Mont Blanc with Chocolate Sauce

This is quite the confection to be served around Christmas, but truly worth the effort. It is a celebration of that season. All the elements of the dish – chestnut purée, meringues, sweetened cream and chocolate sauce – can be prepared in advance for assembly at a later point. The meringues will keep for several days in an airtight container. The chestnut purée can be made the previous day and refrigerated, as can the chocolate sauce. It is not a classic rendition of the pudding, which gets its name from the famous mountain in Switzerland, but contains all the elements, though the addition of decorative myrtle berries or pomegranate seeds is certainly not traditional. I serve this on a large flat platter with lots of holly sprigs to leave one in no doubt that it is indeed the season to be jolly.

When I first cooked sweet chestnut, an ingredient that was completely new to me, we started with the raw nuts, then poached them and went through the torturous process of peeling off the tough skins before passing them through a sieve to achieve the required smooth consistency. After all that I found the flavour to be very strange and did not really enjoy it. It was not until two decades later when my friend, the great Australian cook Skye Gyngell, who is head chef at the beautiful Spring restaurant in London's Somerset House, cooked the dish for me at a dinner in Turin that I got the point and since then I've grown to love the smoky flavour of these nuts. My recollection (cloaked in the mists of time) of Skye's presentation of the dish is of the chestnut rendered to a purée, shaped into a neat dome, covered with lots of sweetened whipped cream and then sprinkled with lots of beautiful glittering candied fruit. It was a revelation. Nowadays the tedious part of cooking and shelling the nuts has been done by someone else and great-quality nuts can be bought ready for use in vacuum-pack containers. Joy.

It is not a classic rendition of the pudding, which gets its name from the famous mountain in Switzerland, but contains all the elements.

Myrtle berries

Serves 10

Meringue
— 200g caster sugar
— 100g egg whites
— 3 teaspoons unsweetened cocoa powder, sieved, plus extra for serving

Chestnut purée
— 180g cooked chestnuts
— 40g caster sugar
— 100ml milk
— 1 tablespoon dark rum
— ½ teaspoon vanilla extract

Chocolate sauce
— 150g chocolate (62% cocoa solids), roughly chopped
— 225ml cream

To serve
— 500ml softly whipped cream
— Pomegranate seeds or myrtle berries

Preheat the oven to 130°C. Line an oven tray with non-stick baking paper.

Place the sugar and egg whites in a spotlessly clean, dry bowl and whisk to a stiff peak. Spread 2 tablespoons of the meringue on the baking paper. This will be ground up to make the meringue 'snow' later. Fold the cocoa carefully but thoroughly into the remaining meringue and using a dessertspoon, shape 10 little blobs onto the baking paper. Use a teaspoon to make a little depression on top of each shape.

Bake in the preheated oven for about 40 minutes. The meringues should lift away easily from the paper when cooked. Turn off the oven and allow the meringues to cool completely, still in the oven, with the door closed.

Place the chestnuts in a small saucepan with the sugar, milk, rum and vanilla. Bring to a simmer and cook for about 8 minutes. Mash the chestnuts with a fork as they cook. They will gradually break down into a coarse purée. Remove from the heat, transfer to a food processor and blend to a smooth purée. Allow to cool completely.

To assemble, place a generous teaspoon of the chestnut purée on top of each meringue. If the purée has become very firm, moisten it with a little milk to a consistency that is soft but will hold its shape. Coat each meringue with a cloak of softly whipped cream. I like to refrigerate the meringues now for up to 2 hours.

Finally, to make the chocolate sauce, place the chocolate and cream in a small saucepan and bring to a bare simmer. Stir until the chocolate has melted completely into the cream and a rich, glossy sauce is achieved. Remove from the heat.

To serve, dust each meringue with cocoa powder and decorate with myrtle berries or pomegranate seeds.

Place the two plain meringues in a mouli légumes or potato ricer and dust the entire confection with a light covering of meringue 'snow'. Serve with the hot chocolate sauce.

Slow Roast Shoulder of Lamb

The cooking world now realises that the shoulder is every bit as good as the more prime cuts, and in some ways is actually better. The hard-working and muscular shoulder has marvellous flavour, but needs long, slow cooking to gently tenderise it so that the flesh becomes sweetly succulent. The cooked lamb in this dish should be soft and melting and will be gently pulled apart for serving rather than carved. You can't rush cooking a shoulder of lamb, but once it is in the oven, there is plenty of time to prepare sauces and vegetables to accompany it.

Serves 8–10
— 1 x 3.6kg whole shoulder of lamb on the bone
— Flaky sea salt and freshly ground black pepper

Preheat the oven to 180°C.

Place the lamb shoulder in a wide roasting tin or oven tray with the skin side up. Score the skin several times to encourage the fat to run out during the cooking and to crisp up the skin. Season with salt and pepper. Roast in the preheated oven for 30 minutes before turning the temperature down to 160°C and cooking for a further 3½ hours.

To test if the lamb is cooked to a melting tenderness, pull the shank bone – it and some of the meat should come away easily from the bone.

When the lamb is cooked, remove it from the oven. There will be plenty of fatty cooking juices. Strain these off the roasting tin through a fine-mesh sieve into a bowl. Keep the lamb warm in the oven with the temperature reduced to 100°C.

When the fat has risen to the surface of the cooking juices, skim it off carefully and thoroughly with a large spoon.

To serve the lamb, a tongs or serving fork and spoon is the best way to remove the meat from the bones. Prise largish pieces off the bones and serve on hot plates with some of the hot cooking juices.

The hard-working and muscular shoulder has marvellous flavour, but needs long, slow cooking to gently tenderise it so that the flesh becomes sweetly succulent.

Pantry
&
Preserves

Pantry and Preserving

This is a rather random collection of items that I find very useful to have to hand. Some of the items will seem a bit eccentric and others will appear more useful – all are valuable to me in my kitchen. They all have the common theme of giving me a feeling of pleasure when I make them and, dare I say it, joy when I use them.

I get immense pleasure from the ease of pushing some tarragon leaves into vinegar and basil leaves into olive oil to preserve for later in the year. I find the simple act of freezing tomatoes and elderflower heads equally satisfying. The mayonnaise, labneh, dukkah and candied peel are more time consuming but they are crucial cornerstones, if you like, of my cooking. Candying rose petals will not be high on most people's list of 'must do' tasks, but the few minutes that are involved in this delicate operation will reward you with an edible decoration for your family and guests that is proof of your devotion to them. In return, I hope they, too, make their devotion to you very clear.

There is, I think, a happy frugality to the general theme of these items. Money and flavour will be saved by preserving items in some of the ways I suggest. I have always loved the idea of a well-stocked store cupboard and most of these items fit into that category. There is also the somewhat sentimental and slightly smug feeling of having extracted the maximum value from an ingredient so that it will come back and visit another day.

Homemade Mayonnaise

I cannot imagine not having mayonnaise in my kitchen. Use good-quality ingredients and you will have one of the most useful and versatile sauces. The cardinal rule is to add the oil to the egg yolks in a very slow dribble or stream while continuously whisking. Once you have made the sauce a couple times, you will find that you can approach the task without the trepidation that is sometimes attached to this sauce. The sauce will keep in your fridge for two weeks in a sealed container.

The cardinal rule is to add the oil to the egg yolks in a very slow dribble or stream while continuously whisking.

Makes 350ml
— 2 egg yolks
— 1 dessertspoon white wine vinegar
— ¼ teaspoon French mustard
— 250ml oil (sunflower, peanut, grapeseed, olive or a mixture – I use about half olive and half sunflower, but use less olive oil if you find my suggested proportion too strong)
— Sea salt and freshly ground black pepper

Place the egg yolks, vinegar, mustard and a pinch of salt and pepper in a bowl. **Drop the oil very slowly** onto the egg mix, whisking all the time. The mixture will gradually start to thicken. You can start to add the oil a little bit more quickly now, but don't get carried away by your success, as caution is needed right up until all the oil has been whisked in. Taste and correct the seasoning.

If the mayonnaise curdles as a result of adding the oil too quickly, it will suddenly become quite thin and oily on top. If this happens, put another egg yolk into a clean bowl and whisk in the curdled mayonnaise a teaspoon at a time until it emulsifies again.

Black Garlic Aioli
For this intensely flavoured and darkly coloured mayonnaise, add six cloves of crushed black garlic to the egg yolks and proceed as in the mayonnaise master recipe above.

whisk
Vigorously

Candied Citrus Peel

In my experience, it is almost impossible to buy candied peel that is as good as what you make at home. Most of what is on sale tastes of very little other than sugar, whereas when you make it yourself, the candy retains the flavour of the particular citrus being used. That deep and true citrus flavour has a dramatic effect on any dish you put it in afterwards. There is definitely a commitment involved here to see the stages of the recipe through, but having made it once you will realise that there is no real mystery involved and that most of the time the fruit is cooking away on its own while you can be getting on with other things.

Various citrus fruits can be used, but I tend to prefer oranges, lemons and grapefruit. I freeze the shells of the fruit that I have previously used for juicing and when I have enough fruit or want to candy some peel, those frozen citrus shells are what I use. I find that freezing the fruit before cooking helps to tenderise and soften the fruit adequately, which is a very important stage of the recipe.

I store the candied peel in sealed jars in my fridge, where in my experience it will keep for a year.

Makes approx. 1kg
— 10 juiced orange, lemon or grapefruit shells (or a mixture)
— 1.3kg granulated or caster sugar
— 850ml water

Day 1
Freeze the juiced orange, lemon or grapefruit shells (or a mixture) the day before you want to make the candied peel (or at some previous time).

Day 2
Place the frozen citrus shells in a saucepan and cover with plenty of cold water. Bring to a simmer and cook, covered, until the peels are completely tender. This can take up to 2 hours or sometimes longer. To test the softness of the peel, I usually take one out of the saucepan and press it under my fingertip – it

Various citrus fruits can be used, but I tend to prefer oranges, lemons and grapefruit. I freeze the shells of the fruit that I have previously used for juicing and when I have enough fruit or want to candy some peel, those frozen citrus shells are what I use.

308

should gently squash under the pressure exerted. This is very important, as if this softness is not achieved at this stage, the addition of the sugar can cause the peel to become very tough.

Drain the shells and allow to cool slightly. With a teaspoon, remove any remaining flesh and membranes from the inside of the shell. Try to keep the white pith and rind intact.

Place the sugar and 850ml of water in a clean saucepan and bring to a simmer. You will need to stir the sugar occasionally to encourage it to dissolve. Add the peels and cook gently until the fruit looks translucent. The cooking time will vary depending on the thickness of the citrus peel, but be prepared to allow it to cook for 45–60 minutes or perhaps longer. To check this, using a fork or tongs, lift up one piece of the fruit and hold it up to the light, where you should see the light coming through as if you were looking through a stained glass window with the sun behind it.

Lift the peels out of the syrup and set aside. Boil the syrup again until it becomes thick and syrupy. To check this stage, dip a spoon into the syrup and lift it out. The syrup falling from the spoon should create a thick and obvious thread. Remove the pan from the heat, return the peels to the syrup and allow to sit for 30 minutes before potting into sterilised jars and covering with the syrup. Cover and store in a cool place. I prefer to keep the jars in the fridge, where the peel will keep for up to a year.

When using, cut the pieces of peel into the size required for the particular recipe.

Dukkah

This is an irresistible toasted blend of nuts, seeds and spices. I find it endlessly useful as a seasoning for meat, fish, vegetables, beans and pulses. I love it with yoghurt-based dishes and particularly with labneh, when it can run off in all directions with further sprinklings of sumac, pomegranate seeds, coriander and mint. It really is magical. Try a little on a hard-boiled or even a scrambled egg. Grill a piece of sourdough bread, kiss it with the lightest rub of garlic, drizzle it with a verdant olive oil, smear it with hummus and sprinkle on the magic that is dukkah and the transportation to a Middle Eastern oasis is immediate. Pop a slice of pink grilled lamb on top of all that and you are on a magic carpet ride.

Toasting the nuts, seeds and spices separately is important, as they cook and colour at different speeds depending on their size and shape. Allowing the toasted ingredients to cool completely before grinding also matters and helps to avoid getting a paste rather than a powder.

Sprinkle on the magic that is dukkah and the transportation to a Middle Eastern oasis is immediate.

Makes approx. 500g
— 50g hazelnuts
— 50g pistachios
— 225g sesame seeds
— 110g coriander seeds
— 50g cumin seeds
— Sea salt and freshly ground black pepper

Preheat the oven to 200°C.

Place the hazelnuts on an oven tray and roast in the preheated oven until the skins start to lift and the nuts are a rich golden colour. Allow to cool. There is no need to peel off the skins. Repeat the process with the pistachios, but only until they crisp and colour lightly.

Place the sesame seeds in a dry frying pan and stir continuously over a medium heat until they start to change colour to a slightly darker shade. Allow to cool.

Toast the coriander and cumin seeds separately on a hot dry pan until they appear lightly toasted and smell aromatic. Allow to cool.

Place the cooled nuts and seeds in a clean coffee or spice grinder and season with a pinch of salt and pepper. Grind until smooth, being careful not to overprocess, by which time they might form a paste. You are looking to achieve a loose grind that will sprinkle easily. You may need to do this in batches depending on the size of your grinding machine. Store in an airtight container.

Picnic

Picnics have always featured in my family. From the youngest age, I remember a picnic rug being a permanent feature in the car. These mobile meals were sometimes put together at the drop of a hat – a simple tea-and-a-slice-of-cake-in-a-basket scenario – while on other occasions the assembly was much more considered and involved multiple hampers and panniers to transport the various elements of the repast. This propensity to eat al fresco when travelling may well have been born out of my mother's need to feed a large brood more economically rather than a deep-seated desire to be en plein air. In any case, being introduced to the joy of outdoor eating – or if not actually exposed to the elements, then certainly at a remove from others (in the car) – and, perhaps most importantly, in a position to control what we chose to eat, left myself and my eight siblings with a love of the picnic.

I find it hard to pinpoint my earliest picnic memory, but the day trips we used to take to Tramore in County Waterford must have happened when I was very young. These outings generated much excitement, as coming from the landlocked county of Laois, we adored the prospect of swimming in the sea. We always swam in our local river and enjoyed it, but Tramore promised a long wide beach with waves, salty water and a carnival atmosphere. We had a favourite spot where we would picnic after our swim (we never ate on the beach). We knew the spot as the 'two little fields', which were away from the town near a landmark known as the Metal Man. We hoped no one else would be in our special little fields, as we somehow felt some ownership of them for our occasional visits. We had no desire to share the moment with others – in fact, a general feature of all picnics was the sometimes protracted drive to get away from others in a desire not to be cheek by jowl with anyone except ourselves. It is not that we were anti-social (did the word even exist then?); it was just that a picnic, especially this seaside picnic, was a special happening and not particularly for sharing.

The assembly of this picnic would have begun the previous day with a cake being baked and iced. Brown soda bread was cooked early in the morning and a chicken was roasted so that it would still be a little warm when we ate it later in the day. I assume there would have been lettuce leaves, tomatoes, hard-boiled eggs, spring onions and so on. Flasks of boiling water would have been included for my mother's cup of tea and a little jar of cream that she also took in her tea instead of the more conventional milk.

The trip from home would have seen us weave a route on the little country roads to Kilkenny, where one essential stop happened. On the corner of the Parade in that lovely town was a shop called Elliot's that sold many delicious things that we regarded as being highly glamorous and a total treat. One of the items was biscuits the size of a euro coin with little rosettes of set coloured icings piped on top. These beauties came in cellophane bags offering a tantalising view of what we knew we could not touch until we had eaten the savoury elements of our picnic. Perhaps we were each given one there and then when my mother got back into the car – regardless, I do remember much procrastination over which colour of icing we each wanted and much frustration as others waited impatiently in line to dip small fingers into the bag. The shop also had a shiny rotisserie, a machine we were entranced by, for roasting whole chickens that they dispensed into foil-lined bags, trapping the delicious cooking juices and heat in the bird. We occasionally got one of these if my mother had not had time to roast a chicken before leaving home. We were mesmerised by the rows of rotating birds, all achieving a rich golden skin that made our mouths water.

There were two other items in the shop that my mother had a controlled weakness for: butterscotch and nougat. My mother did not have a particularly sweet tooth, and that fact combined with having lived through the scarcities of the Second World War meant that she exhibited a beautiful restraint when it came to these sweets. The butterscotch came in tins decorated with Scottish thistles and the nougat in deliciously pretty blue and pink cardboard boxes with grand notices stating the preference of various royals for this particular product. Both of those went into the glove compartment of the car to be kept under lock and key.

At some point during the journey, if we were getting too boisterous or impatient, we were each given a single piece of the butterscotch to individually unwrap and enjoy. Silence would be restored as we watched the countryside whizzing by and passed through little villages whose names amused us, such as Knocktopher and Stoneyford. When we got to the outskirts of Waterford, we knew we were getting close. The nougat did not reappear until we got home late in the evening, our skin tingling from a sunny, salty day. Each of the pieces was cut with a knife into even smaller pieces and doled out with a reverence we grew to respect. We loved the smart starchy silver foil wrappers. Those little joyous and what we considered spoiling moments were in a time when the word 'treat' had much greater meaning than it does now. The notion of a treat cupboard did not exist. In fact, for a person of my mother's generation, I suspect the very idea would have seemed entirely unnecessary and actually offensive. We grumbled, I suppose, as we were enlisted to unpack the now dishevelled picnic.

There were winter picnics too, often in the back of my Aunt Florence's car as we hared around Laois and Kilkenny after various packs of hounds chasing foxes, most of whom I like to think managed to get away. Florence, like my mother, never left home without mobile refreshment and we hoped her famous orange cake would be in the repurposed biscuit tin in the boot of the car.

When we went to boarding school, the picnic took on a whole new significance. Removed from the ambrosial food of home, the contents of the wicker basket were a precious taste of that warm, secure nest we had left. The basket became the motif not only for the food I was missing, but the mother I adored. My mother would visit when possible and I remember at some point thinking that our picnic was a much less smart option than the fare in the local hotels that some of the other boys enjoyed. It seemed much more glamorous to be whisked off to a hotel for high tea. Well, that bubble was abruptly burst when a kind friend's parents asked me to join them for tea at one of the hotels and I quickly realised that what came out of the boot of my mother's car was much more delicious than what the hostelries of County Tipperary had to offer at that time. This was a significant realisation and is one of my earliest memories of making a conscious judgement about the quality of one food over another. I secretly bristled with embarrassment and guilt at my brief disloyalty to my mother's food.

I particularly remember another school picnic when one of my older brothers, David, and his wife Allison came to visit. They had roasted a whole chicken and brought it in a large Thermos and my brother Richard and I nearly fainted at the pleasure of it. A roast chicken, still warm and juicy from the oven on lavishly buttered fresh brown soda bread, is a joy that schoolboys can only dream of. We had driven to a remote and rarely visited part of the farm that surrounded the monastery school to spread out our picnic, and at some point one of the Cistercian monks passed by, prayer book in hand, silently and visibly amused by the unlikely sight of seeing people on a rug on the ground eating warm chicken sandwiches.

We once picnicked on Christmas Day. My mother had been saying for years that it was something she would love to do, so one year we said, okay, let's do it. Cars were packed with crockery, cutlery, glasses, rugs, napkins, crackers, turkey, ham, Uncle Tom Cobley and all. The whole feast came with us the few miles' drive to the top of Cullohill Mountain. We even brought the trifle. The weather was fair to us and a memory of great preciousness was created.

Picnics have happened in the most unlikely surroundings. On one occasion, when travelling with my sister Darina in America, promoting Ireland and its food, we had to take a train trip from New York to Washington, DC. Our hosts had kindly reserved seats for us in the business class carriage. The previous evening we had eaten with the wonderful Indian cook and our dear friend, Madhur Jaffrey, at her Manhattan restaurant, Dawat. Madhur had wanted us to taste as many of the menu items as possible and as a result there was a lot of delicious food on the table that we could not possibly eat. My sister, a confirmed picnicker (her packed meals are legendary), suggested we pack the leftovers into little cartons to bring on our train journey – a perfectly logical solution to the next day's railway luncheon. We duly caught our train and our carriage was for the greater part occupied by rather formal and stiffly suited businessmen. When the refreshment trolley wheeled through, all we needed was a couple of beers to accompany our picnic. The other travellers chose from the heavily packaged sandwiches, muffins and so on and all was smooth and calm as we left New York City.

When after some time our hunger pangs suggested to us that it was time to eat, we lined up our foil containers on our table top. Napkins and cutlery had been kindly proffered by the trolley driver on hearing we would be picnicking. We removed the covers from the packages and immediately unleashed a rather violent aroma of downtown Delhi into the tightly sealed air-conditioned carriage. Yum, said Darina. Where previously the only obvious or noticeable perfume in the carriage had been a subtle whiff of expensive cologne, shoe polish and power, now it was as if we had gone down a slip rail and ended up on the subcontinent. Stiff backs positively went into spasm as the most delicious but undeniably pungent whiff permeated our plushly cushioned and swishly silent surrounds. I suspect neck muscles were torn as heads swivelled to uncomfortable unnatural angles to catch a glimpse of the offending purveyors of this ferocious smell. I, being somewhat sensitive to my co-passengers' Ivy League demeanour, sensed the change of atmosphere and promptly blushed like a tomato. My sister was by then on to her third mouthful of last night's dal and was using her other hand to tear a naan into submission. Without moving her eyes from the food but somehow still managing to notice my heightened colour, she asked me if perhaps I found the food a little too spicy and tore her gaze off the food to throw me a sort of 'man up' glance. Delicious as the picnic was, I am not sure how good it was for my digestion, but despite my discomfort it remains a memory that brings a flushed smile to my face.

Another feature of picnics over the years has been a

chest of sandwiches. This rather brilliant invention was the brainchild of Myrtle Allen at Ballymaloe House. The concept is simple enough, the execution another matter. You take a large loaf of white bread cooked in the old-fashioned 'pan loaf' shape, carefully cut the top open but leaving it hinged on one of the long sides, then with a long, thin, sharp and pointed knife, by a series of precise cuts you lift the bulk of the bread out of its crust in one loaf-shaped piece, leaving you also with a hollow chest. This piece of bread is then cut into long horizontal slices that are buttered, filled with the chosen filling, topped with another slice of bread to create the sandwiches, cut into genteel pieces and carefully placed back into the hollowed-out loaf. The hinged lid is closed and the sandwiches remain fresh and lovely in their chest. Eccentric as all this may sound, it is eminently practical and really a joy. Radishes with leaves attached, small crisp lettuce leaves, cherry tomatoes, tiny spring onions and sprigs of watercress were often also placed under the lid to add a salad element to the picnic and to create a lovely balance of ingredients considering the amount of bread being consumed.

It is difficult to describe the facial expressions and wide-eyed reactions of attendant air and train hosts, fellow passengers and other witnesses on the removal of this plain loaf from its basket. The simple appearance of the bread gives nothing away. However, the opening of the lid for the reveal has been known to draw astonished gasps, disbelief and sometimes delight. To some, the notion of going to so much trouble to keep a sandwich fresh and transportable is sheer lunacy, but to others, such as myself, it is an entirely justified activity – a charming and delicious nonsense with a scrumptious ending.

At the end of the day, a picnic is about the food, simple or otherwise, and the company with whom it is shared. Curiously, whereas I find eating alone in a restaurant to be an uncomfortable business, throwing a rug on the ground or unpacking a little box of goodies on a train or plane causes me none of the same discomfort. The picnic is mostly a simple pleasure and we have learned that in so many ways, those are the ones we remember and cherish the most.

Chicken Stock –
Bone Broth

Chicken stock is indispensable. It is now widely known as bone broth by millennials, and where once it was regarded only as a useful condiment in the kitchen, now it has achieved an exalted status in its own right as the knowledge of its health benefits has become widely known. For making soup, sauces and gravies, it really has no substitute.

There are a few important rules to remember when making chicken stock and they apply to all stock making. Choose a saucepan that the ingredients fit into snugly. If your saucepan is too big, you will have too much water and as a result will end up with a watery stock that is lacking in flavour. Always pour cold water over the ingredients, as the cold water will draw the flavour out of the bones and vegetables as it comes up to the boil. Remember, it is the liquid you are going to eat here, so getting the flavour into that liquid is vital. If you can manage to get giblets to add to the stock, that's great, but don't worry at all if you can't. Sometimes the chicken liver is included in the giblets, but that should never go into the stock, as it gets bitter with prolonged cooking. Keep the liver for adding to a pâté or salad. A perfectly good stock can be made with just the bones.

Bring the contents of the pan slowly to the boil and then only allow the stock to simmer gently as it cooks. If it boils, it will loosen solid particles from the meat and vegetables and your stock will taste rather muddy and look cloudy. The ideal result is a sparklingly clear and well-flavoured liquid. I prefer not to cover the stock when it is cooking, as I feel it can cause the stock to cloud up. A rich and well-flavoured chicken stock can be achieved in 2 hours and I find that cooking the stock for hours on end makes it too strong. The stock will keep in the fridge for a few days or can be frozen.

Choose a saucepan that the ingredients fit into snugly. If your saucepan is too big, you will have too much water and as a result will end up with a watery stock that is lacking in flavour.

319

Makes approx. 3 litres
— 2–3 raw or cooked chicken carcasses (or a mixture of both)
— Giblets from the chicken (neck, heart, gizzard; optional)
— 1 onion, sliced
— 1 leek, split in two
— 1 outside stick of celery
— 1 carrot, sliced
— A few fresh parsley stalks
— 1 sprig of fresh thyme
— 6 black peppercorns
— 3.4 litres cold water (approx.)

Chop or break up the chicken carcasses. Put all the ingredients into a saucepan and cover with the **cold water**. Bring slowly up to the boil and skim the fat off the top with a tablespoon. **Simmer very gently** for 2–3 hours, uncovered. If the heat is too high, the liquid will reduce and you will end up with less stock and also it may be stronger than you need it to be. Strain through a sieve and remove any remaining fat. Allow the stock to become cold before storing in the fridge. Once it has been in the fridge for a few hours, a little more fat may rise to the surface and it is best to skim that off as well.

The stock can also be frozen and I almost always have a few tubs in the freezer for soups, gravies and so on. You can pop frozen stock out of its container and straight into a saucepan to quickly defrost directly over the heat.

If you need a stronger flavour, boil down the liquid in an open pan to reduce by one-third or half the volume. Do not add salt.

Labneh

Labneh once sounded exotic, but most cooks will now know it as a simple dripped yoghurt. It is absolutely easy to make and I have used it in several recipes in this book. The thick consistency of the dripped yoghurt is like a soft cheese and is useful in both the savoury and sweet kitchen. Buy the best thick Greek-style yoghurt you can find, and before you know it you will have made your own homemade cheese.

Serves 4–6
— 500g natural full-fat Greek-style yoghurt
— 1 tablespoon extra virgin olive oil

To make the labneh, take a double-thick square of muslin and place it over a sieve sitting over a bowl. Add the yoghurt and olive oil and tie the four corners of the muslin to make a knot. Secure the knot with some string. You now need to hang the tied muslin bag by the string over the bowl to allow the whey in the yoghurt to drip off, leaving you with your soft cheese. I hang the bag from a cup hook attached to a shelf and that works perfectly. If that all sounds too complicated, just sit the muslin bag in a sieve over a deep bowl and that will also do the job quite successfully. When the whey has all dripped out, simply remove the muslin and chill the cheese, covered, until you are ready to serve it.

Save the whey that dripped out of the yoghurt for another use. I sometimes use it instead of water in homemade lemonade for a drink with a little more bite.

The thick consistency of the dripped yoghurt is like a soft cheese and is useful in both the savoury and sweet kitchen.

BASIL OIL

Keep cooR

Basil Preserved in Olive Oil

This is an excellent way to preserve basil for the times of the year when the herb is out of season. Even after sitting in the oil for months, the flavour of the herb is excellent and the oil will have become wonderfully infused with the herb. I like to make this early in the basil season, before the herb becomes too strong and has lost some of its lovely fragrance, so in my part of the world that will be in June or July. It is important to store the oil in a cool, dark place, such as a garage, cellar or cold pantry. You can also store it in the fridge, but it will take up a little space and the oil will probably solidify with the colder temperature, which is absolutely fine – both the basil and oil are still perfect to use. It is surprising, though, how only a few bottles of a herb like this will get you through most of the year, when the alternative will be getting flown in from some faraway part of the globe.

I like to make this early in the basil season, before the herb becomes too strong and has lost some of its lovely fragrance, so in my part of the world that will be in June or July.

— Fresh basil leaves, dry and unblemished (no need to wash)
— Extra virgin olive oil
— Dark-coloured bottles and lids

Wash and dry the bottles, ensuring they are spotlessly clean. Place the bottles in an oven at 180°C for 5 minutes. Place the lids in a saucepan of water and bring to the boil. Remove the bottles from the oven and the lids from the water and dry thoroughly. Allow the bottles to become completely cold.

Stuff the bottles with basil leaves until they are three-quarters full. Try not to bruise the leaves by being too heavy handed. Pour over the olive oil to generously cover the leaves. Shake the bottles a little to make sure there are no air pockets and that the leaves are completely cloaked in the oil. It is crucial that the leaves are totally covered and submerged in the oil. Screw on the lids and store in a cool, dark place.

The oil is ready to use after two weeks and will keep for a year as long as the storage conditions are correct.

Tarragon Vinegar

What could be easier than putting some tarragon leaves in a jar or bottle and covering them with vinegar? It is that simple to make your own tarragon-infused vinegar, the only caveat being to use good-quality white wine vinegar and fresh French tarragon. The 'French' refers to the variety of tarragon rather than the country of origin. The other notable variety of tarragon is Russian, but its flavour is milder and its scent less aromatic than the French.

This is a great example of how to save an ingredient from going in the bin or the compost heap. It is old-fashioned home economics that yields a flavoured vinegar that can be used in vinaigrette dressings, mayonnaise, pickles and of course in a classic béarnaise sauce.

— Fresh French tarragon leaves
— White wine vinegar
— Jam jars and lids or bottles

Wash and dry the jam jars or bottles, ensuring they are spotlessly clean. Place the jars or bottles in an oven at 180°C for 5 minutes. Place the lids in a saucepan of water and bring to the boil. Remove the jars or bottles from the oven and the lids from the water and dry thoroughly. Allow the jars or bottles to become completely cold.

Place the tarragon leaves in a sterilised bottle or jam jar. The leaves should come up to a minimum of one-third of the height of the container being used. Cover with the vinegar, making sure the herb is completely submerged. I usually fill the containers to the top with vinegar. Put a little label on the containers with the date and store in a cool, dark place, or at least out of direct sunlight. The vinegar will be ready to use after one month and will keep for a year.

To use the vinegar at a later date, just pour it off and use as directed. The leaves, which will have discoloured, can be fished out, chopped and added to the dish you are making.

This is a great example of how to save an ingredient from going in the bin or the compost heap. It is old-fashioned home economics that yields a flavoured vinegar.

Elderflower Vinegar
Make this when elderflower is in season. Follow the directions
for the tarragon vinegar, squashing fresh and perfumed
elderflower heads into the containers and covering completely
with the vinegar.

FREEZE Tomatoes

Frozen Tomatoes

Who knew that this could be a thing? Well, it is, and I think I can say with certainty that this is the easiest preserving recipe I know. You simply freeze tomatoes! There is no need to do anything to them other than popping them in a bag or a container. I suppose if you wanted to you could remove the calyx beforehand, but even that little job is not vital.

As usual with anything this simple, there is the matter of the quality of the ingredient being used – the only important thing here is that the tomatoes are ripe. It does not matter if they are a little soft or even tarnished on the skin. When you come to use the tomatoes at a later stage, you take them from the freezer and pop them into a bowl of cold or tepid water and within a few minutes, the skins will peel off easily. The tomatoes can then be used in sauces, soups, stews – anywhere the tomatoes are going to be cooked. They will still be freezer hard, so do take care when chopping them that they don't go skidding off your chopping board and render the Chihuahua unconscious, or worse!

But really, how marvellous to be able to preserve the flavour of vine-ripened summer tomatoes for other times of the year when the tomatoes that are available are dull in comparison. How great to save a few tomatoes before you go away for the weekend or simply don't feel like eating them. How utterly tremendous for those who grow their own tomatoes and don't want to lose a single one of their crop. Even if you are not a grower, you could buy a box of super-ripe tomatoes from your greengrocer in August or September when they are at their best (and coincidentally, also at their cheapest) and freeze those. These frozen tomatoes will then keep you going in the darker months when imported tinned or bottled tomatoes would be the alternative.

— Tomatoes: Any quantity you like

Directions: Freeze in a freezerproof bag or container.

How marvellous to be able to preserve the flavour of vine-ripened summer tomatoes for other times of the year when the tomatoes that are available are dull in comparison.

Tomato Stew

This simple tomato stew is an immensely useful dish and I consider it to be an essential. It is a simple stew or sauce of cooked melted tomatoes. I use it in many different ways: as a vegetable, as a sauce to serve with grilled meats and fish, as a simple sauce for pasta or as a pizza topping. It also makes an excellent base for a fish or shellfish stew. The addition of a little chilli can spice it up. Finger-sized pieces of chicken breast or pork fillet cook quickly and perfectly in the stew. The choice of herbs used can vary depending on other ingredient additions and in winter a sprig of rosemary or thyme can add a deeper wintery flavour. The time of year determines the tomato being used. The optimum situation is fresh vine-ripened summer and autumn tomatoes, but frozen or tinned tomatoes also yield a lovely result.

Serves 6
— 2 tablespoons extra virgin olive oil or 25g butter
— 115g sliced onions
— 1 garlic clove, peeled and crushed to a paste
— 900g very ripe summer tomatoes, peeled and sliced or chopped, or the same weight of frozen or tinned tomatoes
— Pinch of caster sugar, to taste
— 2 tablespoons of the chopped fresh herb of your choice: basil, mint, marjoram, coriander or a mixture
— Sea salt and freshly ground black pepper

Heat the oil or butter in a saucepan or heavy-based casserole. Add the sliced onions and garlic and toss in the heated oil or melted butter. Cover and cook on a very gentle heat until the onions are really soft – this is the secret of this recipe.

Add the sliced or chopped tomatoes. Season with salt, pepper and a pinch of sugar. Cover again and simmer gently for about 15 minutes. The mixture will now look like a juicy sauce. Now add the chopped herb of your choice. Taste to correct the seasoning.

I use it in many different ways: as a vegetable, as a sauce to serve with grilled meats and fish, as a simple sauce for pasta or as a pizza topping. It also makes an excellent base for a fish or shellfish stew.

If you require a thicker sauce (for a pizza topping or pasta sauce), cook, uncovered, at a simmer and stir regularly for a further 15 minutes or so to reduce the liquid and thicken the consistency.

The sauce can be used immediately or allow it to cool completely and store in the fridge for up to three days or freeze in tightly sealed containers.

give a LIVINg gift

Frozen Elderflowers and Berries

Elderflower has a very particular place in the year when its host, the innocuous-looking elder tree, transforms itself into a creation that surely must have inspired a milliner or two coming up with a showstopper for a wedding or racing at Ascot. The normally shy and retiring tree is suddenly bedecked with big, frothy, lacy blooms that open and spread to the size of a side plate. The tree must feel positively embarrassed having lurked in the wings all year, then suddenly all eyes are pointed in its direction, as for a period it is centre stage in the hedgerows.

Foragers armed with secateurs and sometimes a long ladder will be frantic to harvest the scented blooms for making all manner of muscat-flavoured drinks, pickles, vinegars, shrubs, wines, champagnes, set creams, mousses, soufflés, ices and sorbets ... the list goes on and on. The season is short, so speed is of the essence unless you decide, like here, to freeze some of the heads to preserve them. This is as easy as freezing tomatoes (page 327). Place perfect unblemished flowers picked at the beginning rather than the end of the season in sealed containers and that's it. Later on in the year, remove the frozen flowers from the freezer and pop them immediately into the liquid or food you are trying to infuse with their heady, almost tropical flavour.

In autumn and early winter, beautiful purple, almost black or aubergine-coloured berries grow in clusters where the flowers once were – more mad inspiration for the hatter, perhaps. These tart, almost vinegary flavour bombs can also be frozen just as they are. There is no need to remove the berries from the little branches before freezing, as you can simply shake them off when frozen. The berries, which are full of floral sharpness, are great with some of the foods we associate with the colder months, such as venison and wild duck.

— Elderflower heads in perfect condition or the berried flowers

Freeze in airtight containers.

Dried Red Chillies and Chilli Flakes

This is another one of those simple practices that seems so obvious when you think about it. You have bought too many red chillies and don't want to waste them. What you don't want to do is keep them in the fridge, as they will wilt and eventually decompose. Simply leave your red chillies on your kitchen counter in a little basket, minding their own business, and eventually (it can take a couple of months) they will dry to a crisp tinder. You then have dried chillies, but if you pop them into a mortar and pound them, seeds and all, with the pestle, you have chilli flakes, an ingredient I regard as essential. Grinding them in a food processor is equally successful.

On the subject of chilli flakes, which are the flesh and seeds of the dried chilli, as just explained, there can be some confusion, as in some recipes (though not in this book) they are called red pepper flakes or crushed red pepper.

Simply leave your red chillies on your kitchen counter in a little basket, minding their own business, and eventually (it can take a couple of months) they will dry to a crisp tinder.

Candied Rose Petals

This is another one of those 'life is too short' situations – dried rose petals delicately painted with egg white, dipped in sugar and then allowed to dry. It doesn't sound all that eccentric when you say it like that; in fact, it sounds more like craft-making than cooking. You can almost imagine the lightly sugar-coated petals glistening in a cabinet de curiosité alongside exotic shells and dried bugs. I suppose it is a question of what makes you happy and these sweet, delicately brittle, featherweight vehicles of scented rose are a marvel and always give me a little shiver of pleasure. They keep well in an airtight container, but I think they are most charming eaten within a few days of being made. I use them on buns, cakes, mousses and soufflés. They are sprinkled on lemon ice with stem ginger (page 202) and I have been known to drop a few pomegranate seeds into the hollow of the dried petals to serve alongside strong small coffees. I can never quite decide if that is a bit too show-offy or if it is just spreading the love.

Many other flowers and scented leaves can also be prepared in exactly the same way. Wild dog violets are exquisite, as are the first wild primroses of the year. Dahlia petals are also a favourite. Any edible flower can be used here. Mint, lemon balm and lemon verbena leaves will have a great and definite flavour to match the crispness of the dried sugar-coated leaves.

— 2 egg whites
— Organic scented roses, picked when completely dry and unsprayed
— Caster sugar

Line a tray with non-stick baking paper.

Beat the egg white until it loses its gloopy consistency but before it gets frothy. You are just trying to liquefy the white so that it will coat the petals in a thin but thorough coating.

Separate the rose petals, discarding any damaged or floppy outer ones. You want firm, pert petals to get a perfect result.

Use a small paintbrush or pastry brush to paint the petals.

You can almost imagine the lightly sugar-coated petals glistening in a cabinet de curiosité alongside exotic shells and dried bugs. I suppose it is a question of what makes you happy and these sweet, delicately brittle, featherweight vehicles of scented rose are a marvel and always give me a little shiver of pleasure.

You can also do the job quite successfully just using your fingers. Take one petal at a time and coat each side of the petal with just enough egg white to make it lightly glisten. Excess egg white will result in little splodges of crystallized sugar and will spoil the delicate effect. Look at the coated petal to make sure there are no dry areas, then dip in the caster sugar. I use a teaspoon or table fork to spread the sugar onto the petal, again making sure that the entire surface area is coated. Lift them out of the sugar, give them a gentle shake to get rid of the excess sugar and place them on the baking paper. Continue until you have the number of sugared petals you require.

I place them on my kitchen counter to dry, which in my kitchen usually happens within 2–3 hours. Some people like to pop the tray into a hot press to achieve a similar result. When the petals are completely dry, transfer to a kitchen paper-lined box with a tight-fitting lid.

Dried Herbs

Dried herbs used to be a thing before fresh herbs became available year round. They were used without embarrassment or fear of ridicule. How you feel about the year-round access to some of these well-travelled fresh herbs is your own matter, of course. In the case of dried herbs, there are just a few that I will dry if they promise to yield a flavour that I am happy to use in my kitchen and that might become a good, but invariably different, alternative for an out-of-season fresh herb. It is worth noting that with the rise in global temperatures due to climate change, we can now grow a wide range of herbs year round, albeit under unheated cover in colder months. In my part of the world, we are hardly ever without coriander, marjoram, fennel, dill, chervil, parsley and of course the robust toughies thyme, rosemary and bay. Tarragon, basil, chives, lemon balm and to a large extent mint and verbena disappear out of view in the chillier season.

The classic mix of dried herbes de Provence was once a cautious and carefully curated blend of dried herbs from that region. It was used in a specific way, in equally specific amounts, and was specific in flavour to suit certain traditional dishes. It was not trying to mimic the flavour of fresh herbs. Sadly, nowadays this blend has become a game of chance, as all manner of unsuitable flavourings can end up in the chi-chi ribbon-tied bags that look more like a moth deterrent or something to be put under your pillow to send you off to a deep and scented sleep. Lavender, dried orange peels and fennel seeds are sometimes included in some of these blends, more for their olfactory impact rather than the gastronomic outcomes.

Hence the message here is to keep it simple and only dry herbs for cooking that will be delicious. The flavour of the dried herb is quite different from the fresh ones, and it is that difference of taste that is important. I once happily presented a visiting cook with fresh mint for a Turkish lahmacun, that thin and crisp mince-topped pizza, only to be told in no uncertain terms that fresh mint was completely the wrong flavour and that the different taste of the dried herb was what was required and correct. I scuttled off with my vibrant green sprigs, wiser and redder.

The classic mix of dried herbes de Provence was once a cautious and carefully curated blend of dried herbs from that region. It was used in a specific way, in equally specific amounts, and was specific in flavour to suit certain traditional dishes. It was not trying to mimic the flavour of fresh herbs.

The best herbs for drying are ones picked just before flowering. I simply lay them out on my kitchen counter or tie them up in bunches for hanging and within a few days they will be as dry as tinder and ready to be put into dry sealed containers. Dehydrators are also excellent for the purpose of drying.

There are just three herbs that I dry. I like spearmint (or what is sometimes called Moroccan mint), French tarragon and oregano. The variety of oregano I like to dry is *Origanum syriacum*, and in this case I do like some flowers attached.

Food in the Freezer

This is a list of food that I always try to have in the freezer, in which case I will never be stuck for something to eat tomorrow. Obviously things go in and out of the freezer, so it is a matter of remembering to restock when something vital is running low.

The berries will be what are remaining from freezing the previous summer. I try to use up all the last year's berries before the new season arrives. Rotating ingredients like fish, poultry and meat needs to be done on a regular basis so that the foods don't suffer from having been frozen for too long. The same could be said of any ingredient, but fruit, once frozen in mint condition, keeps remarkably and that is the key to using the freezer to successfully preserve food – if the food does not go in it in perfect condition, it is certainly not going to be any better when it is defrosted and used again.

- Tomatoes
- Chicken stock
- Breadcrumbs
- Chicken drumsticks and thighs and sometimes a whole chicken
- Chicken carcasses for making into stock
- Fish bones and lobster or prawn shells for making stock
- Berries (blackberries, raspberries, blueberries, strawberries)
- Redcurrants
- Elderflower heads
- Basil leaves
- Peas
- A piece or two of puff pastry
- Filo pastry
- A packet of rashers
- 2 portions of fish frozen when spanking fresh
- Butter
- Egg whites for meringues, soufflés and batter
- Kumquats
- A slab of both sweet and savoury freezer biscuits
- Duck legs

give an edible gift

Index

Have a cup of tea